Real-Resumes for Human Resources & Personnel Jobs..
including real resumes used to change careers and transfer skills to other industries

Anne McKinney, Editor

PREP PUBLISHING

FAYETTEVILLE, NC

PREP Publishing
1110½ Hay Street
Fayetteville, NC 28305
(910) 483-6611

Copyright © 2002 by Anne McKinney

All rights reserved under International and Pan-American Copyright Conventions. No part of this book may be reproduced or copied in any form or by any means–graphic, electronic, or mechanical, including photocopying, taping, or information storage and retrieval systems–without written permission from the publisher, except by a reviewer, who may quote brief passages in a review. Published in the United States by PREP Publishing.

Library of Congress Cataloging-in-Publication Data

Real-resumes for human-resources & personnel jobs : including real resumes used to change careers and transfer skills to other industries / Anne McKinney, editor.
      p. cm. -- (Real-resumes series)
  ISBN 1-885288-29-8
     1. Résumés (Employment) 2. Personnel management. 3. Personnel departments--Employees. I. McKinney, Anne, 1948- II. Series.

HF5383 .R39586 2002
650.14'2--dc21
                                                       2002027088
                                                                     CIP

Printed in the United States of America

By PREP Publishing

Business and Career Series:

RESUMES AND COVER LETTERS THAT HAVE WORKED

RESUMES AND COVER LETTERS THAT HAVE WORKED FOR MILITARY PROFESSIONALS

GOVERNMENT JOB APPLICATIONS AND FEDERAL RESUMES

COVER LETTERS THAT BLOW DOORS OPEN

LETTERS FOR SPECIAL SITUATIONS

RESUMES AND COVER LETTERS FOR MANAGERS

REAL-RESUMES FOR COMPUTER JOBS

REAL-RESUMES FOR MEDICAL JOBS

REAL-RESUMES FOR FINANCIAL JOBS

REAL-RESUMES FOR TEACHERS

REAL-RESUMES FOR STUDENTS

REAL-RESUMES FOR CAREER CHANGERS

REAL-RESUMES FOR SALES

REAL ESSAYS FOR COLLEGE & GRADUATE SCHOOL

REAL-RESUMES FOR AVIATION & TRAVEL JOBS

REAL-RESUMES FOR POLICE, LAW ENFORCEMENT & SECURITY JOBS

REAL-RESUMES FOR SOCIAL WORK & COUNSELING JOBS

REAL-RESUMES FOR CONSTRUCTION JOBS

REAL-RESUMES FOR MANUFACTURING JOBS

REAL-RESUMES FOR RESTAURANT, FOOD SERVICE & HOTEL JOBS

REAL-RESUMES FOR MEDIA, NEWSPAPER, BROADCASTING & PUBLIC AFFAIRS JOBS

REAL-RESUMES FOR RETAILING, MODELING, FASHION & BEAUTY JOBS

REAL-RESUMES FOR HUMAN RESOURCES & PERSONNEL JOBS

Judeo-Christian Ethics Series:

SECOND TIME AROUND

BACK IN TIME

WHAT THE BIBLE SAYS ABOUT...Words that can lead to success and happiness

A GENTLE BREEZE FROM GOSSAMER WINGS

BIBLE STORIES FROM THE OLD TESTAMENT

Table of Contents

Introduction: The Art of Changing Jobs...and Finding New Careers 1

PART ONE: SOME ADVICE ABOUT YOUR JOB HUNT 4
Step One: Planning Your Career Change and Assembling the Tools 4
Step Two: Using Your Resume and Cover Letter 6
Step Three: Preparing for Interviews 9
Step Four: Handling the Interview and Negotiating Salary 11
Looking Closer: The Anatomy of a Cover Letter 14

PART TWO: REAL-RESUMES FOR HUMAN RESOURCES & PERSONNEL JOBS 17
Administrative Services Manager for a public relations company 18
Assistant Personnel Administrator for a major kitchen equipment distributor 20
Assistant Personnel Department Supervisor for a major telecommunications company 22
Assistant Personnel Manager for Walgreen Stores 24
Assistant Personnel Supervisor for the Department of Energy 26
Chief of Personnel Management for the Department of the Army 28
Chief of Personnel for Monsanto Chemical 30
Director of Human Resources for Allied Capital, a Fortune 500 company 32
Director of Human Resource Management for the U.S. Department of State 34
Director of Human Resources for Dow Chemical 36
Director of Plans and Operations for Verizon Communications. 38
Director of Training for the Department of the Interior 40
Director of Training and Human Resources for Sara Lee Foods, Inc 42
Director of Training and Personnel Recruiting for General Electric 44
Educational Coordinator for Information Technology Training for a bank 46
Employee Relations Manager for Pfizer Industries 48
Employee Training Benefits Assistant for Wang Computers 50
Executive Personnel Manager for Sears and Roebuck 52
Family and Vocational Counselor for the Veterans Administration 54
Human Resources Student earning degree in Human Resources Management 56
Human Resources Administrator and Regional Operations Manager for Kelly Staffing 58
Human Resources Advisor for General Dynamics 60
Human Resource Analyst for the city of Muncie, IN 62
Human Resources Manager in a manufacturing environment 64
Human Resources Recruiter with previous experience in a Fortune 500 company 66
Human Resources Consultant for a private staffing firm 68
Human Resources Coordinator for the Department of Natural Resources 70
Human Resources Counselor and Case Worker for a career change within a university 72
Human Resources Department Manager for AT&T 74
Human Resources Development Master's Degree Candidate at a major medical center 76
Human Resources Director for Hechts, a prominent retailer 78
Human Resources Manager in a medical environment 80
Human Resources Manager for Reliant Energy 82
Human Resources Vice President for the Fortune 500 company General Technologies 84
Human Services Department Manager for the Alcoa corporation 86
Human Services Program Director for the Eckerds organization 88
Labor Relations Mediator for Boeing Aircraft 90

v

Logistical Support Manager with the Ford Motor Company. 92
Medical Operations Manager for the Davis Medical Staffing Agency 94
Operations Supervisor for E.I. du Pont de Nemours 96
Organizational Development Consultant for a division of Pillsbury 98
Personnel Administration Manager at Wal-Mart 100
Personnel Administration Supervisor for Westinghouse 102
Personnel Administrator and Regional Maintenance Operations Manager for a distributor   104
Personnel and Training Supervisor for International Paper 106
Personnel Assistant in an academic environment at the University of Idaho 108
Personnel Assistant at Tech Data 110
Personnel Director for a major chemical company 112
Personnel Coordinator for a temporary service agency 114
Personnel Drug Testing Administrator for SBC Communications 116
Personnel Manager in a medical environment 118
Personnel Manager and Retention Specialist with Johnson & Johnson 120
Personnel Manager at Monarch Foods 122
Personnel Policy Development Manager for Georgia Pacific Corporation 124
Personnel Recruiter and Training Manager for a staffing service 126
Personnel Recruiter for the Department of Transportation 128
Personnel Recruiter for Sara Lee Products Company 130
Personnel Recruiter and Sales Representative at Hewlett Packard 132
Personnel Recruiting Manager for Prudential Insurance Company 134
Personnel Recruiting Specialist for Proctor & Gamble 136
Personnel Recruiting Supervisor for Haldane Staffing Services 138
Personnel Recruitment Manager and Regional Sales Manager with Costco Wholesale 140
Personnel Recruitment Supervisor with Electronics Staffing Services 142
Personnel Training Administrator for Golden Foods, Inc. 144
Personnel Training Supervisor for Rohr Industries 146
Plans and Contracts Manager seeks to transition into the human resources arena 148
Retirement Services Office Supervisor with the U.S. Department of State 150
School Operations Manager seeks to transition into a business setting 152
Senior Administration Advisor for the Data General Corporation 154
Staff Services Director for a public utilities company. 156
Staffing Specialist with Reliable Staffing 158
Staffing Specialist for Manpower Staffing 160
Support Services Manager for Oscar Meyer Meats 162
Temporary Placement Supervisor for Premier Staffing Services 164
Territory Manager and Recruiter for the Department of Transportation 166
Training Department Manager for Motorola 168
Training Director for Johnson & Johnson 170
Training Manager for Kestler Pharmaceuticals 172
Training Program Manager for Intel Corporation 174
Vice President for Human Resources for a prominent credit union 176

A WORD FROM THE EDITOR:
ABOUT THE REAL-RESUMES SERIES

Welcome to the Real-Resumes Series. The Real-Resumes Series is a series of books which have been developed based on the experiences of real job hunters and which target specialized fields or types of resumes. As the editor of the series, I have carefully selected resumes and cover letters (with names and other key data disguised, of course) which have been used successfully in real job hunts. That's what we mean by "Real-Resumes." What you see in this book are *real* resumes and cover letters which helped real people get ahead in their careers.

The Real-Resumes Series is based on the work of the country's oldest resume-preparation company known as PREP Resumes. If you would like a free information packet describing the company's resume preparation services, call 910-483-6611 or write to PREP at 1110½ Hay Street, Fayetteville, NC 28305. If you have a job hunting experience you would like to share with our staff at the Real-Resumes Series, please contact us at preppub@aol.com or visit our website at http://www.prep-pub.com.

The resumes and cover letters in this book are designed to be of most value to people already in a job hunt or contemplating a career change. If we could give you one word of advice about your career, here's what we would say: Manage your career and don't stumble from job to job in an incoherent pattern. Try to find work that interests you, and then identify prosperous industries which need work performed of the type you want to do. Learn early in your working life that a great resume and cover letter can blow doors open for you and help you maximize your salary.

> This book is dedicated to those seeking jobs in the human resources and personnel field. We hope the superior samples will help you manage your current job campaign and your career so that you will find work aligned to your career interests.

Real-Resumes for Human Resources & Personnel Jobs...
including real resumes used to change careers
and transfer skills to other industries

Anne McKinney, Editor

Introduction: The Art of Changing Jobs... and Finding New Careers

As the editor of this book, I would like to give you some tips on how to make the best use of the information you will find here. Because you are considering a career change, you already understand the concept of managing your career for maximum enjoyment and self-fulfillment. The purpose of this book is to provide expert tools and advice so that you *can* manage your career. Inside these pages you will find resumes and cover letters that will help you find not just a job but the type of work you want to do.

Overview of the Book
Every resume and cover letter in this book actually worked. And most of the resumes and cover letters have common features: most are one-page, most are in the chronological format, and most resumes are accompanied by a companion cover letter. In this section you will find helpful advice about job hunting. Step One begins with a discussion of why employers prefer the one-page, chronological resume. In Step Two you are introduced to the direct approach and to the proper format for a cover letter. In Step Three you learn the 14 main reasons why job hunters are not offered the jobs they want, and you learn the six key areas employers focus on when they interview you. Step Four gives nuts-and-bolts advice on how to handle the interview, send a follow-up letter after an interview, and negotiate your salary.

The cover letter plays such a critical role in a career change. You will learn from the experts how to format your cover letters and you will see suggested language to use in particular career-change situations. It has been said that "A picture is worth a thousand words" and, for that reason, you will see numerous examples of effective cover letters used by real individuals to change fields, functions, and industries.

The most important part of the book is the Real-Resumes section. Some of the individuals whose resumes and cover letters you see spent a lengthy career in an industry they loved. Then there are resumes and cover letters of people who wanted a change but who probably wanted to remain in their industry. Many of you will be especially interested by the resumes and cover letters of individuals who knew they definitely wanted a career change but had no idea what they wanted to do next. Other resumes and cover letters show individuals who knew they wanted to change fields and had a pretty good idea of what they wanted to do next.

Whatever your field, and whatever your circumstances, you'll find resumes and cover letters that will "show you the ropes" in terms of successfully changing jobs and switching careers.

Before you proceed further, think about why you picked up this book.
- Are you dissatisfied with the type of work you are now doing?
- Would you like to change careers, change companies, or change industries?
- Are you satisfied with your industry but not with your niche or function within it?
- Do you want to transfer your skills to a new product or service?
- Even if you have excelled in your field, have you "had enough"? Would you like the stimulation of a new challenge?
- Are you aware of the importance of a great cover letter but unsure of how to write one?
- Are you preparing to launch a second career after retirement?
- Have you been downsized, or do you anticipate becoming a victim of downsizing?
- Do you need expert advice on how to plan and implement a job campaign that will open the maximum number of doors?
- Do you want to make sure you handle an interview to your maximum advantage?

- Would you like to master the techniques of negotiating salary and benefits?
- Do you want to learn the secrets and shortcuts of professional resume writers?

Using the Direct Approach

As you consider the possibility of a job hunt or career change, you need to be aware that most people end up having at least three distinctly different careers in their working lifetimes, and often those careers are different from each other. Yet people usually stumble through each job campaign, unsure of what they should be doing. Whether you find yourself voluntarily or unexpectedly in a job hunt, the direct approach is the job hunting strategy most likely to yield a full-time permanent job. The direct approach is an active, take-the-initiative style of job hunting in which you choose your next employer rather than relying on responding to ads, using employment agencies, or depending on other methods of finding jobs. You will learn how to use the direct approach in this book, and you will see that an effective cover letter is a critical ingredient in using the direct approach.

The "direct approach" is the style of job hunting most likely to yield the maximum number of job interviews.

Lack of Industry Experience Not a Major Barrier to Entering New Field

"Lack of experience" is often the last reason people are not offered jobs, according to the companies who do the hiring. If you are changing careers, you will be glad to learn that experienced professionals often are selling "potential" rather than experience in a job hunt. Companies look for personal qualities that they know tend to be present in their most effective professionals, such as communication skills, initiative, persistence, organizational and time management skills, and creativity. Frequently companies are trying to discover "personality type," "talent," "ability," "aptitude," and "potential" rather than seeking actual hands-on experience, so your resume should be designed to aggressively present your accomplishments. Attitude, enthusiasm, personality, and a track record of achievements in any type of work are the primary "indicators of success" which employers are seeking, and you will see numerous examples in this book of resumes written in an all-purpose fashion so that the professional can approach various industries and companies.

Using references in a skillful fashion in your job hunt will inspire confidence in prospective employers and help you "close the sale" after interviews.

The Art of Using References in a Job Hunt

You probably already know that you need to provide references during a job hunt, but you may not be sure of how and when to use references for maximum advantage. You can use references very creatively during a job hunt to call attention to your strengths and make yourself "stand out." Your references will rarely get you a job, no matter how impressive the names, but the way you use references can boost the employer's confidence in you and lead to a job offer in the least time.

You should ask from three to five people, including people who have supervised you, if you can use them as a reference during your job hunt. You may not be able to ask your current boss since your job hunt is probably confidential.

A common question in resume preparation is: "Do I need to put my references on my resume?" No, you don't. Even if you create a references page at the same time you prepare your resume, you don't need to mail, e-mail, or fax your references page with the resume and cover letter. Usually the potential employer is not interested in references until he meets you, so the earliest you need to have references ready is at the first interview. Obviously there are exceptions to this standard rule of thumb; sometimes an ad will ask you to send references with your first response. Wait until the employer requests references before providing them.

An excellent attention-getting technique is to take to the first interview not just a page of references (giving names, addresses, and telephone numbers) but an actual letter of reference written by someone who knows you well and who preferably has supervised or employed you. A professional way to close the first interview is to thank the interviewer, shake his or her hand, and then say you'd like to give him or her a copy of a letter of reference from a previous employer. Hopefully you already made a good impression during the interview, but you'll "close the sale" in a dynamic fashion if you leave a letter praising you and your accomplishments. For that reason, it's a good idea to ask supervisors during your final weeks in a job if they will provide you with a written letter of recommendation which you can use in future job hunts. Most employers will oblige, and you will have a letter that has a useful "shelf life" of many years. Such a letter often gives the prospective employer enough confidence in his opinion of you that he may forego checking out other references and decide to offer you the job on the spot or in the next few days.

> With regard to references, it's best to provide the names and addresses of people who have supervised you or observed you in a work situation.

Whom should you ask to serve as references? References should be people who have known or supervised you in a professional, academic, or work situation. References with big titles, like school superintendent or congressman, are fine, but remind busy people when you get to the interview stage that they may be contacted soon. Make sure the busy official recognizes your name and has instant positive recall of you! If you're asked to provide references on a formal company application, you can simply transcribe names from your references list. In summary, follow this rule in using references: If you've got them, flaunt them! If you've obtained well-written letters of reference, make sure you find a polite way to push those references under the nose of the interviewer so he or she can hear someone other than you describing your strengths. Your references probably won't ever get you a job, but glowing letters of reference can give you credibility and visibility that can make you stand out among candidates with similar credentials and potential!

The approach taken by this book is to (1) help you master the proven best techniques of conducting a job hunt and (2) show you how to stand out in a job hunt through your resume, cover letter, interviewing skills, as well as the way in which you present your references and follow up on interviews. Now, the best way to "get in the mood" for writing your own resume and cover letter is to select samples from the Table of Contents that interest you and then read them. A great resume is a "photograph," usually on one page, of an individual. If you wish to seek professional advice in preparing your resume, you may contact one of the professional writers at Professional Resume & Employment Publishing (PREP) for a brief free consultation by calling 1-910-483-6611.

Part One: Some Advice About Your Job Hunt

STEP ONE: Planning Your Career Change and Assembling the Tools

What if you don't know what you want to do?
Your job hunt will be more comfortable if you can figure out what type of work you want to do. But you are not alone if you have no idea what you want to do next! You may have knowledge and skills in certain areas but want to get into another type of work. What *The Wall Street Journal* has discovered in its research on careers is that most of us end up having at least three distinctly different careers in our working lives; it seems that, even if we really like a particular kind of activity, twenty years of doing it is enough for most of us and we want to move on to something else!

That's why we strongly believe that you need to spend some time figuring out *what interests you* rather than taking an inventory of the skills you have. You may have skills that you simply don't want to use, but if you can build your career on the things that interest you, you will be more likely to be happy and satisfied in your job. Realize, too, that interests can change over time; the activities that interest you now may not be the ones that interested you years ago. For example, some professionals may decide that they've had enough of retail sales and want a job selling another product or service, even though they have earned a reputation for being an excellent retail manager. We strongly believe that interests rather than skills should be the determining factor in deciding what types of jobs you want to apply for and what directions you explore in your job hunt. Obviously one cannot be a lawyer without a law degree or a secretary without secretarial skills; but a professional can embark on a next career as a financial consultant, property manager, plant manager, production supervisor, retail manager, or other occupation if he/she has a strong interest in that type of work and can provide a resume that clearly demonstrates past excellent performance in *any* field and *potential* to excel in another field. As you will see later in this book, "lack of exact experience" is the last reason why people are turned down for the jobs they apply for.

Figure out what interests you and you will hold the key to a successful job hunt and working career. (And be prepared for your interests to change over time!)

"Lack of exact experience" is the last reason people are turned down for the jobs for which they apply.

How can you have a resume prepared if you don't know what you want to do?
You may be wondering how you can have a resume prepared if you don't know what you want to do next. The approach to resume writing which PREP, the country's oldest resume-preparation company, has used successfully for many years is to develop an "all-purpose" resume that translates your skills, experience, and accomplishments into language employers can understand. What most people need in a job hunt is a versatile resume that will allow them to apply for numerous types of jobs. For example, you may want to apply for a job in pharmaceutical sales but you may also want to have a resume that will be versatile enough for you to apply for jobs in the construction, financial services, or automotive industries.

Based on more than 20 years of serving job hunters, we at PREP have found that your best approach to job hunting is **an all-purpose resume** and **specific cover letters tailored to specific fields** rather than using the approach of trying to create different resumes for every job. If you are remaining in your field, you may not even need more than one "all-purpose" cover letter, although the cover letter rather than the resume is the place to communicate your interest in a narrow or specific field. An all-purpose resume and cover letter that translate your experience and accomplishments into plain English are the tools that will maximize the number of doors which open for you while permitting you to "fish" in the widest range of job areas.

Your resume will provide the script for your job interview.
When you get down to it, your resume has a simple job to do: Its purpose is to blow as many doors open as possible and to make as many people as possible want to meet you. So a well-written resume that really "sells" you is a key that will create opportunities for you in a job hunt.

This statistic explains why: The typical newspaper advertisement for a job opening receives more than 245 replies. And normally only 10 or 12 will be invited to an interview.

But here's another purpose of the resume: it provides the "script" the employer uses when he interviews you. If your resume has been written in such a way that your strengths and achievements are revealed, that's what you'll end up talking about at the job interview. Since the resume will govern what you get asked about at your interviews, you can't overestimate the importance of making sure your resume makes you look and sound as good as you are.

Your resume is the "script" for your job interviews. Make sure you put on your resume what you want to talk about or be asked about at the job interview.

So what is a "good" resume?
Very literally, your resume should motivate the person reading it to dial the phone number or e-mail the screen name you have put on the resume. When you are relocating, you should put a local phone number on your resume if your physical address is several states away; employers are more likely to dial a local telephone number than a long-distance number when they're looking for potential employees.

If you have a resume already, look at it objectively. Is it a limp, colorless "laundry list" of your job titles and duties? Or does it "paint a picture" of your skills, abilities, and accomplishments in a way that would make someone want to meet you? Can people understand what you're saying? If you are attempting to change fields or industries, can potential employers see that your skills and knowledge are transferable to other environments? For example, have you described accomplishments which reveal your problem-solving abilities or communication skills?

The one-page resume in chronological format is the format preferred by most employers.

How long should your resume be?
One page, maybe two. Usually only people in the academic community have a resume (which they usually call a *curriculum vitae*) longer than one or two pages. Remember that your resume is almost always accompanied by a cover letter, and a potential employer does not want to read more than two or three pages about a total stranger in order to decide if he wants to meet that person! Besides, don't forget that the more you tell someone about yourself, the more opportunity you are providing for the employer to screen you out at the "first-cut" stage. A resume should be concise and exciting and designed to make the reader want to meet you in person!

Should resumes be functional or chronological?
Employers almost always prefer a chronological resume; in other words, an employer will find a resume easier to read if it is immediately apparent what your current or most recent job is, what you did before that, and so forth, in reverse chronological order. A resume that goes back in detail for the last ten years of employment will generally satisfy the employer's curiosity about your background. Employment more than ten years old can be shown even more briefly in an "Other Experience" section at the end of your "Experience" section. Remember that your intention is not to tell everything you've done but to "hit the high points" and especially impress the employer with what you learned, contributed, or accomplished in each job you describe.

STEP TWO: Using Your Resume and Cover Letter

Once you get your resume, what do you do with it?
You will be using your resume to answer ads, as a tool to use in talking with friends and relatives about your job search, and, most importantly, in using the "direct approach" described in this book.

When you mail your resume, always send a "cover letter."
A "cover letter," sometimes called a "resume letter" or "letter of interest," is a letter that accompanies and introduces your resume. Your cover letter is a way of personalizing the resume by sending it to the specific person you think you might want to work for at each company. Your cover letter should contain a few highlights from your resume—just enough to make someone want to meet you. Cover letters should always be typed or word processed on a computer—never handwritten.

Never mail or fax your resume without a cover letter.

1. Learn the art of answering ads.
There is an "art," part of which can be learned, in using your "bestselling" resume to reply to advertisements.

Sometimes an exciting job lurks behind a boring ad that someone dictated in a hurry, so reply to any ad that interests you. Don't worry that you aren't "25 years old with an MBA" like the ad asks for. Employers will always make compromises in their requirements if they think you're the "best fit" overall.

What about ads that ask for "salary requirements?"
What if the ad you're answering asks for "salary requirements?" The first rule is to avoid committing yourself in writing at that point to a specific salary. You don't want to "lock yourself in."

What if the ad asks for your "salary requirements?"

There are two ways to handle the ad that asks for "salary requirements."
First, you can ignore that part of the ad and accompany your resume with a cover letter that focuses on "selling" you, your abilities, and even some of your philosophy about work or your field. You may include a sentence in your cover letter like this: "I can provide excellent personal and professional references at your request, and I would be delighted to share the private details of my salary history with you in person."

Second, if you feel you must give some kind of number, just state a range in your cover letter that includes your medical, dental, other benefits, and expected bonuses. You might state, for example, "My current compensation, including benefits and bonuses, is in the range of $30,000-$40,000."

Analyze the ad and "tailor" yourself to it.
When you're replying to ads, a finely tailored cover letter is an important tool in getting your resume noticed and read. On the next page is a cover letter which has been "tailored to fit" a specific ad. Notice the "art" used by PREP writers of analyzing the ad's main requirements and then writing the letter so that the person's background, work habits, and interests seem "tailor-made" to the company's needs. Use this cover letter as a model when you prepare your own reply to ads.

6 Part One: Some Advice About Your Job Hunt

Date

Mr. Arthur Wise
National Careers, Inc.
9439 Goshen Lane
Dallas, TX 22105

Dear Mr. Wise:

I would appreciate an opportunity to show you in person, soon, that I am the energetic, dynamic individual you are looking for as the Manager for your personnel placement office in Dallas.

Here are just three reasons why I believe I am the effective young professional you seek:

- *I am a proven salesperson* with a demonstrated ability to "prospect" and produce sales. In my current job as a sales representative, I contact more than 150 business professionals per week and won my company's annual award for outstanding sales performance.

- *I enjoy traveling and am eager to assist in the growth of your business.* I am fortunate to have the natural energy, industry, and enthusiasm required to put in the long hours necessary for effective sales performance. I am also single (never married) with no dependents.

- *I understand the personnel placement business and enjoy training other individuals in the "habits of effective personnel specialists."* As you will see from my enclosed resume, I offer experience in both the temporary placement business and the permanent placement field.

You will find me, I am certain, a friendly, good-natured person whom you would be proud to call part of your "team." I would enjoy the opportunity to share my proven sales techniques and extensive knowledge with other junior sales professionals in a management and development position.

I hope you will call or write me soon to suggest a convenient time when we might meet to discuss your needs further and how I might serve them.

Yours sincerely,

Your Name

Employers are trying to identify the individual who wants the job they are filling. Don't be afraid to express your enthusiasm in the cover letter!

2. Talk to friends and relatives.
Don't be shy about telling your friends and relatives the kind of job you're looking for. Looking for the job you want involves using your network of contacts, so tell people what you're looking for. They may be able to make introductions and help set up interviews.

About 25% of all interviews are set up through "who you know," so don't ignore this approach.

3. Finally, and most importantly, use the "direct approach."
More than 50% of all job interviews are set up by the "direct approach." That means you actually mail, e-mail, or fax a resume and a cover letter to a company you think might be interesting to work for.

> The "direct approach" is a strategy in which you choose your next employer.

To whom do you write?
In general, you should write directly to the *exact name* of the person who would be hiring you: say, the vice-president of marketing or data processing. If you're in doubt about to whom to address the letter, address it to the president by name and he or she will make sure it gets forwarded to the right person within the company who has hiring authority in your area.

How do you find the names of potential employers?
You're not alone if you feel that the biggest problem in your job search is finding the right names at the companies you want to contact. But you can usually figure out the names of companies you want to approach by deciding first if your job hunt is primarily geography-driven or industry-driven.

In a **geography-driven job hunt,** you could select a list of, say, 50 companies you want to contact **by location** from the lists that the U.S. Chambers of Commerce publish yearly of their "major area employers." There are hundreds of local Chambers of Commerce across America, and most of them will have an 800 number which you can find through 1-800-555-1212. If you and your family think Atlanta, Dallas, Ft. Lauderdale, and Virginia Beach might be nice places to live, for example, you could contact the Chamber of Commerce in those cities and ask how you can obtain a copy of their list of major employers. Your nearest library will have the book which lists the addresses of all chambers.

In an **industry-driven job hunt,** and if you are willing to relocate, you will be identifying the companies which you find most attractive in the industry in which you want to work. When you select a list of companies to contact **by industry,** you can find the right person to write and the address of firms by industrial category in *Standard and Poor's, Moody's,* and other excellent books in public libraries. Many Web sites also provide contact information.

Many people feel it's a good investment to actually call the company to either find out or double-check the name of the person to whom they want to send a resume and cover letter. It's important to do as much as you feasibly can to assure that the letter gets to the right person in the company.

On-line research will be the best way for many people to locate organizations to which they wish to send their resume. It is outside the scope of this book to teach Internet research skills, but librarians are often useful in this area.

What's the correct way to follow up on a resume you send?
There is a polite way to be aggressively interested in a company during your job hunt. It is ideal to end the cover letter accompanying your resume by saying, "I hope you'll welcome my call next week when I try to arrange a brief meeting at your convenience to discuss your current and future needs and how I might serve them." Keep it low key, and just ask for a "brief meeting," not an interview. Employers want people who show a determined interest in working with them, so don't be shy about following up on the resume and cover letter you've mailed.

STEP THREE: Preparing for Interviews

But a resume and cover letter by themselves can't get you the job you want. You need to "prep" yourself before the interview. Step Three in your job campaign is "Preparing for Interviews." First, let's look at interviewing from the hiring organization's point of view.

What are the biggest "turnoffs" for potential employers?
One of the ways to help yourself perform well at an interview is to look at the main reasons why organizations *don't* hire the people they interview, according to those who do the interviewing.

Notice that "lack of appropriate background" (or lack of experience) is the *last* reason for not being offered the job.

The 14 Most Common Reasons Job Hunters Are Not Offered Jobs (according to the companies who do the interviewing and hiring):

1. Low level of accomplishment
2. Poor attitude, lack of self-confidence
3. Lack of goals/objectives
4. Lack of enthusiasm
5. Lack of interest in the company's business
6. Inability to sell or express yourself
7. Unrealistic salary demands
8. Poor appearance
9. Lack of maturity, no leadership potential
10. Lack of extracurricular activities
11. Lack of preparation for the interview, no knowledge about company
12. Objecting to travel
13. Excessive interest in security and benefits
14. Inappropriate background

It pays to be aware of the 14 most common pitfalls for job hunters.

Department of Labor studies have proven that smart, "prepared" job hunters can increase their beginning salary while getting a job in *half* the time it normally takes. (4½ months is the average national length of a job search.) Here, from PREP, are some questions that can prepare you to find a job faster.

Are you in the "right" frame of mind?
It seems unfair that we have to look for a job just when we're lowest in morale. Don't worry *too* much if you're nervous before interviews. You're supposed to be a little nervous, especially if the job means a lot to you. But the best way to kill unnecessary

fears about job hunting is through 1) making sure you have a great resume and 2) preparing yourself for the interview. Here are three main areas you need to think about before each interview.

Do you know what the company does?
Don't walk into an interview giving the impression that, "If this is Tuesday, this must be General Motors."

> Research the company before you go to interviews.

Find out before the interview what the company's main product or service is. Where is the company heading? Is it in a "growth" or declining industry? (Answers to these questions may influence whether or not you want to work there!)

Information about what the company does is in annual reports, in newspaper and magazine articles, and on the Internet. If you're not yet skilled at Internet research, just visit your nearest library and ask the reference librarian to guide you to printed materials on the company.

Do you know what you want to do for the company?
Before the interview, try to decide how you see yourself fitting into the company. Remember, "lack of exact background" the company wants is usually the last reason people are not offered jobs.

Understand before you go to each interview that the burden will be on you to "sell" the interviewer on why you're the best person for the job and the company.

How will you answer the critical interview questions?
Put yourself in the interviewer's position and think about the questions you're most likely to be asked. Here are some of the most commonly asked interview questions:

> Anticipate the questions you will be asked at the interview, and prepare your responses in advance.

Q: *"What are your greatest strengths?"*
A: Don't say you've never thought about it! Go into an interview knowing the three main impressions you want to leave about yourself, such as "I'm hard-working, loyal, and an imaginative cost-cutter."

Q: *"What are your greatest weaknesses?"*
A: Don't confess that you're lazy or have trouble meeting deadlines! Confessing that you tend to be a "workaholic" or "tend to be a perfectionist and sometimes get frustrated when others don't share my high standards" will make your prospective employer see a "weakness" that he likes. Name a weakness that your interviewer will perceive as a strength.

Q: *"What are your long-range goals?"*
A: If you're interviewing with Microsoft, don't say you want to work for IBM in five years! Say your long-range goal is to be *with* the company, contributing to its goals and success.

Q: *"What motivates you to do your best work?"*
A: Don't get dollar signs in your eyes here! "A challenge" is not a bad answer, but it's a little cliched. Saying something like "troubleshooting" or "solving a tough problem" is more interesting and specific. Give an example if you can.

Q: "What do you know about this organization?"
A: Don't say you never heard of it until they asked you to the interview! Name an interesting, positive thing you learned about the company recently from your research. Remember, company executives can sometimes feel rather "maternal" about the company they serve. Don't get onto a negative area of the company if you can think of positive facts you can bring up. Of course, if you learned in your research that the company's sales seem to be taking a nose-dive, or that the company president is being prosecuted for taking bribes, you might politely ask your interviewer to tell you something that could help you better understand what you've been reading. Those are the kinds of company facts that can help you determine whether or not you want to work there.

> Go to an interview prepared to tell the company why it should hire you.

Q: "Why should I hire you?"
A: "I'm unemployed and available" is the wrong answer here! Get back to your strengths and say that you believe the organization could benefit by a loyal, hard-working cost-cutter like yourself.

In conclusion, you should decide in advance, before you go to the interview, how you will answer each of these commonly asked questions. Have some practice interviews with a friend to role-play and build your confidence.

STEP FOUR: Handling the Interview and Negotiating Salary

Now you're ready for Step Four: actually handling the interview successfully and effectively. Remember, the purpose of an interview is to get a job offer.

> A smile at an interview makes the employer perceive of you as intelligent!

Eight "do's" for the interview
According to leading U.S. companies, there are eight key areas in interviewing success. You can fail at an interview if you mishandle just one area.

1. **Do wear appropriate clothes.**
   You can never go wrong by wearing a suit to an interview.

2. **Do be well groomed.**
   Don't overlook the obvious things like having clean hair, clothes, and fingernails for the interview.

3. **Do give a firm handshake.**
   You'll have to shake hands twice in most interviews: first, before you sit down, and second, when you leave the interview. Limp handshakes turn most people off.

4. **Do smile and show a sense of humor.**
   Interviewers are looking for people who would be nice to work with, so don't be so somber that you don't smile. In fact, research shows that people who smile at interviews are perceived as more intelligent. So, smile!

5. **Do be enthusiastic.**
   Employers say they are "turned off" by lifeless, unenthusiastic job hunters who show no special interest in that company. The best way to show some enthusiasm for the employer's operation is to find out about the business beforehand.

6. **Do show you are flexible and adaptable.**
   An employer is looking for someone who can contribute to his organization in a flexible, adaptable way. No matter what skills and training you have, employers know every new employee must go through initiation and training on the company's turf. Certainly show pride in your past accomplishments in a specific, factual way ("I saved my last employer $50.00 a week by a new cost-cutting measure I developed"). But don't come across as though there's nothing about the job you couldn't easily handle.

7. **Do ask intelligent questions about the employer's business.**
   An employer is hiring someone because of certain business needs. Show interest in those needs. Asking questions to get a better idea of the employer's needs will help you "stand out" from other candidates interviewing for the job.

8. **Do "take charge" when the interviewer "falls down" on the job.**
   Go into every interview knowing the three or four points about yourself you want the interviewer to remember. And be prepared to take an active part in leading the discussion if the interviewer's "canned approach" does not permit you to display your "strong suit." You can't always depend on the interviewer's asking you the "right" questions so you can stress your strengths and accomplishments.

> Employers are seeking people with good attitudes whom they can train and coach to do things their way.

An important "don't": Don't ask questions about salary or benefits at the first interview.
Employers don't take warmly to people who look at their organization as just a place to satisfy salary and benefit needs. Don't risk making a negative impression by appearing greedy or self-serving. The place to discuss salary and benefits is normally at the second interview, and the employer will bring it up. Then you can ask questions without appearing excessively interested in what the organization can do for you.

Now…negotiating your salary
Even if an ad requests that you communicate your "salary requirement" or "salary history," you should avoid providing those numbers in your initial cover letter. You can usually say something like this: "I would be delighted to discuss the private details of my salary history with you in person."

Once you're at the interview, you must avoid even appearing *interested* in salary before you are offered the job. Make sure you've "sold" yourself before talking salary. First show you're the "best fit" for the employer and then you'll be in a stronger position from which to negotiate salary. **Never** bring up the subject of salary yourself. Employers say there's no way you can avoid looking greedy if you bring up the issue of salary and benefits before the company has identified you as its "best fit."

> Don't appear excessively interested in salary and benefits at the interview.

Interviewers sometimes throw out a salary figure at the first interview to see if you'll accept it. You may not want to commit yourself if you think you will be able to negotiate a better deal later on. Get back to finding out more about the job. This lets the interviewer know you're interested primarily in the job and not the salary.

When the organization brings up salary, it may say something like this: "Well, Mary, we think you'd make a good candidate for this job. What kind of salary are we talking about?" You may not want to name a number here, either. Give the ball back to the interviewer. Act as though you hadn't given the subject of salary much thought and respond something like this: "Ah, Mr. Jones, I wonder if you'd be kind enough to tell me what salary you had in mind when you advertised the job?" Or … "What is the range you have in mind?"

Don't worry, if the interviewer names a figure that you think is too low, you can say so without turning down the job or locking yourself into a rigid position. The point here is to negotiate for yourself as well as you can. You might reply to a number named by the interviewer that you think is low by saying something like this: "Well, Mr. Lee, the job interests me very much, and I think I'd certainly enjoy working with you. But, frankly, I was thinking of something a little higher than that." That leaves the ball in your interviewer's court again, and you haven't turned down the job either, in case it turns out that the interviewer can't increase the offer and you still want the job.

Salary negotiation can be tricky.

Last, send a follow-up letter.
Mail, e-mail, or fax a letter right after the interview telling your interviewer you enjoyed the meeting and are certain (if you are) that you are the "best fit" for the job. The people interviewing you will probably have an attitude described as either "professionally loyal" to their companies, or "maternal and proprietary" if the interviewer also owns the company. In either case, they are looking for people who want to work for *that* company in particular. The follow-up letter you send might be just the deciding factor in your favor if the employer is trying to choose between you and someone else. You will see an example of a follow-up letter on page 16.

A follow-up letter can help the employer choose between you and another qualified candidate.

A cover letter is an essential part of a job hunt or career change.
Many people are aware of the importance of having a great resume, but most people in a job hunt don't realize just how important a cover letter can be. The purpose of the cover letter, sometimes called a **"letter of interest,"** is to introduce your resume to prospective employers. The cover letter is often the critical ingredient in a job hunt because the cover letter allows you to say a lot of things that just don't "fit" on the resume. For example, you can emphasize your commitment to a new field and stress your related talents. The cover letter also gives you a chance to stress outstanding character and personal values. On the next two pages you will see examples of very effective cover letters.

A cover letter is an essential part of a career change.

Please do not attempt to implement a career change without a cover letter such as the ones you see in Part Two of this book. A cover letter is the first impression of you, and you can influence the way an employer views you by the language and style of your letter.

Special help for those in career change
We want to emphasize again that, especially in a career change, the cover letter is very important and can help you "build a bridge" to a new career. A creative and appealing cover letter can begin the process of encouraging the potential employer to imagine you in an industry other than the one in which you have worked.

As a special help to those in career change, there are resumes and cover letters included in this book which show valuable techniques and tips you should use when changing fields or industries. The resumes and cover letters of career changers are identified in the table of contents as "Career Change" and you will see the "Career Change" label on cover letters in Part Two where the individuals are changing careers.

Looking Closer: The ANATOMY OF A COVER LETTER

Addressing the Cover Letter: Get the exact name of the person to whom you are writing. This makes your approach personal.

First Paragraph: This explains why you are writing.

Second Paragraph: You have a chance to talk about whatever you feel is your most distinguishing feature.

Third Paragraph: You bring up your next most distinguishing qualities and try to sell yourself.

Fourth Paragraph: Here you have another opportunity to reveal qualities or achievements which will impress your future employer.

Final Paragraph: She asks the employer to contact her. Make sure your reader knows what the "next step" is.

Alternate Final Paragraph: It's more aggressive (but not too aggressive) to let the employer know that you will be calling him or her. Don't be afraid to be persistent. Employers are looking for people who know what they want to do.

Date

Exact Name of Person
Title or Position
Name of Company
Address (no., street)
Address (city, state, zip)

Dear Exact Name of Person: (or Dear Sir or Madam if answering a blind ad)

    I would appreciate an opportunity to talk with you soon about how I could contribute to your organization through my versatile skills related to human resources and personnel administration as well as management and budget analysis.

    Although I live in Evansville with my husband (we are recently married), I currently work for the city of Muncie in its Human Resources Department. Even though I thoroughly enjoy my job and the people with whom I work, I am seeking an employer close to Evansville that can use my exceptionally strong human resources, public relations, budgeting, and finance skills.

    My current job was considered a lateral promotion into the human resources field from the finance and budgeting area, where I previously worked. In the city of Muncie's Budget Office, I played a key role in numerous cost-reduction programs which are saving the city thousands of dollars. I made vital input into difficult resourcing decisions and cost-benefit analyses related to matters such as whether to buy or rent uniforms, how to manage the maintenance of a fleet of vehicles, and other similar issues. I am skilled in thinking about costs in creative and resourceful ways, and I believe my thrifty approach to problem-solving and practical cost-cutting style could benefit any organization.

    I am a versatile and adaptable person who is known for my professionalism and high personal standards as well as for my reliability and patience. A second-generation native of Evansville, I can offer outstanding personal and professional references from academic, government, and business professionals throughout the Evansville area. I am a loyal person by nature, and I am attempting to find an organization that I can grow with and contribute to over the long range. I feel certain you would find me to be a very capable person who could become a valuable addition to your team.

    I hope you will welcome my call soon to arrange a brief meeting at your convenience to discuss your current and future needs and how I might serve them. Thank you in advance for your time.

                                                   Sincerely yours,

                                                   Amy June Bard-Wilkes

Alternate Final Paragraph:
    I hope you will contact me soon to arrange a brief meeting at your convenience to discuss your current and future needs and how I might serve them. Thank you in advance for your time.

Date

Exact Name of Person
Exact Title
Exact Name of Company
Address
City, State, Zip

Dear Exact Name of Person: (or Dear Sir or Madam if answering a blind ad)

    With the enclosed resume, I would like to make you aware of my experience in office administration and customer service as well as in the management of services related to human resources and personnel administration.

    In my current job as Personnel Coordinator, I manage 25 professionals who perform recruiting, hiring, and contract negotiations with client organizations who utilize Manpower Temporaries to find employees. Known for my tact and discretion, I maintain personnel files and prepare reports on turnover, absenteeism, and productivity. I am proud of the role I have played in enriching numerous organizations through the quality employees which Manpower has provided, and numerous clients have praised my dedicated efforts and organizational skills.

    In all of my jobs I have expertly utilized a computer with numerous software applications in order to maintain databases, write reports, compile statistics, and track data. I am highly computer literate and offer an ability to rapidly master new programs.

    In my previous job at Star Companies, I excelled in a "track record" of advancement to increasing responsibilities within a diversified corporate environment. I pride myself on my strong customer service orientation, and I believe my professional customer service attitude is inspired by my sincere desire to help others. I have discovered that my attention to detail and organizational skills have helped me be of service to numerous people on many occasions.

    I would like to become a part of an organization that can use a hard-working and disciplined young professional who aims for excellence in all I do. If you can use my considerable skills and talents, please contact me to suggest a time when we might meet to discuss your needs and how I might serve them. Thank you in advance for your time.

                                                Yours sincerely,

                                              Barbara L. Polaski

CC: Jason Phelps

Semi-blocked Letter

Date
Three blank spaces

Address

Salutation
One blank space

Body

One blank space

Signature

cc: Indicates you are sending a copy of the letter to someone

Date

Exact Name of Person
Title or Position
Name of Company
Address (number and street)
Address (city, state, and zip)

Follow-up Letter

A great follow-up letter can motivate the employer to make the job offer, and the salary offer may be influenced by the style and tone of your follow-up letter, too!

Dear Exact Name:

I am writing to express my appreciation for the time you spent with me on 9 December, and I want to let you know that I am sincerely interested in the position of Controller which you described.

I feel confident that I could skillfully interact with your 60-person work force in order to obtain the information we need to assure expert controllership of your diversified interests, and I would cheerfully travel as your needs require. I want you to know, too, that I would not consider relocating to Salt Lake City to be a hardship! It is certainly one of the most beautiful areas I have ever seen.

As you described to me what you are looking for in a controller, I had a sense of "déjà vu" because my current boss was in a similar position when I went to work for him. He needed someone to come in and be his "right arm" and take on an increasing amount of his management responsibilities so that he could be freed up to do other things. I have played a key role in the growth and profitability of his multi-unit business, and he has come to depend on my sound financial and business advice as much as my day-to-day management skills. Since Christmas is the busiest time of the year in the restaurant business, I feel that I could not leave him during that time. I could certainly make myself available by mid-January.

It would be a pleasure to work for a successful individual such as yourself, and I feel I could contribute significantly to your construction business not only through my accounting and business background but also through my strong qualities of loyalty, reliability, and trustworthiness. I am confident that I could learn Quick Books rapidly, and I would welcome being trained to do things your way.

Yours sincerely,

Jacob Evangelisto

PART TWO
REAL-RESUMES FOR HUMAN RESOURCES & PERSONNEL JOBS

In this section, you will find resumes and cover letters of human resources and personnel professionals—and of people who want to work in those fields. How do they differ from other job hunters? Why should there be a book dedicated to people seeking jobs in these areas? Based on more than 20 years of experience in working with job hunters, this editor is convinced that resumes and cover letters which "speak the lingo" of the field you wish to enter will communicate more effectively than language which is not industry specific. This book is designed to help people (1) who are seeking to prepare their own resumes and (2) who wish to use as models "real" resumes of individuals who have successfully launched careers in the human resources and personnel field or who have advanced in the field. You will see a wide range of experience levels reflected in the resumes in this book. Some of the resumes and cover letters were used by individuals seeking to enter the field; others were used successfully by senior professionals to advance in the field.

Newcomers to an industry sometimes have advantages over more experienced professionals. In a job hunt, junior professionals can have an advantage over their more experienced counterparts. Prospective employers often view the less experienced workers as "more trainable" and "more coachable" than their seniors. This means that the mature professional who has already excelled in a first career can, with credibility, "change careers" and transfer skills to other industries.

Newcomers to the field may have disadvantages compared to their seniors. Almost by definition, the inexperienced professional—the young person who has recently earned a college degree, or the individual who has recently received certifications respected by the industry—is less tested and less experienced than senior managers, so the resume and cover letter of the inexperienced professional may often have to "sell" his or her potential to do something he or she has never done before. Lack of experience in the field she wants to enter can be a stumbling block to the junior manager, but remember that many employers believe that someone who has excelled in anything—academics, for example—can excel in many other fields.

Some advice to inexperienced professionals...
If senior professionals could give junior professionals a piece of advice about careers, here's what they would say: Manage your career and don't stumble from job to job in an incoherent pattern. Try to find work that interests you, and then identify prosperous industries which need work performed of the type you want to do. Learn early in your working life that a great resume and cover letter can blow doors open for you and help you maximize your salary.

Special help for career changers...
For those changing careers, you will find useful the resumes and cover letters marked "Career Change" on the following pages. Consult the Table of Contents for page numbers showing career changers.

> Human resources and personnel professionals might be said to "talk funny." They talk in lingo specific to their field, and you will find helpful examples throughout this book.

Date

Exact Name of Person
Title or Position
Name of Company
Address (no., street)
Address (city, state, zip)

ADMINISTRATIVE SERVICES MANAGER
for a public relations company

Dear Exact Name of Person (or Dear Sir or Madam if answering a blind ad):

I would appreciate an opportunity to talk with you soon about how I could contribute to your organization through my reputation as a quick learner who is known for handling pressure, applying creativity to find more productive operational methods, and displaying a strong human resources orientation.

As you will see from my resume, I am now a Personnel and Administrative Services Manager at Kinnard Public Relations. After being recruited for this position, I spent several months helping this new company organize its personnel and administrative functions. After bringing operations from chaos to a high state of productivity, I was promoted to manage the continued success of this department. I have been honored with the opportunity to oversee the Human Resources Management portion of a unit self-assessment study based on the criteria from the Malcolm Baldridge Award for Quality.

In a previous position as Assistant Personnel Manager, I applied my organizational skills while ably handling programs including newcomers' orientation and various benefits programs. I rewrote many personnel procedures for this company which became the standard. I gained experience in various aspects of human relations and personnel administration including counseling personnel for advanced training programs and developing/delivering employee presentations.

I would enjoy the opportunity to meet with you and talk about how my enthusiasm, creativity, and talents could be applied to ensure the continuing productivity of your organization, too.

I hope you will welcome my call soon to arrange a brief meeting at your convenience to discuss your current and future needs and how I might serve them. Thank you in advance for your time.

Sincerely yours,

Jana Burke-White

Alternate last paragraph:
I hope you will call or write me soon to suggest a time convenient for us to meet and discuss your current and future needs and how I might serve them. Thank you in advance for your time.

JANA BURKE-WHITE

1110½ Hay Street, Fayetteville, NC 28305 • preppub@aol.com • (910) 483-6611

OBJECTIVE To apply my experience in personnel/human resources management and public relations to an organization that will benefit from my superb organizational and planning abilities as well as my customer-service and problem-solving skills.

EXPERIENCE **PERSONNEL AND ADMINISTRATIVE SERVICES MANAGER.** Kinnard Public Relations, Dayton, OH (2003-present). After several months of organizing and implementing the administrative functions for a newly founded office of this national public relations company, created "from scratch" and then managed all personnel programs. Provide administrative support and advice to a chief executive; trained and supervise two employees.
- Determined that many employees were being inadequately evaluated and redesigned the system to ensure all personnel were being fairly evaluated by their direct supervisor.
- Earned nomination for "Personnel Manager of the Year" and numerous awards for exceptional performance.

ASSISTANT PERSONNEL MANAGER. Bailey Manufacturing, Cincinnati, OH (2000-2002). Applied my organizational skills while ably handling programs including a newcomers' orientation and vacation record keeping and verification.
- Evaluated the effectiveness of each program, made improvements, and rewrote standard operating procedures guidelines to help smooth training for new personnel.
- Reorganized the newcomer orientation program so that it provided necessary information in an interesting and informative manner, but in a shorter period of time.

PUBLIC RELATIONS SPECIALIST. Jones Public Relations Agency, Dayton, OH (1999-00). Upon college graduation, was recruited for this position. Broadened my knowledge of public relations activities while planning and coordinating visits of clients.
- Became known for my ability to think on my feet and consistently be able to act with maturity and grace under pressure.
- Honed my communication skills preparing scripts and presenting presentations.
- Developed public relations campaigns for a manufacturing business, a hospital, and a medical practice.

INFORMATION SERVICES SPECIALIST. Lyons Advertising, Inc., Dayton, OH (1995-99). Excelled in providing information both on the phone and in writing about this busy advertising agency. Planned, coordinated, and conducted presentations to new and prospective clients.

SALES CLERK. Dewey's Department Store, Dayton, OH (1993-94). Worked in this job after high school. Learned how to deal with the public in a courteous and gracious manner.
- Worked in this position while earning my associate's degree at night.

EDUCATION & TRAINING **A.A., Personnel Administration**, Dayton Community College, Dayton, OH, September 1999. Excelled in more than 600 hours of training in the areas of Total Quality Management, instruction techniques, information systems management, and personnel management.

COMPUTER SKILLS Offer experience with a variety of computer software including Windows, Word, Word Perfect, and various other software.

PERSONAL Contribute to professional organization and have held elected offices including president, treasurer, and secretary.

CAREER CHANGE

Date

Exact Name of Person
Type of position
Name of Company
Address (no., street)
Address (city, state, zip)

ASSISTANT PERSONNEL SUPERVISOR

for Kitchen Equipment, Inc., a major kitchen equipment distributor

Dear Exact Name of Person (or Dear Sir or Madam if answering a blind ad):

I would appreciate an opportunity to talk with you soon about how I could contribute to your organization through my proven management skills and human resources education. As you will see from my resume, I have recently earned a master's degree in Human Resources from the University of California at Santa Barbara. I am interested in applying my human resources knowledge within an organization that use an experienced manager.

Currently I am serving as Assistant Personnel Supervisor for a kitchen equipment distributor with 1250 employees where I am responsible for all aspects of personnel administration. I have excelled in initiating new projects, such as a newsletter for employees, and I have been praised for my "foresight, keen analytical mind, and enthusiastic leadership."

In previous positions, I served in several challenging and unique leadership positions in the law enforcement community. As the captain of a police force in Santa Barbara, I supervised a work force that included 14 officers and 42 other personnel while overseeing a fleet of 30 vehicles, over 100 weapons, a dining facility, and over 80 pieces of communications equipment totaling $4.5 million with zero losses.

I feel certain you will find me to be a congenial individual who enjoys working as part of a highly professional team and who is known for high levels of personal initiative, reliability, and integrity. I can provide outstanding references upon request.

I hope you will call or write me soon to suggest a time that is convenient for both of us to meet and discuss your current and future needs and how I might serve them. Thank you in advance for your time.

Sincerely yours,

Donovan Bright

DONOVAN BRIGHT

1110½ Hay Street, Fayetteville, NC 28305 • preppub@aol.com • (910) 483-6611

OBJECTIVE   I want to contribute to an organization that can use an experienced manager with a state-of-the-art education related to human resources.

EDUCATION   **M.A.** in Human Resources, Foothill College, Los Altos, CA, 2003.
B.S. in Political Science, Vincennes University, Vincennes, IN, 1996.

LANGUAGE   Proficient in Spanish

EXPERIENCE   **ASSISTANT PERSONNEL SUPERVISOR.** Kitchen Equipment, Inc., Glendale, CA (2003-present). Direct all aspects of personnel management and administrative support for a major kitchen equipment distributor with 1250 employees.
- Edit and publish a newsletter designed to boost morale and instill pride in employees.
- Directly supervise three mid-level managers and three junior support employees.
- Oversee all aspects of personnel administration including financial and payroll administration, the provision of legal and counseling services, and the administration of job assignments and promotions.

DEPARTMENT MANAGER. Major Manufacturing, San Jacinto, CA (2000-02). Was praised in a formal evaluation for the "foresight, keen analytical mind, and enthusiastic leadership" I displayed in a job which required me to demonstrate m expertise in personnel management while supporting fast-paced production. Accounted for a half million-dollar inventory.
- Supervised nine mid-level managers and five junior employees.

POLICE CAPTAIN. Santa Barbara, CA (1998-99). After leaving the military as a Major, joined the police force of the City of Santa Barbara. Was specially selected to manage a work force that included 14 officers and 42 other personnel while overseeing a fleet of 30 vehicles, 80 pieces of communications equipment, and 100 weapons totaling $4.5 million with zero losses.
- Oversaw the training of personnel in 18 separate police/support specialties.
- Supervised the management of a dining facility serving 300 meals daily to 700 people.
- On a special assignment, played a key role in establishing and operating six migrant camps with a population of more than 12,000 Mexicans.
- Developed camp physical security and civil disturbance plan for six migrant camps.

Highlights of prior military experience:
OPERATIONS & TRAINING OFFICER. U.S. Army, Ft. Bragg, NC (1992-97). In three separate assignments at the world's largest U.S. military base, provided leadership in the areas of operations management and training.
- Provided military police combat support during the war in the Middle East.

CHIEF OF POLICE OPERATIONS. U.S. Army, Germany (1990-92). Functioned as the police chief in an international community; enforced military laws and regulations, supported counterterrorist activities, prevented and investigated crimes, apprehended and incarcerated offenders, and oversaw the security of buildings, people, equipment, and documents.
- Supervised 21 military and 21 civilian personnel; administered a budget of $100,000.
- Established innovative procedures for guard posts, police patrols, and vehicle registrations; acquired new computers which greatly enhanced police response capability.

PERSONAL   Won numerous awards and medals for exceptional performance. Take great pride in the fact that I have served my country with distinction and achieved the rank of Major.

Date

Exact Name of Person
Title or Position
Name of Company
Address (no., street)
Address (city, state, zip)

ASSISTANT PERSONNEL DEPARTMENT SUPERVISOR

for Sprint, Inc., a major telecommunications company

Dear Exact Name of Person (or Dear Sir or Madam if answering a blind ad):

I would appreciate an opportunity to talk with you soon about how I could contribute to your organization through my experience related to personnel and administrative operations as well as through my reputation for thoroughness, honesty, and dedication.

As you will see by my enclosed resume, during my approximately eight years with the Sprint organization, I became quite successful in stepping into substandard operations and finding ways to transform them into top-notch ones. Very persistent and unwilling to accept substandard performance from myself or my subordinates, I am dedicated to excellence.

At personnel administration support centers in locations including NJ, TN, TX, Fl, GA, and CA, I was handpicked to take on the challenging jobs and excelled in roles normally reserved for more experienced and higher-ranking managers.

My education has included a B.S. degree in Business Administration, and my professional training emphasized leadership development as well as courses in personnel administration procedures, total quality management, technical computer operations, and logistics.

One of my greatest strengths is my ability to guide others to exceed expected standards through my example and motivational skills. I am a responsible, dependable professional with a strong work ethic and reputation for integrity.

I hope you will welcome my call soon to arrange a brief meeting at your convenience to discuss your current and future needs and how I might serve them. Thank you in advance for your time.

Sincerely yours,

Randy S. Topaz

Alternate last paragraph:
I hope you will call or write me soon to suggest a time convenient for us to meet and discuss your current and future needs and how I might serve them. Thank you in advance for your time.

RANDY S. TOPAZ

1110½ Hay Street, Fayetteville, NC 28305 • preppub@aol.com • (910) 483-6611

OBJECTIVE To apply my superior organizational and managerial skills to a business that can benefit from my experience related to personnel and administrative operations as well as through my reputation as a flexible professional with a strong work ethic.

EXPERIENCE *Built a reputation as a professional who could be counted on to take over substandard operations and turn them into models of efficiency, Sprint, Inc.:*
2003-present: ASSISTANT PERSONNEL DEPARTMENT SUPERVISOR. Lavergne, TN. Handpicked ahead of 13 others for a position usually reserved for a more experienced supervisor, provided support for a 556-person organization and supervised 15 people.
- Coordinated maintenance and operation of $150,000 in automation equipment.
- Transformed a poorly functioning personnel center into one maintaining a 97% accuracy rate — far exceeding the standard of 90% and the previous 72% rating.
- Frequently praised for my ability to counsel employees and serve as an example for them, motivated employees to exceed set standards.
- Managed functions including promotions, performance reports for employees at all levels, publications, and personnel availability and status figures.
- Set up regular cross-training and skills enhancement programs which resulted in continually high quality of service and levels of productivity.
- Achieved the highest skill test scores in the parent organization and finished in the top 13% of all PAC supervisors in the entire Southeast.

2000-2003: ASSISTANT PERSONNEL CENTER MANAGER. Chesterfield, NJ. Was promoted on the basis of my performance in supervising five employees involved in processing personnel actions and administrative support functions for a 556-person organization.
- Received a 100% error-free rating of personnel actions during a major inspection.
- Reorganized the center's physical layout in order to maximize working space.

1998-1999: PERSONNEL CENTER SUPERVISOR. Dallas, TX. Provided advice and supervision for a wide range of administrative actions ranging from performance reports, to financial support, to disciplinary actions.
- Was cited for achieving an error-free and on-time rate for all personnel documents.

1996-1997: SENIOR ADMINISTRATIVE SPECIALIST. Lakeland, FL. Trained and supervised three people while handling the details of inputting and controlling data for a headquarters operation.
- Prepared monthly statistical reports for executives and briefed them on personnel strength and projected shortages in specific career fields.
- Was cited for professionalism and willingness to give time to develop my subordinates.
- Received praise during a major audit for my expertise in training and building a team of qualified workers and instilling pride in their performance.
- Revamped the operating procedures for improved efficiency and productivity.

EDUCATION **Bachelor of Science (B.S.)**, Business Administration, Pierce College, Lakewood, WA, 1996. Excelled in numerous executive development courses and programs sponsored by Sprint emphasizing personnel administrative procedures, total quality management, technical computer operations, and logistics.

PERSONAL Persistent and dedicated. Handle stress, pressure, and deadlines well. Can be counted on to come up with a solution and make it work! Willing to relocate.

Date

Exact Name of Person
Title or Position
Name of Company
Address (number and street)
Address (city, state, and zip)

ASSISTANT PERSONNEL MANAGER

for Walgreen Stores

Dear Exact Name of Person: (or Dear Sir or Madam if answering a blind ad)

Can you use a hard-working and energetic young professional who offers outstanding office operations and management skills with an especially strong background in customer service and data entry?

As you will see by my enclosed resume, I most recently applied my abilities in the administrative offices of the Walgreen Store's location in Tampa, FL. As the Assistant Personnel Manager, I have played a role in setting up the procedures for and organizing the personnel department. Currently I oversee the management of personnel records, time cards, and scheduling for around 150 employees with direct supervision over six people.

In earlier jobs, I was cited for my customer service and managerial abilities and placed in positions of responsibility usually reserved for older, more experienced managers. For instance, at The Lounge of the Hilton Hotel in downtown Savannah, GA, I directed a staff of 18 people at one of the hotel's popular restaurants. In a subsequent job with the Environmental Protection Agency (EPA), I used state-of-the-art automated equipment to maintain personnel records for over 15,000 people.

I feel that I offer exceptional organizational, motivational, and communication skills. With a reputation as a fast learner, I am proficient in using computer systems and rapidly master new software.

I hope you will welcome my call soon to arrange a brief meeting at your convenience to discuss your current and future needs and how I might serve them. Thank you in advance for your time.

Sincerely yours,

Kimberly Sue Addison

Alternate last paragraph:
I hope you will call or write me soon to suggest a time convenient for us to meet and discuss your current and future needs and how I might serve them. Thank you in advance for your time.

KIMBERLY SUE ADDISON

1110½ Hay Street, Fayetteville, NC 28305   •   preppub@aol.com   •   (910) 483-6611

OBJECTIVE   To contribute through my reputation as a hard-working, enthusiastic, and energetic young professional with a broad base of experience related to data entry, computer operations, personnel management, and customer service.

COMPUTERS   Proficient with Power Point, Access, Excel, and WordPerfect using Windows

EXPERIENCE   **ASSISTANT PERSONNEL MANAGER.** Walgreen Stores, Tampa, FL (2003-present). Was cited for my planning and organizational skills as well as my detail orientation while contributing to the smooth operation of internal personnel activities and providing excellent customer service for this business in its first year in this city.
- Directly supervise six people; maintain personnel records for over 150 employees along with scheduling, timekeeping, and preparing the payroll.
- Contribute to the store's reputation for customer service by seeing that rain checks were issued promptly when advertised merchandise became available and while assisting with check cashing.
- Played an important role in the establishment of personnel department organization and setup.
- Learned ISIS and HOST computer systems which are specialized systems with pricing, e-Mail, and merchandising information for the retail industry.

ADMINISTRATIVE ASSISTANT. Environmental Protection Agency, Tampa, FL (2000-02). Fine-tuned my general office, administrative, and customer service skills while handling dual roles as an Administrative Assistant and **Personnel Information Systems Management Specialist** in a department maintaining personnel records for more than 15,000 people.
- Received, analyzed, and entered data into a data base at a personnel headquarters.
- Was singled out for my exceptional public relations skills demonstrated while assisting customers with various needs.
- Applied writing, proofreading, and typing/word processing abilities while preparing correspondence, documentation to explain awards, and narratives for personnel reports.

ASSISTANT MANAGER. The Lounge of the Hilton Hotels, Savannah, GA (1999-00). Was hired at the age of 20 to manage a staff of 18 people and a wide range of daily activities in the restaurant of a major downtown hotel.
- Learned what to look for and how to investigate any overages or shortages in cash drawers or in stock and supply levels. Trained, scheduled, and supervised employees.

ASSISTANT MANAGER. McDonalds, Detroit, MI (1997-98). Originally hired as a Cashier, was soon promoted on the basis of my maturity and ability to lead others and contribute to the sense of team work that is necessary in the fast-paced environment of fast food.
- Supervised nine people while overseeing day-to-day activities including an emphasis on quick, friendly customer service.

EDUCATION   Completed three years of college course work in Biology.
Excelled in approximately 724 hours of professional development training in the areas of computer systems in information analysis and personnel information systems management.

PERSONAL   Am a quick learner who strongly believes in always giving 100%. Have an outgoing personality and well-developed motivational abilities. Excellent references on request.

CAREER CHANGE

Date

Exact Name of Person
Exact Title or Position
Company Name
Company Address (street and number)
Company Address (city, state, and zip)

ASSISTANT PERSONNEL SUPERVISOR
for the Department of Energy

Dear Exact Name (or Dear Sir or Madam if answering a blind ad):

With the enclosed resume, I would like to express my interest in receiving consideration for employment with your organization.

From my enclosed resume, you will see that I am an articulate and highly self-motivated young professional with a strong background in human resources and administrative services and support. I offer a proven ability to easily master new ideas and procedures. I am currently completing a bachelor's degree in Business Administration in my spare time.

Currently serving in the position of Assistant Personnel Administration Center Supervisor at the Department of Energy, I have demonstrated leadership abilities and a level of initiative which led to my selection for management positions in the personnel administrative services area. In my most recent assignment, I became the "internal expert" on a new software system which provides automated support for human services administration for 3,000 people.

If you can use an adaptable professional with strong management and problem-solving skills, I hope you will contact me to suggest a time when we might meet to discuss your needs. I can provide excellent personal and professional references.

Sincerely,

Pedro Jacinto

PEDRO JACINTO

1110½ Hay Street, Fayetteville, NC 28305 • preppub@aol.com • (910) 483-6611

OBJECTIVE	To offer experience and education related to management and human resources to an organization that can use a young professional with a special talent for planning and prioritizing activities along with strong computer operations skills.
EDUCATION & TRAINING	Completing B.A. in **Business Administration,** American University, Washington, DC. Received extensive training in leadership, personnel supervision, and administrative management.
SPECIAL KNOWLEDGE	**Languages:** Fully bilingual in English and Spanish. **Computers:** Proficient with Microsoft Excel, PowerPoint, and Word

EXPERIENCE

Received several awards while advancing in leadership roles in personnel administrative operations with the Department of Energy, Washington DC:

2003-present: ASSISTANT PERSONNEL SUPERVISOR. In a position usually held by a more experienced supervisor, provided support services for more than 3,000 people and became the "internal expert" on a new software system which provides automated support for human resources administration.

- Was strongly encouraged to remain in civil service and assured of continued rapid advancement; however, I have decided to seek employment in the private sector.
- Held the position as Acting Personnel Center (PAC) Supervisor for nearly one year while the search was conducted for my supervisor; subsequently trained my supervisor.
- Supervise six individuals; earned the respect of my superiors for my ability to motivate others to excel and for effectiveness in training, counseling, and supervising junior personnel.
- On my own initiative, dedicated long hours to ensuring the success of a program for personnel reporting which earned an impressive 100% accuracy rate.
- Was praised in official evaluations as having sound management and problem-solving skills. Provided leadership which led to a 100% pass rate for department personnel during regular audits.

2000-02: PERSONNEL ADMINISTRATIVE SPECIALIST. Excelled in providing timely and thorough customer service while processing a full range of personnel functions, benefits, performance evaluations, promotions, and awards.

- Stepped into a vacated leadership role and acted independently for a two-month period; was singled out for "meritorious professionalism."

1999: PROJECT LEADER. Was specially selected because of my people skills to staff a new office in California which was to study solar energy usage.

1996-98: CLERK. Consistently cited for my initiative and ability to deal with people, was chosen for the Project Leader position after working in the Personnel Department for two years. Earned respect and praise from my superiors for my performance.

Other experience: QUALITY CONTROL TECHNICIAN. Johnson & Andrews Architects, Colorado Springs, CO (1994-95). Applied strong organizational, planning, and computer operations skills while performing light auditing, data input, and administrative support for an architectural engineering company; utilized PowerPoint and Excel.

PERSONAL	Strong manager of time and scarce resources. Outstanding references.

CAREER CHANGE

Date

Exact Name of Person
Exact Title
Exact Name of Company
Address
City, State, Zip

CHIEF OF PERSONNEL MANAGEMENT
for the Department of the Army

Dear Exact Name of Person: (or Dear Sir or Madam if answering a blind ad):

I would appreciate an opportunity to talk with you soon about how I could contribute to your organization through my versatile experience and education as well as through my reputation as a bright, articulate, and energetic young professional.

As you will see from my enclosed resume, I am working for the Department of the Army where I have been handpicked for jobs in the finance and personnel administration field. As Chief of Personnel Management for a personnel and finance center serving 34 offices, I provide support for a wide range of operational areas including records management, computer applications, distribution support, and quality assurance. I was selected for this job on the basis of my performance as a supervisor in a finance and accounting center.

I earned both a B.S. degree in Business Administration and Certification as a Human Resources Assistant from Temple College, Temple, TX. While excelling in temporary positions with a hospital, management corporation, and government administrative center, I was aggressively recruited by the Department of the Army, where I have received extensive specialized training and advanced to jobs usually held by senior professionals.

Highly proficient with computers and with the ability to quickly master new software and applications, I offer a wide range of skills in professional office administration and operations. Although I am highly regarded and in line for advancement in civil service, I have decided to explore employment opportunities in the private sector.

If you can use a versatile and adaptable young professional with a reputation for integrity, dedication to excellence, and a positive, enthusiastic attitude, I hope you will write or call me soon to suggest a time when we might meet to discuss your needs and goals and how my background might serve them. I can provide outstanding references at the appropriate time.

Sincerely,

Myrna B. Coates

MYRNA B. COATES

1110½ Hay Street, Fayetteville, NC 28305 • preppub@aol.com • (910) 483-6611

OBJECTIVE To offer my versatility and diverse skills to an organization that can benefit from my experience and knowledge of human resources, office operations, and computer software as well as my reputation as a bright, articulate, and enthusiastic professional.

EDUCATION & TRAINING Earned the following degree and professional certifications, Temple College, Temple, TX:
Bachelor of Science degree in **Business Administration** with a concentration in Marketing awarded May 1993: minor in Speech Communication and Pre-Law.
Human Resources Specialist Certification awarded June 1999.
Aggressively recruited by the Department of the Army, was selected to receive specialized training:

Finance School – was selected as class leader	Accounting Specialist Course
Accounting Supervisor/Technician Course	Driver's Course
Defense Hazardous Material /Waste Handling Course	Emergency Lifesaving
The Defense Reutilization and Marketing System	Numerous computer courses

SPECIAL SKILLS Highly proficient with computers in both Windows and Macintosh environments; familiar with various systems and software including: Windows, Word, Excel, and PowerPoint.

EXPERIENCE *Am earning a reputation as a skilled professional, Department of the Army:*
CHIEF OF PERSONNEL MANAGEMENT. Baltimore, MD (2003-present). Handpicked for a position usually reserved for a senior professional, supervise 12 people while handling paperwork and compiling information for hundreds of people in a finance/personnel administration center.
- Coordinate the arrangements for a monthly management conference.
- Coordinate, plan, and conduct personnel assistance visits to 34 personnel offices.
- Provide administrative support for operational areas which include records management, computer applications, distribution and driving support, and suspense tracking.
- Earned Certificates of Appreciation for customer service excellence, preparing and presenting briefings, and preparing for successful inspections.

ACCOUNTING SPECIALIST and **SUPERVISOR.** Temple, TX (1999-01). Ensured timely and accurate processing of incoming and departing management personnel, supervisors, and employees in the Southwest division.
- Processed advance payments for relocation and travel expenses for senior executives.
- Daily coded pay documents to Defense Finance and Accounting Service (DFAS).
- Received an award in recognition of "dedication and attention to detail" which resulted in reducing travel voucher processing time to one day from three and for contributions which led to excellent results in technical proficiency inspections.
- Was recognized for contributing many hours of my own time to load new codes into an upgraded travel system and help establish standard operating procedures.
- Selected ahead of my peers to brief and process two general officers.

Gained experience in professional office environments in earlier temporary jobs:
STAFF ASSISTANT. Health Management Corporation, Philadelphia, PA (1998). Maintained case files while handling administrative and office support.
OFFICE MANAGER. National Oceanic and Atmospheric Administration, Silver Spring, MD (1994-97). Provided data input/formatting, proofreading, and editing support.

PERSONAL Was entrusted with a Secret security clearance. Am an American Red Cross volunteer and member of Alpha Kappa Alpha Sorority. Excellent references on request.

Date

Exact Name of Person
Title or Position
Name of Company
Address (no., street)
Address (city, state, zip)

CHIEF OF PERSONNEL

for Monsanto Chemical

Dear Exact Name of Person: (or Dear Sir or Madam if answering a blind ad)

I would appreciate an opportunity to talk with you soon about how I could contribute to your organization through my proven expertise in motivating, counseling, training, and supervising employees as well as through my planning and organizational skills.

During my career I have specialized in the areas of personnel and training program management.

In my current position as Chief of Personnel Administration and Training, I handle activities which include advising a chief executive, managing dining facilities serving 2,000 people, and counseling/training/supervising a staff of 50 managers providing training to 1,500 employees in all Monsanto plants across the country.

As you will see from my resume, my background is predominantly in the areas of personnel and training operations management. I am known for my ability to lead and motivate others and encourage them to discover their own strengths and make the most of them.

I hope you will welcome my call soon to arrange a brief meeting at your convenience to discuss your current and future needs and how I might serve them. Thank you in advance for your time.

Sincerely yours,

Tony W. Vitello

Alternate last paragraph:
I hope you will call or write soon to suggest a time convenient for us to meet and discuss your current and future needs and how I might serve them. Thank you in advance for your time.

TONY W. VITELLO

1110½ Hay Street, Fayetteville, NC 28305 • preppub@aol.com • (910) 483-6611

OBJECTIVE   To supply my outstanding motivational, training, managerial, and supervisory abilities to a business that can use a proven mature professional who offers a broad background of success in large-scale project planning and management.

EDUCATION   M.A. degree in **Personnel Management,** Point Park College, Pittsburgh, PA, 1994.
B.S. degree in **Public Administration**, Franklin University, Columbus, OH, 1990.

TRAINING   Extensive training in human relations, diversity planning, equal opportunity, benefits administration, and counseling sponsored by Proctor & Gamble, Monsanto Chemical, and Johnson & Johnson.

EXPERIENCE   **CHIEF OF PERSONNEL ADMINISTRATION AND TRAINING.** Monsanto Chemical, St. Louis, MO (2003-present). Reorganized operational procedures for the headquarters of this major chemical company and acted as the senior advisor to a chief executive on the status of training operations.
- Counsel, supervise, and train 50 managers conducting training programs for Monsanto plants across the country.
- Supervise management of a dining facility which serves three meals a day to as many as 2,000 people.
- Applied effective management techniques which reduced disciplinary problems among staff members by one-fifth.
- Developed several training programs for new employees.
- Revised several company policies relating to personnel functions.

SUPPORT SERVICES MANAGER. Proctor & Gamble, Cincinnati, OH (2000-02). Managed a diverse range of support services for 5,000 people, including supervision of both executive and employee dining rooms.
- Supervised 12 persons, including the employee benefits manager.
- Excelled in conducting training which resulted in more productive employees.
- Reorganized the benefits and compensation packages for employees which resulted in increased employee morale as well as financial savings for the company.

ASSISTANT SUPPORT SERVICES MANAGER. Proctor & Gamble, Cincinnati, OH (1997-99). Served in this position as senior advisor to a chief executive on all aspects of training.
- Developed a revised employee orientation presentation.
- Excelled in dealing with day-to-day personnel counseling and administration for this organization.

TRAINING OPERATIONS ADMINISTRATOR. Johnson & Johnson, Pittsburgh, PA (1994-96). Managed personnel training at headquarters and provided administrative support and record-keeping for three branches of this organization. Supervised a six-person staff.
- Planned and managed an annual performance evaluation program.
- Initiated and set up an automated recordkeeping system which was used throughout the parent organization and all company branches.

PERSONAL   Feel that my strongest abilities are in helping others and encouraging them to do their best. Offer a broad background in personnel management and training.

Date

Exact Name of Person
Title or Position
Name of Company
Address (no., street)
Address (city, state, zip)

DIRECTOR OF HUMAN RESOURCES
for Allied Capital, a Fortune 500 company

Dear Exact Name of Person: (or Dear Sir or Madam if answering a blind ad)

I would appreciate an opportunity to talk with you soon about how I could contribute to your organization through the management, analytical, problem-solving, and decision-making expertise I have refined during my career.

In every position I have held, I have been consistently evaluated as "one of the very best young managers I have ever worked with" by numerous executives who have been impressed with my performance and capabilities. I am especially experienced and skillful at seeing all aspects of a situation, diagnosing the problem areas, and then developing and implementing effective solutions. In 2003, I was recruited for my current position as Director of Human Resources for Allied Capital. Although I am excelling in my job and can provide excellent references at the appropriate time, I am selectively exploring opportunities in other companies.

I offer a reputation as a professional who can be counted on to step into the tough jobs, take over where others have failed, and transform substandard operations into ones which "set the standards" for productivity and efficiency.

I hope you will welcome my call soon to arrange a brief meeting at your convenience to discuss your current and future needs and how I might serve them. Thank you in advance for your time.

Sincerely yours,

Maria S. Sanchez

Alternate last paragraph:
I hope you will call or write soon to suggest a time convenient for us to meet and discuss your current and future needs and how I might serve them. Thank you in advance for your time.

MARIA S. SANCHEZ

1110½ Hay Street, Fayetteville, NC 28305 • preppub@aol.com • (910) 483-6611

OBJECTIVE To apply my superior managerial, written and verbal communication, and motivational skills to an organization in need of a professional who excels in solving problems through exceptional analytical and planning skills.

EXPERIENCE **DIRECTOR OF HUMAN RESOURCES.** Allied Capital, Richmond, VA (2003-present). Was recruited by Allied Capital to take charge of its Human Resources Department; provide a senior executive with advice and guidance on matters requiring the most advantageous use of available human resources in a 22,000-person corporate division.
- Manage 25 personnel specialists and provide expertise to three human resource managers.
- Have reduced employee turnover and strengthened morale through a new pension plan I designed which was approved by the board of directors.

HUMAN AND MATERIAL RESOURCES MANAGER. Caterpillar, Des Moines, IA (2000-02). Earned a reputation as a "quick thinker with extremely sound and mature judgment" while directing a 30-person staff providing administrative and personnel support for this major manufacturer.
- Became known as the "resident expert" on developing and implementing procedures for reducing manpower without serious losses in productivity.
- Developed the policy and procedures for enhancing a wide range of functional areas from labor relations to expanded benefits.

Previous military experience with the U.S. Army includes:
PERSONNEL ADMINISTRATIVE ACTIONS MANAGER. Ft. Dix, NJ (1998-00). As "second-in-command" of a training center's administrative operations center, directed the performance of specialists preparing all correspondence, reports, and awards for 8,000 new trainees passing through two separate processing centers each year.
- Refined my executive management skills providing guidance to five junior managers.
- Implemented improvements which reduced processing time, improved productivity, and were successfully accepted with minimum disruption.

GENERAL MANAGER. Ft. Richardson, AK (1996-97). Learned "total" management techniques while building a personnel services company "from scratch" and then developing 85 employees into a team which supported 4,500 people by providing "consistently outstanding" service without expert guidance from outside sources.
- Was cited for "sound judgment, high personal standards, and excelling under pressure."

SPECIAL SUPPLY OPERATIONS MANAGER. Germany (1994-95). Was handpicked to control documents used to issue and manage rationed items for 18,000 military personnel as well as government workers and contractors in 150 separate units.

GENERAL MANAGER. Ft. Campbell, KY (1992-94). Supervised 45 employees in a personnel administration center processing an average of 12,000 new employees a year; oversaw operations including dining, supply, and training.
- Refined my verbal communication skills presenting frequent briefings to executives.

EDUCATION/ TRAINING **B.A., English**, Winthrop College, Rock Hill, SC, 1990.
Excelled in more than a year of administrative/management training for executives.

PERSONAL Was honored with the Alexander Macomb Award for "outstanding achievements."

CAREER CHANGE

Date

Exact Name of Person
Exact Title
Exact Name of Company
Address
City, State, Zip

DIRECTOR OF HUMAN RESOURCE MANAGEMENT
for the U.S. Department of State

Dear Exact Name of Person (or Dear Sir or Madam if answering a blind ad):

I would like to take this opportunity to make you aware of my distinguished background and broad base of experience in human resources management, administration, and policy development gained in international settings.

As you will see from my enclosed resume, I offer a proven track record along with a reputation as a results-oriented professional who excels in enhancing cultural diversity and awareness. In my present position as the Director of Human Resource Management for an international organization with more than 8,500 employees, I control a $14 million annual operating budget. Credited with developing vital and vigorous new programs, I support the worldwide missions of the State Department and affiliated organizations with human resource services. Although I have enjoyed my career in government service, I have decided to pursue opportunities in the corporate world.

I have enjoyed a rewarding career with the U.S. Government and advanced to the GS-15 level in management roles while developing and directing personnel administration programs for large organizations in Europe. As a government liaison for labor relations in an ethnically diverse workforce, I carried out a wide range of services including consulting, interpreting, developing, and managing human resource programs for organizations with as many as 26,000 employees while working closely with representatives of various government ministries, organizations, and departments.

With a Master of Education (M.Ed.) degree and bachelor's degree in Psychology, I also have completed extensive executive-level training which has emphasized the areas of labor-management relations, EEO, ADP utilization, and international labor relations.

If you can use a mature, articulate, and results-oriented executive with a special interest in and knowledge of building human resources programs emphasizing equal opportunity and cultural awareness, I hope you will write me soon to suggest a time when we might have a brief discussion of how I could contribute to your organization. I will provide excellent professional and personal references at the appropriate time.

Sincerely,

Donald T. Justice

DONALD T. JUSTICE

1110½ Hay Street, Fayetteville, NC 28305 • preppub@aol.com • (910) 483-6611

OBJECTIVE To offer a track record of accomplishments to an organization that can use a results-oriented executive with expertise in developing and implementing personnel management/human resources policies while enhancing cultural diversity and awareness.

EDUCATION & TRAINING **Masters in Education and Psychology (M.Ed.),** Washington State Univ., Pullman, WA.
B.S., Psychology, Washington State University, Pullman, WA.
Have completed extensive management training programs in areas which have included:

    Administration of Public Policy   Total Quality Management
    Economics and Public Policy   Congressional Briefings for Executives
    ADP Utilization and Information   International Labor Relations

EXPERIENCE *Advanced to the GS-15 level in management roles in the personnel administration and human resources field with the U.S. Government in worldwide locations:*

DIRECTOR OF HUMAN RESOURCE MANAGEMENT. U.S. Department of State, Washington, DC (2003-present). Control a $14 million annual operating budget and develop vital new programs and services while managing 190 employees in a headquarters and five field offices which provide total human resources services for 8,500 people worldwide.

- Established and implemented an executive development program emphasizing competencies, organizational development, and workforce planning.
- Developed the policy and procedures for enhancing a wide range of functional areas from security, to family-friendly programs, to labor relations, to diversity programs, to expanded benefits, to customer service.
- Led the way to the development and rapid expansion of a formal mentoring program.

INTERNATIONAL LABOR & PERSONNEL MANAGEMENT SPECIALIST. London, England (1999-02). Held dual responsibilities as the Chief of International Labor Relations and Director of the Department of State's Civilian Support Agency. Served as chief negotiator with international labor unions for developing, interpreting, and implementing U.S. and foreign national labor policies.

- Represented the U.S. in policy negotiations with the European Trade Unions in discussions of such areas as wage and salaries, general employment conditions, fringe benefits, pension arrangements, and separation settlements.

REGIONAL PERSONNEL OFFICE DIRECTOR. London, England (1996-98). Received the highest award granted to a Department of State employee for my accomplishments in simultaneous roles in consulting and management. Managed a large-scale reduction in personnel due to drawdowns, which resulted in elimination of 7,000 out of 24,000 positions.

Highlights of earlier experience: Advanced to the GS-12 level; held positions as Supervisory Personnel Management Specialist, Employee Relations Specialist, Personnel Management Specialists, Personnel Assistant, and Personnel Clerk.

HONORS Consistently singled out for "Exceptional Ratings/Performance Awards" as well as numerous Superior Civilian Service, Special Service, and Meritorious Service Awards. Presented the "Decoration for Exceptional Civilian Service" by the Secretary of State.

AFFILIATIONS International Personnel Management Association (IPMA) and Council on Leadership.

PERSONAL Fluent in English; knowledgeable of Spanish; and speak conversational German.

Date

Exact Name of Person
Title or Position
Name of Company
Address (no., street)
Address (city, state, zip)

DIRECTOR OF HUMAN RESOURCES

for Dow Chemical

Dear Exact Name of Person: (or Dear Sir or Madam if answering a blind ad)

I would appreciate an opportunity to talk with you soon about how I could contribute to your organization through my extensive experience in managing human resources and developing cost-effective solutions to administrative problems.

Having attained the position of Director of Human Resources at Dow Chemical, I offer a "track record" of selection to high-visibility positions requiring analytical, administrative, communication, and organizational abilities. I also have an M.S. in management and administration, which provides a strong basis for managing any position in the field of human resources.

As you will see from my resume, I excel in short-term and long-range planning and have applied my expertise to reduce costs and manhours while improving efficiency and performance standards in every position I have held.

I hope you will welcome my call soon to arrange a brief meeting at your convenience to discuss your current and future needs and how I might serve them. Thank you in advance for your time.

Sincerely yours,

John W. Li

Alternate last paragraph:
I hope you will call or write soon to suggest a time convenient for us to meet and discuss your current and future needs and how I might serve them. Thank you in advance for your time.

JOHN W. LI

1110½ Hay Street, Fayetteville, NC 28305 • preppub@aol.com • (910) 483-6611

OBJECTIVE To benefit an organization that can use an experienced manager of human and fiscal resources who has displayed superior motivational, organizational, and planning abilities in a distinguished career in the field of human resources.

EDUCATION **M.S. in Management and Administration,** Faulkner University, Montgomery, AL, 1995.
B.A. in Business Administration, University of Alabama, Huntsville, AL, 1991.

EXPERIENCE **Advanced to a senior position with Dow Chemical's human resources team:**
2003-present: DIRECTOR OF HUMAN RESOURCES. Dow Chemical, Chicago, IL. Selected in tough competition for this position, am excelling in researching requirements in order to determine goals for 50 people providing personnel and training support for this major chemical company.
- Developed an employee orientation presentation.
- Wrote a policy manual to assure unified procedures in all departments.
- Established a new standardized training program.
- Initiated several employee recognition programs.

2000-2002: PERSONNEL MANAGER. Dow Chemical, Chicago, IL. Interviewed for and filled vacancies in staff; counseled employees. Prepared detailed information for quarterly committee meetings where determinations were made on promotions.
- Reduced expenses $75,000 annually by decreasing approval processing times.
- Singled out for my excellent communication skills and "polish," was promoted to the position of Director of Human Resources.

Highlights of previous experience:
CHIEF OF PERSONNEL MANAGEMENT. Hallmark Corporation, Gainesville, TX (1996-99). Increased efficiency ratings to the 90 to 94% range from an earlier 70% as the manager of 40 employees providing administrative support to this greeting card manufacturer.
- Automated office operations by integrating a state-of-the-art system.

STORE MANAGER. J.C. Penney, Huntsville, AL (1993-95). Controlled $1.2 million budget while overseeing training/performance of 350 employees. Interviewed prospective employees.

HUMAN SERVICES MANAGER. A & S Department Store, Westfield, AL (1990-92). Managed a diverse range of support services for 5,000 people, including supervision of both executive and employee dining rooms. Supervised 12 people including the employee benefits manager.
- Excelled in conducting training which resulted in more productive employees.
- Reorganized the benefits and compensation packages for employees which resulted in increased employee morale as well as financial savings for the company.
- Advanced to this position after beginning with the company as an Administrative Assistant in a part-time job while I was completing my college degree; was groomed by the Human Services Manager to take over her job when she retired.

PERSONAL Known for my outgoing personality as well as my strong analytical and problem-solving abilities. Experienced in using computer software for word processing and graphics. Will cheerfully travel and relocate as my employer's needs require.

CAREER CHANGE

Date

Exact Name of Person
Title or Position
Name of Company
Address (no., street)
Address (city, state, zip)

DIRECTOR OF PLANS AND OPERATIONS for Verizon Communications. Very often human resources and personnel professionals find themselves "multi-tasking," with the responsibility for human resources being only one of their activities!

Dear Exact Name of Person: (or Dear Sir or Madam if answering a blind ad)

I would appreciate an opportunity to talk with you soon about how I could contribute to your organization through my experience and special abilities in project planning and coordination and employee supervision as well as my broad base of knowledge in instructing and counseling employees.

During my professional career, I advanced in a "track record" of accomplishments and earned rapid promotions. I have been singled out for praise for my superior abilities as a communicator, instructor, planner, and supervisor.

In my present position as the Director of Plans and Operations, I advise a senior executive on personnel matters while establishing policy, assigning mid-level managers, directing facilities maintenance and upkeep, and supervising a 20-person staff. Although I enjoy my current position and am being groomed for further rapid promotion, I feel that my career path within Verizon Communications is in production operations rather than personnel management, and I wish to concentrate my career energies in the human resources and personnel administration field. Therefore, I am selectively exploring opportunities in the human resources arena with other companies.

I offer a highly effective style of management based on true concern for my employees and am known as a fair supervisor who "leads by example."

I hope you will welcome my call soon to arrange a brief meeting at your convenience to discuss your current and future needs and how I might serve them. Thank you in advance for your time.

Sincerely yours,

Irving H. Larson

Alternate last paragraph:
I hope you will call or write soon to suggest a time convenient for us to meet and discuss your current and future needs and how I might serve them. Thank you in advance for your time.

38 Part Two: Real-Resumes for Human Resources & Personnel Jobs

IRVING HOWARD LARSON

1110½ Hay Street, Fayetteville, NC 28305 • preppub@aol.com • (910) 483-6611

OBJECTIVE I want to apply my expertise as a planner, supervisor, and manager to an organization that can use a professional with a reputation for superior verbal and written communication skills and effectiveness as a leader.

EXPERIENCE **DIRECTOR OF PLANS AND OPERATIONS.** Verizon Communications, Milwaukee, WI (2003-present). Supervise 20 employees while serving as the senior advisor to the chief executive of a 5,510-person organization and keeping her informed of factors which could affect employee performance, training, safety, and morale.
- Reduced expenses $250,000 a year by reorganizing/relocating a mid-level management training program.
- Establish personnel policies as the senior advisor for 5,510 employees. Determine specific assignments for mid-level managers.
- Direct maintenance/upkeep of eight buildings while overseeing safety and security for recreation areas and food service.

PERSONNEL/OPERATIONS MANAGER. 3M Company, St. Paul, MN (2001-02). Cited as a "superb leader and mentor," achieved outstanding results in every measurable area of employee performance after being handpicked for a role usually held by a more senior professional.
- Rewrote the policy regarding attendance, and created a schedule in which people could flex their time. This new attendance policy has saved the company $.5 million annually while dramatically reducing turnover and boosting employee morale.
- Developed training classes for all levels of the organization and continuously evaluated and improved training.

OPERATIONS AND TRAINING MANAGER. Bassett Furniture, Wichita, KS (1998-00). Oversaw nine employees while planning and scheduling frequent training programs for 2,500 employees. Managed a budget of $3.5 million.
- Supervised the services of employee benefits, personnel, and labor relations managers.
- Prepared and distributed instructions to support departments including coordinating with the personnel manager. Maintained records on absenteeism and safety and made recommendations to management for improvements.
- Conducted negotiations with labor union officials regarding company policies.

PERSONNEL MANAGER. Dynergy, Racine, WI (1995-97). Supervised seven mid-level managers and directed training, counseling, and performance of up to 125 employees.
- Planned the short-term and long-range training objectives while making determinations on promotions and selection for further schooling. Was honored for my "technical competence, remarkable problem-solving skills, and personal concern for employees."

ASSISTANT PERSONNEL MANAGER. Xerox Corporation, Baltimore, MD (1992-94). Initiated a variety of programs designed to boost employee morale which include sending birthday cards and initiating a "red phone" for anonymous tips.
- Coordinated employee meetings, produced a company newsletter, and created special bulletin boards. Established clear productivity measures.

EDUCATION **B.A., Business Administration,** Salisbury State University, Salisbury, MD, 1992.

PERSONAL Have been singled out for my caring leadership style. Excellent references upon request.

CAREER CHANGE

Date

Exact Name of Person
Exact Title or Position
Company Name
Company Address (street and number)
Company Address (city, state, and zip)

DIRECTOR OF TRAINING
for the Department of the Interior

Dear Exact Name (or Dear Sir or Madam if answering a blind ad):

With the enclosed resume, I am formally advising you of my interest in the position of Executive Director for Warner County Partnership for Children which you recently advertised in the Alexandria Gazette.

As I believe you will see from my resume, I appear to possess all the qualifications and attributes you are seeking. Although I am excelling in my current job and enjoy the people I work with, I would very much like to get back into a job in which I would be managing a staff and directing daily operations. I have had extensive experience in planning and administering budgets of all sizes, and I am skilled at writing proposals that justify and validate the use of funds.

I offer extensive experience in implementing "from scratch" education programs, and that responsibility required me to supervise the acquisition of facilities and development of curricula as well as the recruiting, interviewing, and evaluating of instructors.

Known as an astute strategic thinker with the ability to "see the big picture" while managing the minute details, I believe my main strength is my ability to work with people at all levels and motivate them to work toward common goals. I believe in leadership by example.

I can provide outstanding personal and professional references, and I hope you will give me a chance to meet with you in person to demonstrate that I am the creative and hard-working professional you are looking for. Thank you in advance for your time.

Yours sincerely,

Susan R. Arnold

SUSAN R. ARNOLD

1110½ Hay Street, Fayetteville, NC 28305 • preppub@aol.com • (910) 483-6611

OBJECTIVE To contribute to an organization that can use a resourceful strategist and problem-solver who offers exceptional planning, communication, and coordinating skills which have been refined through extensive experience in managing people, programs, projects, and finances.

EDUCATION & TECHNICAL TRAINING

Earned **Master's** degree in Business Administration (M.B.A.) degree, Indiana University, South Bend, IN, 1992.

Hold a **Bachelor of Science (B.S.)** degree, Aurora University, Aurora IN, 1988.

Completed other extensive graduate-level training programs for executive related to:
- strategic management
- equal employment opportunity
- finance and budgeting
- prevention of sexual harassment
- total quality management
- operational planning

Received NC Life & Health Insurance license after extensive training in investments, estate planning, business insurance; learned to use leading financial software to create profiles.

EXPERIENCE

DIRECTOR OF TRAINING. Department of the Interior, Washington, DC (2003-present). Coordinate and schedule industrial and municipal environmental training.
- Interview prospective employees to be trained to assist companies and cities in their projects as well as hire Washington office staff.
- Review salary and promotion policies annually to ensure they are up-to-date.

STAFFING COORDINATOR & PROJECT MANAGER. Compaq Computer, Atlanta, GA (2000-02). Provided personnel from the headquarters office to establish other offices for Compaq at various locations. Counseled employees and reviewed wage and benefit packages.
- Managed a $14.7 million budget which I had to validate annually and justify quarterly.
- Implemented the Total Quality Management process within this diversified and spread-out organization.

MANAGER OF TRAINING & PERSONNEL. Intel, Peoria, IL (1997-00). Directed training of 2,000 people while personally managing a $10 million budget. Prepared a revised employee orientation presentation, and published an updated employee manual.
- Proposed and supervised preparation of a new employee lounge to improve morale.
- Oversaw a facility that provided state-of-the-art audiovisual training aids.

PERSONNEL ASSISTANT. Albertson's, Glen Ellyn, IL (1994-96). In charge of interviewing applicants for employment at Albertson's. Was the "right arm" to the Personnel Director, who described me as reliable, fair, and with "great communication and people skills."

PERSONNEL CLERK. Wal-Mart, Marion, IN (1992-93). In the Personnel Department, made appointments for interviews, filed applications, and prepared other related paperwork.

SALES CLERK. Goody's Department Store, Aurora, IN (1990-92). While attending college, worked in the Women's Fashion Department at Goody's.
- Became skilled at dealing with all types of people with tact and courtesy.

PERSONAL Have helped transform several organizations into "the best" of their kind. Offer a reputation as a "diplomat" and possess proven communication skills. Outstanding references.

Date

Exact Name of Person
Title or Position
Name of Company
Address (number and street)
Address (city, state, and zip)

DIRECTOR OF TRAINING & HUMAN RESOURCES for Sara Lee Foods, Inc.

Dear Exact Name of Person: (or Sir or Madam if answering a blind ad)

    Can you use an astute professional with proven skills related to human resources management?

    In my current position as Director of Training & Human Resources for Sara Lee Foods, I have initiated and implemented improvements which dramatically improved productivity. After taking over as HR Chief in an organization with deep-seated labor-management problems, I have established a cooperative relationship with labor union representatives and have directed all phases of a comprehensive training program.

    During previous employment, I excelled in full-time management positions while utilizing my leisure time in creative ways to refine my communication skills. In a previous job as Personnel Manager for Cisco Systems, I introduced an employee incentive plan which resulted in lower turnover. Prior to that, as Training and Administrative Manager at Compaq computers, I integrated automated systems and personnel systems/procedures into a comprehensive support system.

    As you see on my resume, I earned my master's degree in Human Resources with a 3.94 GPA. My B.A. degree is in Economics. I am highly proficient in using computers and offer a knack for mastering new software.

    If you can use a versatile and resourceful self-starter with proven management abilities, excellent communication and public relations skills, I would enjoy meeting you in person to discuss your needs. I hope you will call or write me soon to suggest a time when we might meet. Thank you in advance for your time.

                                                                 Sincerely,

                                                                 David S. Webster

Alternate last paragraph:
    I hope you will welcome my call soon to suggest a time convenient for us to meet and discuss your current and future needs and how I might serve them. Thank you in advance for your time.

DAVID S. WEBSTER

1110½ Hay Street, Fayetteville, NC 28305 • preppub@aol.com • (910) 483-6611

OBJECTIVE To contribute to an organization that can benefit from my management abilities and problem-solving skills as well as through my experience in finance and investing, training management and personnel administration, and computer operations.

COMPUTERS Am familiar with Windows and Microsoft Office, Word, and Quicken software.
- Offer a proven knack for rapidly mastering new software and for utilizing programs to enhance profitability and decision making.

EDUCATION & TRAINING
M.A., Human Resources, Wittenberg University, Springfield, OH, 1992.
- Achieved a 3.94 GPA.

B.A., Economics, Malone College, Canton, OH, 1988.

EXPERIENCE **DIRECTOR OF TRAINING & HUMAN RESOURCES.** Sara Lee Foods, Inc., Cedar Rapids, IA (2002-present). Initiated and implemented improvements which dramatically improved the productivity of an office providing training and administrative support for 5,000 people; supervise 35 employees and control an $8 million budget.
- Perform detailed planning in order to provide 24-hour operations in the plant.
- Established a cooperative relationship with labor union representatives.
- Direct all phases of a comprehensive training program including scheduling personnel for professional development schools and informal classes, tracking and analyzing personnel statistics, and administering awards and promotions.
- Initiated procedures for correcting problems so that personnel actions are initiated within 72 hours.
- Created new internal forms that streamlined management decision making.

PERSONNEL MANAGER. Cisco Systems, Lawrence, KS (2000-02). Supervised 18 employees in the personnel department. Responsible for providing training and maintaining an up-to-date employee manual.
- Wrote and produced an audiovisual employment presentation.
- Introduced an employee incentive plan which resulted in a lower turnover and increased productivity.

TRAINING AND ADMINISTRATIVE MANAGER. Compaq Computers, Inc., Dallas, TX (1997-00). Integrated automated systems, training policies, and personnel systems/procedures into a comprehensive support system for this major manufacturer.
- Utilized the Windows operating systems in personnel administration.
- Developed short-term and long-range goals which clarified strategy and facilitated operational improvements.

PURCHASING AGENT. Coca-Cola Bottling Plant, Miami, FL (1993-96). Played an important role in scheduling, planning, and providing logistical support which ensured the organization was adequately supplied and equipped.
- Became skilled in negotiating contracts.
- Ensured the availability of basic products needed both in the office and in the plant

PERSONAL Offer exceptional analytical, communication, and management skills. Can provide excellent references upon request.

CAREER CHANGE

Date

Exact Name of Person
Title or Position
Name of Company
Address (no., street)
Address (city, state, zip)

DIRECTOR OF TRAINING & PERSONNEL RECRUITING for General Electric

Dear Exact Name of Person: (or Dear Sir or Madam if answering a blind ad)

I would appreciate an opportunity to talk with you soon about how I could contribute to your organization through my training in electromechanical maintenance and my ability to motivate, train, and manage others. It is my strong desire to benefit a company which can use my technical knowledge as well as my demonstrated ability to motivate, manage, and train others. It is my goal to make a permanent career in the human resources field with a company that can use a human resources professional who can "talk technical" and understand technical concepts.

As you will see from my resume, I hold a degree in Human Resources and have completed numerous training programs which have refined my ability to relate effectively to others. Subsequently I strengthened my technical knowledge as I completed 3,200 shop hours and 60 classroom hours in an apprenticeship program sponsored by the Ball State University, IN. During my apprenticeship at Lowell Plastics in Mason, IL, I learned solid state and conventional wiring and performed maintenance on hydraulic equipment using blueprints and schematics.

With strong communication skills along with a sincere desire to achieve the highest goals, I have distinguished myself as a top performer in versatile areas. While involved in sales and personnel recruiting, I have earned numerous honors and awards for exceeding goals as well as for my efforts in training and molding personnel into top-notch sales teams.

Known as a mature and dependable leader and manager, I also offer a reputation as an enthusiastic and highly energetic individual with a creative mind and the ability to think on my feet. I am a skilled public speaker with a talent for motivating and encouraging others to perform to high standards.

I hope you will welcome my call soon to arrange a brief meeting at your convenience to discuss your current and future needs and how I might serve them. Thank you in advance for your time.

Sincerely yours,

Alan J. Winthrop

Alternate last paragraph:
I hope you will call or write me soon to suggest a time convenient for us to meet and discuss your current and future needs and how I might serve them. Thank you in advance for your time.

ALAN J. WINTHROP

1110½ Hay Street, Fayetteville, NC 28305 • preppub@aol.com • (910) 483-6611

OBJECTIVE To contribute my exceptional sales abilities, outstanding technical electronics skills, and talent for motivating others to an organization that can use an enthusiastic and energetic professional known as a creative thinker with a keen intellect and decision-making skills.

EDUCATION & TRAINING Completed more than 3,200 shop hours and 60 semester hours of class work in an Electro-mechanical Maintenance Apprenticeship Program, Bell State University, Muncie, IN, 2002.
Earned **Associate's degree in Human Resources,** Anderson University, Anderson, IN, 1993.
Excelled in over 1,500 hours of training in programs such as the following:
- An 800-hour advanced management training program which emphasized leadership, supervisory, and organizational skills
- A 500-hour program for personnel recruiters which emphasized sales, market analysis, and motivational techniques
- Additional courses in physical fitness and nutrition, electrical wiring, and hydraulics
- A Zig Zigler sales and motivational program

EXPERIENCE *Consistently set the standards for others to attempt to meet and advanced rapidly in managerial and supervisory roles with General Electric:*
2003-present: DIRECTOR OF TRAINING & PERSONNEL RECRUITING. Muncie, IN. Developed and implemented improvements which greatly boosted the productivity of more than 300 sales professionals in 42 offices located throughout Indiana, Illinois, Wisconsin, and Michigan.
- Established training programs and operating procedures which allowed me to produce highly effective sales and administrative professionals.
- Developed a test program which has been very effective in evaluating sales personnel.

2000-02: DIRECTOR OF TRAINING. Dayton, OH. Developed and oversaw training programs for a sales force of more than 200 people; the programs' goals varied from refining the skills of executives to training new personnel.
- Gained a broad base of experience in setting up and managing sales conferences and developing sources for requisitioning technical materials and equipment.

1998-00: AREA SALES MANAGER and **PERSONNEL MANAGER.** Chicago, IL. Supervised and guided the efforts of 28 sales representatives from seven offices which covered a total of 28,000 square miles. Guided seven sales managers to increase their productivity 30% and earned recognition as the top company manager after my first year in charge.

1997-98: SALES MANAGER. Baltimore, MD. Sharpened my supervisory techniques and was highly effective in selling qualified young people on the advantages of a career at General Electric. Was honored as the **Top Salesman** two consecutive years in an office which was the most productive in the region.

Highlights of other experience:
SALES MANAGER and **SALES REPRESENTATIVE.** Gained experience in conducting market analysis and developing well-trained sales professionals while earning numerous awards for my expertise and results achieved.
ELECTRO-MECHANICAL MAINTENANCE APPRENTICE. Completed a Journeyman experience.

PERSONAL Am able to read electrical schematics and blueprints and perform troubleshooting techniques.

Date

Exact Name of Person
Exact Title
Exact Name of Company
Address
City, State, Zip

EDUCATIONAL COORDINATOR

for Information Technology Training for a bank

Dear Exact Name of Person: (or Dear Sir or Madam if answering a blind ad)

With the enclosed resume, I would like to make you aware of my exceptional communication, organizational, and supervisory skills. I offer a track record of success in challenging human resources, training, and property management positions which I could put to work for your company.

As you will see from my resume, I maintained a 3.75 GPA while completing my Master of Arts at the University of Minnesota at Duluth, where I previously finished my Bachelor of Arts in Business Administration six months early despite working full time through most of my collegiate career. The exceptional organizational and time management skills that I developed during this period have served me well in my professional endeavors.

Currently I am excelling as Educational Coordinator for Information Technology Training with the Duluth corporate headquarters of a large national bank, overseeing all administrative and organizational aspects of this extensive training program. Although I am highly regarded by my employer and can provide exceptional personal and professional references at the appropriate time, I am from Minneapolis originally and have decided to permanently relocate to be closer to my friends and family. I am currently exploring career opportunities in the area, and I feel that there may be a good fit between my versatile abilities and your company's needs.

Throughout most of my collegiate career, I worked in full- or part-time positions with the University of Minnesota Department of Housing and Residence Life. As a Graduate Assistant Residence Coordinator and Resident Advisor for a four-building area serving 500 students, I performed duties which combined human resources, supervision, training, public relations, events coordination, and property management skills. I interviewed, hired, trained, and supervised as many as 40 employees, managing human resources, operations and administrative support as well as housekeeping and security.

If you can use an energetic and articulate professional whose skills have been proven in a variety of challenging environments, I look forward to hearing from you soon.

Sincerely,

Dawn B. Wake

DAWN B. WAKE

1110½ Hay Street, Fayetteville, NC 28305 • preppub@aol.com • (910) 483-6611

OBJECTIVE To benefit an organization that can use an articulate, poised young professional with exceptional organizational skills who offers a background of excellence in human resources, training, and property management in corporate and academic environments.

EDUCATION **Master of Arts** in **Human Resources**, University of Minnesota at Duluth, Duluth, MN, 2002; maintained a **3.75 cumulative GPA**.
Bachelor of Arts in **Business Administration**, University of Minnesota at Duluth, MN, 2000; graduated with a **3.7 GPA** in my major, 3.2 overall, while completing this rigorous degree program in only 3½ years.

COMPUTERS Proficient with many popular computer operating systems and software, including Windows, Word, Excel, Access, and PowerPoint, and WordPerfect; have used and maintained Internet and Intranet servers.

EXPERIENCE **EDUCATIONAL COORDINATOR FOR INFORMATION TECHNOLOGY TRAINING.** Duluth National Bank, Duluth, MN (2002-present). Work without supervision, managing all administrative and organizational aspects of the Information Technologies Training program.
- Coordinated with three on-site instructors and two outside contractors that provided training to company personnel; assisted trainers in setting up courses as well as developing and distributing the quarterly class schedule to participants.
- Maintain Local Area Network (LAN) and Mainframe Computer-Based Training (CBT) programs, handling system security, issuing passwords, setting access levels, and providing technical support to Duluth National employees involved in the training program.
- Oversee ordering, inventory control, updating, and maintenance for an extensive library of technical training materials in computer database, videotape, and print formats.

With the University of Minnesota at Duluth Department of Housing and Residence Life, advanced in the following "track record" of increasing responsibilities:
2000-2002: GRADUATE ASSISTANT RESIDENCE COORDINATOR. Supervised as many as 40 employees including Resident Advisors, Desk Receptionists, Housekeeping, and Security while managing human resources, operations, and administrative support for a residential area comprised of four buildings and serving more than 500 residents.
- Interviewed, hired, and trained up to 32 employees, providing supervision and performing periodic evaluations for all personnel; oversaw all occupancy and maintenance issues.
- Developed and implemented a number of programs and events; managed an operational budget for the residence area; served as co-instructor, teaching a Communication Skills class for students striving to become effective speakers and leaders.

1999: **CONFERENCE COORDINATOR.** Interviewed, hired, and trained 10 Conference Assistants, as well as participating in the planning and implementation of numerous conferences held at the University for organizations such as the Junior Olympics.

1997-98: **RESIDENT ADVISOR.** Performed a wide variety of administrative, planning and organizational, mentoring, and counseling duties as well as managing discipline issues for as many as 500 resident students.

PERSONAL Excellent personal and professional references are available upon request.

Date

Exact Name of Person
Title or Position
Name of Company
Address (number and street)
Address (city, state, and ZIP)

EMPLOYEE RELATIONS MANAGER
for Pfizer Industries

Dear Exact Name of Person (or Sir or Madam if answering a blind ad):

I would appreciate an opportunity to talk with you soon about how I could contribute to your organization through the application of my extensive experience in a distinguished career with Pfizer Industries.

While advancing ahead of my peers I have consistently been selected for positions usually reserved for a higher-ranking and more experienced professional. In every instance I have excelled and set the standard in all aspects of performance and operational accomplishments in numerous positions in the field of human resources.

Handpicked for my present job as the Employee Relations Manager for one of the largest drug manufacturing companies, I direct the activities and provide leadership for 120 people in the Personnel Department. Since taking over this position, I have been effective in leading the company to achieve commendable productivity rates and a reduction in turnover.

I hope you will welcome my call soon to arrange a brief meeting to discuss your current and future needs and how I might serve them. Thank you in advance for your time.

Sincerely,

Frederick L. Johns

Alternate last paragraph:
I hope you will call or write me soon to suggest a time convenient for us to meet and discuss your current and future needs and how I might serve them. Thank you in advance for your time.

FREDERICK LEE JOHNS

1110½ Hay Street, Fayetteville, NC 28305 • preppub@aol.com • (910) 483-6611

OBJECTIVE   To offer expertise in project planning and management to an organization that can benefit from my ability to provide effective human, fiscal, and resource management as well as my specialized experience in ensuring security for personnel and material resources.

EXPERIENCE   *Advanced to managerial and supervisory roles ahead of my peers in a distinguished career with the Pfizer Industries, Boston, MA:*

2003-present: **EMPLOYEE RELATIONS MANAGER.** Cited as "a superb leader and mentor," achieved outstanding results in every measurable area of employee performance after being handpicked for a role usually held by a more senior professional.

- Revised the wage and salary schedules to reflect current economic situation, which resulted in cost savings for Pfizer.
- Direct the employee training and orientation programs for all departments, which have increased productivity.
- Initiated a new attendance policy which saved the company a half million dollars annually while reducing turnover and improving morale.

2002: **SENIOR TRAINING PLANNER.** Managed a 20-person section which prepared, administered, and coordinated training for both individuals and managers.

2000-02: **SUPPORT SERVICES COORDINATOR.** In a position usually reserved for a more experienced manager, supervised employee benefits, personnel, and labor relations managers. Scheduled monthly meetings for performance reviews of those departments. Ensured compliance with government policies in hiring new personnel.

- Recognized as the subject matter expert on government policies pertaining to employment, such as Affirmative Action and the EEO Act.
- Was considered an expert in smoothly settling labor union demands.

Other experience:
PERSONNEL SUPERVISOR. Johnson & Johnson, Scranton, PA (1997-99). Was sought for my advice by peers and supervisors alike as leader and manager of a 15-person staff. Reviewed on a regular basis company policies on wage scale, absenteeism, insurance and benefits.

- Updated the company manual and scripted a new employee orientation presentation.
- Cited for my understanding of Affirmative Action and EEO policies.
- Initiated the remodeling of the employee dining facilities.

TRAINING MANAGER. Alcoa, Erie, PA (1994-96). Planned and managed employee training programs. Praised by a senior executive for the orientation program for new employees which I created. Initiated special workshops for various groups of employees to improve productivity.

- Was credited with achieving accident-free operations with an average of 99% attendance while motivating personnel to excel in every evaluated aspect of performance.

INSTRUCTOR, TECHNICAL WRITER, AND PROGRAM DEVELOPER. State Farm Insurance, Hartford CT (1991-93). Earned a reputation as a thoroughly knowledgeable instructor with a strong grasp of subject matter and the ability to develop high standards for classroom and practical training.

EDUCATION   **B.S.** in **Human Relations** with a minor in Personnel, Trinity College, Hartford, CT.

PERSONAL   Highly computer proficient. Hold memberships in the VFW and the American Legion.

Date

Exact Name of Person
Title or Position
Name of Company
Address (number and street)
Address (city, state, and zip)

EMPLOYEE TRAINING AND BENEFITS ASSISTANT
for Wang Computers

Dear Exact Name of Person: (or Sir or Madam if answering a blind ad)

I would appreciate an opportunity to talk with you soon about how I could contribute to your organization through my expert secretarial skills and my extensive knowledge of the human resources field. I am responding to your ad in <u>The Hempstead Gazette</u> for a Human Resources Assistant.

As you will see from my resume, I appear to possess all the qualifications you are seeking in the successful candidate for this job. In my job as an Employee Training and Benefits Assistant for Wang Computers, I expertly performed all secretarial duties while becoming increasingly specialized in the human resources area of the company's operations. I have worked extensively on projects pertaining to personnel, employee training, labor efficiency, employee policies and procedures, and personnel forms design.

On my own initiative, I became involved in formal training programs which permitted me to institute training programs at Wang Computers for both management and support personnel. We emphasized computer training for all employees, and I personally conducted workshops on Affirmative Action, on the Americans with Disabilities Act of 1990, on Sexual Harassment, and on correct interviewing procedures. I have completed extensive training myself related to Word, D-Base, and Excel.

You would find me to be an energetic self-starter who works well with employees at all levels. I can provide outstanding personal and professional references upon request, and I would cheerfully travel in this job as your needs require.

In the hope that we can get together in person to discuss this job further, I will telephone your office in the coming week to see if your schedule permits setting up a brief meeting. I believe you would be impressed with the enthusiasm, skills, and knowledge I could bring to your organization.

Sincerely,

Marianne C. Bosley

MARIANNE C. BOSLEY

1110½ Hay Street, Fayetteville, NC 28305 • preppub@aol.com • (910) 483-6611

OBJECTIVE To contribute to an organization that can use an experienced professional who offers outstanding oral and written communication skills, excellent secretarial and office administration abilities, along with extensive knowledge of the human resources field.

EDUCATION & COMPUTER TRAINING Earned **Bachelor of Arts** (B.A.) degree in Human Resources, Dowling College, Oakdale, NY. At Broome Community College, Binghamton, NY, excelled in computer classes related to Excel, Microsoft Word, PageMaker, and D-Base.

EXPERIENCE **EMPLOYEE TRAINING & BENEFITS ASSISTANT.** Wang Computers, Hempstead, NY (2002-present). Gained broad experience in the human resources field while excelling in performing secretarial duties for this large manufacturer.

- *Personnel*: Initiated, revised, and administered personnel procedures which enabled the company to become more competitive in employment recruitment and retention.
- *Employee training*: On my own initiative, instituted training programs for management and support personnel related to computer operations and other areas; personally conducted workshops on Affirmative Action guidelines, Americans with Disabilities Act of 1990, sexual harassment, correct interviewing procedures, and other human resources areas; emphasized computer training for employees.
- *Policy and procedures*: Revised the company policy manual, wage progression, job descriptions, semiannual job reviews, and employee application form to abide with all state and federal laws and regulations.
- *Forms design*: Designed and implemented new in-house Attendance Records, Employee Warning Notices, Leave of Absence Requests, and other internal forms.
- *Employee morale surveys*: Was responsible for in-house morale survey and compiled summary of results for top management; orally briefed top management on results and made recommendations.
- *Health insurance and Workers' Compensation*: Analyzed and assisted in selecting a medical health insurance benefits plan, the Workers' Compensation carrier, and all other employee benefits.
- *Purchasing*: Am responsible for purchasing office computers, printers, software, and business office equipment.
- *Labor efficiency contributions*: Worked with outside consultants over a three-year period to develop and implement a Labor Efficiency Bonus program and a companion computer program to track labor efficiency; then played a key role in "selling" to employees a new concept which altered their traditional pay system.

Other experience: In prior experience, worked briefly as a **Substitute Teacher** for Oakdale City School System; **Retail Buyer** for Wright Brothers Department Store; **Office Auditor** for the Internal Revenue Service, and **Clerk** for the U.S. Treasury Department.

CIVIC INVOLVEMENT Believe in making contributions to my community, and have served as a "Trustee" for the Smith County Public Library, **President** of the Oakdale Junior High School P.T.A., and **President** and **Vice President** of the Oakdale Junior Service League. Was founder and organizer of the Oakdale "Reading is Fundamental" (RIF) Program. Coordinated performances for the Oakdale Little Symphony and for drama presented in Oakdale public schools.

PERSONAL Will provide outstanding references upon request. Will travel as needed.

CAREER CHANGE

Date

Exact Name of Person
Title or Position
Name of Company
Address (no., street)
Address (city, state, zip)

EXECUTIVE PERSONNEL MANAGER

for Sears & Roebuck. This individual seeks a career change from retailing to a nonprofit environment.

Dear Exact Name of Person: (or Dear Sir or Madam if answering a blind ad)

I would appreciate an opportunity to talk with you soon about how I could contribute to your organization. Years of leadership experience have honed my abilities as a manager, communicator, trainer and instructor, and planner. My professional trademarks are completing assigned or implied projects on time, to standard, and building a winning team.

Consistently excelling in jobs requiring a mature leader who could manage complex projects, I have specialized in successfully forecasting long-range objectives to produce a targeted end state. Fully trained as a Personnel Management Specialist, I offer expertise in operations, plans, management, and program development.

As you will see from my resume I am completing requirements for a master's degree in **Business Administration** and I already hold a B.A. in **Economics**. I offer a combination of experience and education which would make me a valuable asset to your company.

Although I have excelled in managing personnel programs in retail as well as automotive environments, I am exploring management opportunities in nonprofit organizations. If my skills and experience interest you, please call or write to suggest a time for us to meet. I look forward to discussing your current and future needs and how I may serve them. Thank you in advance for your time and attention.

Sincerely yours,

Isaac Goldstein

ISAAC GOLDSTEIN

1110½ Hay Street, Fayetteville, NC 28305 • preppub@aol.com • (910) 483-6611

OBJECTIVE To apply my leadership and team building skills to an organization that can benefit from human resources, training, and project management expertise.

EDUCATION & TRAINING Completed two management programs for executives sponsored by Sears.
M.S., Business Administration, Capital University, Columbus, OH, 1986.
B.S., Economics, Kent State University, Kent, OH, 1982.

EXPERIENCE **EXECUTIVE PERSONNEL MANAGER.** Sears & Roebuck, Cincinnati, OH (2002-present). Oversee a seven-person staff as the senior planner, developer, and author of personnel plans and programs. Analyzed and selected a new medical health insurance plan.
- Redesigned the employee evaluation system to ensure fairness. Rewrote standard company policy regarding attendance which resulted in a reduction in absences.
- Am known for my excellent communication skills and enthusiastic leadership ability.
- Managed functions including promotions, performance reports for employees at all levels, and personnel availability and status figures. Revitalized employee recognition programs.

PERSONNEL MANAGER. Ford Motor Company, Detroit, MI (1998-2001). Was in charge of personnel policies, training, and labor relations for this Fortune 500 company.
- Developed management training programs for which I was praised. Oversaw the benefits program manager. Established a new-employee orientation presentation.

ASSISTANT PERSONNEL MANAGER. General Motors, Dearborn, MI (1995-97). Planned, implemented, and refined human resource support efforts. Was assigned to oversee refurbishing of employee lounge and dining room.
- Redesigned the employee evaluation program.

INSTRUCTOR/STUDENT ADVISOR. Capital University, Columbus, OH (1993-95). Conducted classroom instruction for 120 undergraduate students while counseling students.

While serving my country in the U.S. Army, held these positions and a Top Secret clearance:
GENERAL MANAGER. Ft. Lewis, WA (1991-92). As a company commander, controlled a $1.2 million dollar annual budget while managing 125 employees; maintained 38 vehicles and other equipment valued at over $14 million.
- Developed company-wide training, maintenance, and deployment programs.
- Awarded Army Commendation Medal for leadership.

PLANS AND OPERATIONS MANAGER. Ft. Gordon, GA (1989-1990). Served as the senior operations planner at the headquarters of the 14,000-person 82nd Airborne Division and inspected personnel programs throughout the command.
- Developed quarterly professional development seminars for mid-level executives from 22 affiliated organizations. Handpicked for responsibility as a company commander.

PERSONAL
- **Leadership:** Possess the ability to build a team and produce results on tough projects within a relatively short time.
- **Decision making:** Assimilate concepts rapidly and react creatively to varying levels of experience and knowledge.
- **Training:** Offer extensive experience in teaching, refining, evaluating, and sustaining both basic and advanced technical skills; have designed training programs for organizations varying in size from 30 people to more than 3,600 individuals.

CAREER CHANGE

Date

Exact Name of Person
Title or Position
Name of Company
Address (no., street)
Address (city, state, zip)

FAMILY AND VOCATIONAL COUNSELOR

for the Veterans Administration with prior experience in private industry. This individual desires to return to corporate employment.

Dear Exact Name of Person: (or Dear Sir or Madam if answering a blind ad)

I would appreciate an opportunity to talk with you soon about how I could contribute to your organization through my experience in the area of human resource management which has included activities related to interviewing, managing, counseling, training, and planning.

In my current position as a Counselor at the Veterans Administration, I am consistently evaluated as a proactive, dedicated, caring, and focused performer who can be counted on to handle tough assignments with professionalism and pride. My previous position as Human Resource Program Manager involved planning and completing the personnel utilization, reassignment, and support for the closure of one of the U.S. Steel plants. I developed ideas for the smooth transition of personnel which became "the model" for U.S. Steel. Although I have enjoyed my service with the Veterans Administration, I am eager to return to the fast pace of the corporate world!

Earlier I was involved in manpower utilization and personnel administration at Enron, where I was singled out by the Vice President as a "top performer" because of my creativity and problem-solving ability. I received several prestigious awards and widespread recognition for my management skills and depth of knowledge of the personnel actions field.

You would find me to be a well-educated and trained professional who is truly concerned with helping others and your organization move ahead by ensuring people are properly placed in the right job so that their talents and experience are maximized.

I hope you will welcome my call soon to arrange a brief meeting at your convenience to discuss your current and future needs and how I might serve them. Thank you in advance for your time.

Sincerely yours,

Fresca T. Gonzalez

Alternate last paragraph:
I hope you will call or write soon to suggest a time convenient for us to meet and discuss your current and future needs and how I might serve them. Thank you in advance for your time.

FRESCA T. GONZALEZ

1110½ Hay Street, Fayetteville, NC 28305 • preppub@aol.com • (910) 483-6611

OBJECTIVE To benefit an organization seeking a results-oriented human resource management professional skilled in planning and implementing large-scale projects, maximizing fiscal resources, and ensuring quality results.

EXPERIENCE **FAMILY & VOCATIONAL COUNSELOR**. Veterans Administration, Pittsburgh, PA (2003-present). Provide vocational, educational, family, and drug and alcohol counseling while assisting transitioning service members in finding jobs and/or developing plans for education.

HUMAN RESOURCE PROGRAM MANAGER. U.S. Steel, Baltimore, MD (2001-02). At a critical point when the economy dictated U.S. Steel to drastically "downsize," was selected for a "hotseat" job that involved planning and directing the closure of a branch plant in Memphis, Tennessee; authored the personnel section of the plant closure guidelines which was cited as fulfilling Total Quality Management (TQM) principles.
- Supervised 48 people in the personnel department.
- Introduced new computer equipment that **doubled** customer service efficiency.
- Earned a reputation as one of the company's foremost authorities in the field of organizational development and organizational effectiveness.

CHIEF OF PERSONNEL OPERATIONS. Enron, Ann Arbor, MI (2000-01). Was singled out by the Vice President as one of the organization's "Top Performers" because of the creativity and problem-solving ability I demonstrated in reorganizing the personnel department.
- Through ruthless attention to detail, identified/corrected over 800 errors in the personnel database. Received two respected awards for developing and implementing procedures for evaluating employees and revising the promotion policy.
- Cited by executives as accomplishing the "best ever seen" personnel action plans.

PERSONNEL DIRECTOR. Pfizer Corporation, Charleston, SC (1998-00). While supervising 18 people, was the Project Officer for a feasibility study which determined the best placement for 176 computers in a new system that, for the first time, provided key managers with access to personnel data.
- Became known as an expert in dealing with tough decisions regarding personnel policies.
- Continuously was involved in making plans for the unexpected and for the "worst case."

PERSONNEL MANAGER. Merck Corporation, Montgomery, AL (1996-98). On my own initiative, implemented a new employee evaluation system; while pioneering this new system, cut personnel turnover, thereby saving thousands of dollars annually.
- Used quality control programs to strengthen personnel policies and procedures.

CHIEF — AIR TRAFFIC CONTROL OPERATIONS. U.S. Air Force, Randolph AFB, TX (1993-96). After excelling as **Senior Air Traffic Control Manager** from 1991-92, was promoted to manage 40 air traffic controllers and $4 million in high-tech equipment.

EDUCATION & TRAINING M.S. degree in **Business Management**, University of Maine, Orono, ME, 1990.
B.S. in **Management**, University of New Hampshire, Durham, NH, 1988.
Excelled in executive training in TQM techniques, human resource/personnel management, motivation, counseling, and international relations.

PERSONAL Secret security clearance. Member, National Association for Female Executives.

Date

Exact Name of Person
Exact Title
Exact Name of Company
Address
City, State, Zip

HUMAN RESOURCES STUDENT

earning degree in Human Resources Management

Dear Exact Name of Person: (or Dear Sir or Madam if answering a blind ad)

With the enclosed resume, I would like to make you aware of my skills and education related to human resources administration and express my interest in exploring employment opportunities with your organization.

Currently completing my B.A. in Human Resources Administration, I have provided human resources support in the medical, financial, as well as the benefits and promotions areas. While serving in the U.S. Army, I gained my earliest exposure to human resources administration as I worked in a Personnel Administration Center supporting 1,200 people. I also became experienced in handling payroll administration for 250 people weekly with a perfect 100% on-time accuracy rate. My experience in human resources and personnel administration while in the U.S. Army was what motivated me to seek my Associate's and Bachelor's degree in this area.

In one position after leaving the military, I supported human resources needs of a medical nature while working with insurance companies and physicians to coordinate physical exams for insured corporate clients. I have refined my communication skills working in customer service positions in a telemarketing firm as well as in the banking industry.

You will notice that I maintained a 3.7 GPA while obtaining an A.A. degree in Human Resources, and I have a 3.6 GPA in my B.A. curriculum. I am seeking a full-time position in a company which can utilize my strengths related to serving customers, assuring the quality of human services provided, and contributing to the company's bottom line.

I can assure you that I am a totally dedicated individual who always makes an effort to excel in all I do, and I have made valuable contributions to every employer for whom I have worked. If my skills and talents interest you, I hope you will contact me to suggest a time when we might meet to discuss your needs.

Sincerely,

Cynthia E. Waters

CYNTHIA E. WATERS

1110½ Hay Street, Fayetteville, NC 28305 • preppub@aol.com • (910) 483-6611

OBJECTIVE To offer my background and education related to human resources to an organization that can use a resourceful young professional who offers exceptional time management and communication skills along with a talent for helping others identify and resolve problems.

EDUCATION & TRAINING Completing **B.A. in Human Resources Management,** Augusta State University, Augusta, GA.
- Am maintaining 3.6 GPA; named to the university's Dean's List in recognition of my "outstanding academic performance."

Earned an **A.A. in Human Resources Management,** Samford University, Birmingham, AL, 1998; maintained a 3.7 GPA.

Received training in computer applications, management, and personnel services.

COMPUTERS Proficient with WordPerfect, MS Word, Excel, and Access.

EXPERIENCE **FULL-TIME STUDENT.** Augusta State University, Augusta, GA (2003-present).

MEDICAL RECORDS CLERK. Executive Insurance Co., Florence, SC (1998-02). Provided human resources support of a medical nature while working for a company which conducts physical exams for insured corporate clients, processed requests for medical records from insurance companies.
- Polished already-effective communication skills dealing with agents and physicians while handling sensitive medical records and maintaining their confidentiality.
- Maintained files and payments; prepared correspondence; made follow-up calls to check on file and payment status; coordinated physical exams.
- Maintained a 100% on-time processing rate for weekly status reports required in my capacity as Attending Physician's Statement or APS Clerk.

CUSTOMER SERVICE REPRESENTATIVE. Hallmark Bank, Birmingham, AL (1997-98). Learned teller and customer service responsibilities in the 24-hour-a-day customer service operations center of this banking institution prior to a reorganization caused by a corporate buy-out; I decided to seek another position rather than stay with the acquiring company.
- Opened and closed accounts, IRAs, CDs, and saving bonds.

ASSISTANT MANAGER. Certain Weight Loss Clinic, Florence, SC (1997). Managed four sales and customer service associates while motivating people to reach their personal goals of weight loss and improved health; left this job because the weight loss product sold by the company, Phen Fen, was taken off the market and the company closed.
- Handled administrative tasks including scheduling, controlling inventory and ordering stock, maintaining files, and making bank deposits.
- Counseled clients on various methods of weight loss and sold individualized diet programs as well as products such as vitamins and dietary foods and supplements.

CUSTOMER SERVICE REPRESENTATIVE. Korman Telemarketing, Tulsa, OK (1996). While enrolling customers in Blue Cross and Blue Shield health insurance programs, assisted in finding health care providers and advised callers of benefits and options available.

Other experience: U.S. Army. Worked in a Personnel Administration Center.

PERSONAL Operate all standard office equipment including multi-line phone systems, fax machines, and copiers. Can provide excellent references.

Date

Exact Name of Person
Exact Title
Exact Name of Company
Address
City, State, Zip

HUMAN RESOURCE ADMINISTRATOR & REGIONAL OPERATIONS MANAGER
for Kelly Staffing Services

Dear Exact Name of Person: (or Dear Sir or Madam if answering a blind ad)

With the enclosed resume, I would like to make you aware of my interest in exploring employment opportunities with your organization and introduce you to my background related to your business. My academic credentials include an M.S. in Management and a B.A. in Human Resources Administration.

As you will see from my resume, I offer expertise in all aspects of human resources administration, ranging from employee recruiting and placement to reduction-in-force management. For the past four years I have excelled in a track record of advancement with Kelly Staffing, Inc. After increasing the profitability of the company's office in Syracuse, NY, I was specially selected for an internal auditing position which involved conducting audits of 26 offices in NY. Through the leadership and problem solving I provided, the company improved its compliance with federal and state regulations while avoiding problems with the INS. Subsequently promoted to Regional Operations Manager in Eastern NY, I played a key role in developing and implementing a new reduction-in-force policy that permitted the company to downsize several profit centers. I also reduced worker's compensation payments through new safety programs and aggressive case management. A new staffing process I instituted allowed the company to lower costs while improving customer satisfaction.

In previous employment, after beginning as an Assistant Student Supervisor, I rose to the position of Director of Food Services at the same college where I earned my Associate's degree. While managing 30 employees and directing all aspects of a 24/7 service operation which included a catering service, snack bars, and cafeteria service, I earned respect as a skillful mediator and negotiator. I served on the committee which conducted comprehensive position analyses of all administrative posts at the college, and we made recommendations that eliminated many positions while restructuring others. I also played a key role in negotiating a three-year labor contract with support personnel.

Single and available for worldwide relocation and extensive travel as needed, I can provide excellent references. If my background and skills interest you, I hope you will contact me to suggest a time when we could meet in person to discuss your needs. Thank you.

Yours sincerely,

Illena G. Hai

ILLENA G. HAI

1110½ Hay Street, Fayetteville, NC 28305 • preppub@aol.com • (910) 483-6611

OBJECTIVE   I want to positively impact the "bottom line" of an organization through my expertise related to corporate staffing, employee training and development, internal auditing and quality assurance, reduction-in-force management, and human resources administration.

CERTIFICATIONS   Certified Temporary Staffing Specialist (CTSS). Certified in Drug Screening Procedures. Recognized Trainer for National Association of Personnel Services.

EDUCATION   **M.S. in Management,** excelled academically, Fordham University, New York, NY, 1997.
B.A. in Human Resources Administration, *summa cum laude,* Dowling College, Oakdale, NY, 1995.
A.A.S. in Food Service Management, *magna cum laude*, Herkimer County Community College, Herkimer, NY, 1993.

EXPERIENCE   **Excelled in the following track record of advancement with Kelly Staffing, Inc.:**
2002-present: HUMAN RESOURCE ADMINISTRATOR & REGIONAL OPERATIONS MANAGER. Eastern New York. Was promoted to the responsibility of planning, implementing, and directing support activities for seven regional profit centers and six on-site industrial accounts in eastern NY.
- Played a key role in developing and implementing a new reduction-in-force policy that permitted the company to downsize several profit centers.
- Lowered costs and improved customer satisfaction through implementing a new staffing process. Reduced worker's compensation payments through new safety programs.
- Designed, developed, and conducted training programs that improved employee performance; established a new performance development process that improved teamwork, and implemented new team-building training evaluated as the company's "best ever." Developed recruiting programs that placed thousands of employees in jobs.

2000-01: QUALITY ASSURANCE COORDINATOR (INTERNAL AUDITOR). Albany, NY. Was specially selected for this newly created internal auditing position. Conducted internal audits of 26 offices.
- Evaluated forms management, worker's compensation, business management, case management, personnel file management, computer documentation requirements, as well as the interviewing and orientation process in all 26 offices. Retrained employees in proper procedures. Improved compliance with federal and state regulations.

1998-00: BRANCH MANAGER. Syracuse, NY. Supervised two staffing specialists and one front office employee while managing the Syracuse profit center.

Other experience: DIRECTOR OF FOOD SERVICES. At the same college where I earned my associate's degree, began my employment as an Assistant Student Supervisor and then excelled in a track record of promotion to Cafeteria Manager and Director of Food Services with Herkimer County Community College, Herkimer, NY.
- Directed 30 employees while managing the overall operation of a food service department that served three meals a day to 500 customers; wrote the organization's first Employee Handbook and implemented employee training programs that improved productivity.
- Served on numerous college committees including an Administrative Negotiation Team that negotiated a three-year labor contract with support personnel.

PERSONAL   Excellent references. Am single and available for worldwide relocation. Will travel as needed.

Date

Exact Name of Person
Title or Position
Name of Company
Address (no., street)
Address (city, state, zip)

HUMAN RESOURCES ADVISOR for General Dynamics

Dear Exact Name of Person: (or Dear Sir or Madam if answering a blind ad.)

I would appreciate an opportunity to talk with you soon about how I could contribute to your organization through the abilities I have gained related to the management, motivation, counseling, and training of personnel.

As you will see from my enclosed resume, I have consistently advanced with General Dynamics in Harrisburg, PA. This "fast track" career progression was accomplished by dedicating myself to being a strong, concerned, and fair leader who could be counted on to exceed organizational goals.

I excel in building morale and team spirit by setting the standard for my co-workers and peers and by displaying the highest caliber of personal and professional ethics in every aspect of my life. A well-organized individual, I can manage multiple complex tasks simultaneously. This trait has allowed me to complete an Associate Degree, a Bachelor's Degree in Psychology with a minor in Business, and 9 hours toward a Master's Degree in Human Services.

My experience includes serving as an advisor for organizations with up to 2,000 employees. I was handpicked for my current job as the Human Resources Advisor for a 2,000-person work force where I oversee support ranging from training, to promotions and awards, to personnel reassignments, to quality of life issues.

I believe that I am an intelligent, assertive, and talented individual who can offer expertise to any organization looking for a skilled human resources professional.

I hope you will welcome my call soon to arrange a brief meeting at your convenience to discuss your current and future needs and how I might serve them. Thank you in advance for your time.

Sincerely yours,

John A. Cho, Jr.

Alternate last paragraph:
I hope you will call or write me soon to suggest a time convenient for us to meet and discuss your current and future needs and how I might serve them. Thank you in advance for your time.

JOHN A. CHO, JR.

1110½ Hay Street, Fayetteville, NC 28305 • preppub@aol.com • (910) 483-6611

OBJECTIVE   To utilize my expertise in motivating, managing, training, and counseling employees to benefit an organization that has a need for an executive with a proven background of success in personnel management, equal opportunity, and in effectively maximizing human resources.

EDUCATION & EXECUTIVE TRAINING

Have completed 9 hours toward a master's degree in **Human Services**, Jefferson College, Hillsboro, MO.

B.S., Psychology with a minor in Business, Benedict College, Columbia, SC, 1991.

A.S., Psychology with a minor in Business, Furman University, Greenville, SC, 1989.

Excelled in more than one year of training with an emphasis on leadership, personnel management, counseling, and motivational techniques.

EXPERIENCE

Demonstrated human services and managerial expertise which resulted in progressive success with General Dynamics, Harrisburg, PA in the following positions:

2003-present: HUMAN RESOURCES ADVISOR. Harrisburg, PA. Handpicked to advise the senior executive in charge of personnel, maintain administrative control over training, promotions, awards, and quality of life issues for a 2,000-person work force.

- Developed a superior training program for supervisory personnel.

2000-02: HUMAN RESOURCES CONSULTANT. Provided exceptional leadership and guidance during a period of downsizing. Praised for my tact; oversaw the personnel department.

- Handled the details of relocating the headquarters facility of this organization.
- Known for my emphasis on training and constant attention to safety, made every contact with less experienced personnel a chance to provide training and guidance.
- Guided the organization to the highest personnel retention percentage rate in 10 years.

Other experience:

PERSONNEL MANAGER. National Association of Manufacturers, Washington, DC (1998-00). Directed professional development in a 200-person organization as the chief advisor for employees, supervisors, and management personnel; oversaw personnel administration, job performance evaluation, and awards activities.

- Applied my excellent communication abilities to persuade management to approve an awards program for Employee of the Month, Quarter, and Year.
- Brought about a 298% increase in enrollment in educational programs!

TRAINING CONSULTANT. Georgetown University, Washington, DC (1995-97). Provided direct daily counseling and supervision over 47 instructors and staff members in the business department of this prestigious college which provides intensive management development programs for mid-level managers.

- Managed administration of programs for approximately 2,360 students a year, maintenance of $2 million worth of buildings and equipment, and a $178,000 budget.

PERSONNEL AND TRAINING MANAGER. Anheuser-Busch, Milwaukee, WI (1991-94). Instilled self-discipline and motivation in 130 people while overseeing their training and professional development. Achieved improvement in absenteeism through an innovative incentive program. Developed a comprehensive and highly effective counseling program.

PERSONAL   Earned a commendation for my superior leadership skills and professional accomplishments. Offer an optimistic outlook and a sense of humor. Outstanding references.

Date

Exact Name of Person
Title or Position
Name of Company
Address (no., street)
Address (city, state, zip)

HUMAN RESOURCES ANALYST for the city of Muncie, IN. This letter gives some idea of what to say when you are relocating.

Dear Exact Name of Person: (or Dear Sir or Madam if answering a blind ad)

I would appreciate an opportunity to talk with you soon about how I could contribute to your organization through my versatile skills related to human resources and personnel administration as well as management and budget analysis.

Although I live in Evansville with my husband (we are recently married), I currently work for the city of Muncie in its Human Resources Department. Even though I thoroughly enjoy my job and the people with whom I work, I am seeking an employer close to Evansville that can use my exceptionally strong human resources, public relations, budgeting, and finance skills.

My current job was considered a lateral promotion into the human resources field from the finance and budgeting area, where I previously worked. In the city of Muncie's Budget Office, I played a key role in numerous cost-reduction programs which are saving the city thousands of dollars. I made vital input into difficult resourcing decisions and cost-benefit analyses related to matters such as whether to buy or rent uniforms, how to manage the maintenance of a fleet of vehicles, and other similar issues. I am skilled in thinking about costs in creative and resourceful ways, and I believe my thrifty approach to problem-solving and practical cost-cutting style could benefit any organization.

I am a versatile and adaptable person who is known for my professionalism and high personal standards as well as for my reliability and patience. A second-generation native of Evansville, I can offer outstanding personal and professional references from academic, government, and business professionals throughout the Evansville area. I am a loyal person by nature, and I am attempting to find an organization that I can grow with and contribute to over the long range. I feel certain you would find me to be a very capable person who could become a valuable addition to your team.

I hope you will welcome my call soon to arrange a brief meeting at your convenience to discuss your current and future needs and how I might serve them. Thank you in advance for your time.

Sincerely yours,

Amy June Bard-Wilkes

AMY JUNE BARD-WILKES

1110½ Hay Street, Fayetteville, NC 28305 • preppub@aol.com • (910) 483-6611

OBJECTIVE   I would like to contribute to the success of an organization that can use a versatile young professional with a background in human resources, budgeting, and management analysis.

EDUCATION   Earned **Master of Public Affairs** (M.P.A.) degree, concentrating in financial management, Ball State University, Muncie, IN, 1996.
Received **Bachelor of Arts** (B.A.) degree majoring in Psychology with a concentration in Business, University of Evansville, Evansville, IN, 1994.
- Was elected President of the Honor Society.

EXPERIENCE   **HUMAN RESOURCES ANALYST**. City of Muncie Human Resources Department, Muncie, IN (2003-present). As a member of a 17-person department, handle a wide range of analytical, investigative, and public relations responsibilities for a city employing 1,800 people.
- Interview and place employees in job assignments; conduct exit interviews.
- Monitor employee grievance process; coordinate employee suggestion program.
- Verify employment status for Employment Security Commission (ESC); prepare ESC quarterly reports and represent the city in ESC hearings.
- Have been commended for my ability to rapidly analyze, understand, and then apply my knowledge of the guidelines and regulations imposed by ordinances and agencies.

MANAGEMENT/BUDGET ANALYST. City of Muncie Budget Office, IN (2000-02). On my own initiative, played a key role in several cost-reduction programs that are saving the city thousands of dollars: conducted a study that determined that the city should buy rather than rent uniforms; and helped develop the fleet maintenance vehicle program that will lower vehicle costs.
- Worked as part of a team in the ongoing administration of the city's budget, and was known for my practical and innovative recommendations during an era when the city had "zero-growth" or reduction budgets.
- Prepared operating budgets for these and other city activities:
  Fleet Maintenance Fund — $1.8 million   Police Budget — $20.8 million
  Emergency Services — $3.3 million   Planning — $3 million
  Real Estate/Cemeteries — $1 million   Finance — $2.7 million
  Parks and Recreation — $8 million   Civic Center Fund — $1.9 million
- Coordinated all phases of the Impact Fee Ordinance Program.
- Assisted in the preparation of the Capital Improvements Budget.
- Made and presented recommendations of funding levels to the City Council.

HUMAN RESOURCES SECRETARY. V.A. Medical Center, Muncie, IN (1996-99). Learned medical terminology while compiling information on incoming and departing employees and patients; handled admissions procedures and coordinated medical services.
- Recorded and communicated physicians' orders; prepared charts for patient discharge.
- Verified medical eligibility and authorizations for procedures to be performed.

HUMAN RESOURCES INTERN. Wiley County, Evansville, IN (1995). In a college internship, worked in city personnel department projects.
- Studied the "adverse impact" of county hiring procedures; conducted a follow-up survey of a new personnel policy; researched advertising formats for announcing job vacancies.
- Became acquainted with human resources policies and procedures in government.

PERSONAL   Patient and dependable person. Member, International Personnel Management Association.

Date

Exact Name of Person
Title or Position
Name of Company
Address (number and street)
Address (city, state, and ZIP)

HUMAN RESOURCES MANAGER

in a manufacturing environment

Dear Exact Name of Person: (or Dear Sir or Madam if answering a blind ad)

I would appreciate an opportunity to talk with you soon about how I could contribute to your organization through my well-developed planning skills, attention to detail, customer service orientation, and knowledge of personnel management and scheduling in manufacturing environments.

Known for my dedication to high quality, I have always been effective in supervising production workers and leading them to reach or exceed production quotas while keeping costs down. As you will see from my resume, I have excelled as a Production Supervisor and Shipping Supervisor for several area manufacturing firms.

A quick learner who easily becomes familiar with new procedures and methods, I derive satisfaction from passing my knowledge on to others. Highly effective in developing subordinates, I have often been recognized for my ability to provide an example of fairness and honesty for others to follow and for being able to pass my own high performance standards and ethics on to others.

I hope you will welcome my call soon to arrange a brief meeting at your convenience to discuss your current and future needs and how I might serve them. Thank you in advance for your time.

Sincerely yours.

Miranda L. Tempest

Alternate last paragraph:
I hope you will call or write me soon to suggest a time convenient for us to meet and discuss your current and future needs and how I might serve them. Thank you in advance for your time.

MIRANDA L. TEMPEST

1110½ Hay Street, Fayetteville, NC 28305 • preppub@aol.com • (910) 483-6611

OBJECTIVE To offer strong planning and organizational skills to a business that can use a mature individual who excels in jobs that require the ability to develop and maintain good public relations as well as motivate employees to provide outstanding customer service and high levels of productivity.

EXPERIENCE **HUMAN RESOURCES MANAGER.** West Manufacturing, Danville, IL (2003-present). For this 30-year-old steel manufacturing company, handle a wide range of administrative functional areas in order to support a staff of 150 employees and serve as the trusted advisor to the owner who relies on me to react quickly to solve problems as they arise.
- Handle the entire process of interviewing, screening, and hiring employees as well as setting up pre-employment tests, and handling the Workmen's Compensation program.
- Enforce DOT requirements and ensure that truck drivers have proper licensing.
- Oversee internal safety including the hearing protection and respiration programs.
- Am widely recognized for being fair and impartial and for treating all employees with dignity in a company with a high turnover rate. Became especially skilled in reacting quickly to defuse difficult situations and solve multiple problems simultaneously.

PRODUCTION SUPERVISOR. Addison Apparel Company, Addison, IL (1994-02). Earned a reputation as an effective supervisor with the ability to produce high quality products and keep costs down while monitoring the work flow of 40 employees.
- Hired, trained, and supervised employees; then evaluated employee skills and assigned them according to their strong points and capabilities.
- Applied knowledge of quality control standards while corresponding with contract buyers and ensuring compliance in the orders they had received.
- Polished my analytical, mathematical, and reasoning skills.

SHIPPING SUPERVISOR. Elmhurst Sportswear, Inc., Elmhurst, IL (1991-93). For a manufacturer of leisure wear, handled day-to-day activities ranging from production scheduling, to supervising 25 employees involved in tagging and packing merchandise for shipment to distributors, to processing correspondence with contract buyers.
- Applied my attention to detail and math skills while processing invoices for shipping and receiving as well as during the preparation of quarterly tax returns.
- Kept track of employee time cards and tallied payroll figures for 100 employees.
- Refined my communication and human resource management skills while earning recognition for my dedication to producing quality products.

Highlights of earlier experience: As the **PRODUCTION SUPERVISOR** for Peggy Sue Manufacturing, Inc., Elmhurst, IL (1985-91), oversaw quality control support while training/ supervising 25 employees and leading them to reach production levels for this manufacturer.
- Assigned employees to work areas so that production goals could be met.
- Was promoted on the basis of my dedication and dependability after going to work for this company at age 17 and being trained to operate an industrial sewing machine.

TRAINING Completed a computer applications course at Danville Community College, Danville, IL.

PERSONAL Have a reputation for being very fair and not expecting others to do more than I can do myself. Am very quality conscious and dedicated to achieving results. Thrive on challenges. Am known for my ability to handle pressure and deadlines with poise.

Date

Exact Name of Person
Title or Position
Name of Company
Address (no., street)
Address (city, state, zip)

HUMAN RESOURCES RECRUITER

for Megaforce Staffing with previous experience in a Fortune 500 company

Dear Exact Name of Person: (or Dear Sir or Madam if answering a blind ad)

I would appreciate an opportunity to talk with you soon about how I could contribute to your organization through my versatile skills related to human resources and personnel administration as well as management and budget analysis.

I excel in building morale and team spirit by setting the standard for my peers and by displaying the highest caliber of personal and professional ethics in every aspect of my life. A well-organized individual, I can manage multiple complex tasks simultaneously.

My experience includes serving as Human Resources Recruiter for a major temporary placement agency. In my current position I direct a 115-person staff supporting 3,000 "salesmen" performing personnel recruiting throughout 17 states in the U.S. In a previous position, I was a Personnel Manager for United Technologies, managing a personnel administration center. For Manpower, Inc, I administered human resources for a 14-state territory covered by 1,800 personnel recruiters, where I guided the organization to unprecedented production results. I have also worked for Kelly Staffing Services.

I am an intelligent, assertive, and talented individual who can offer expertise to any organization looking for a skilled human resources professional.

I hope you will welcome my call soon to arrange a brief meeting at your convenience to discuss your current and future needs and how I might serve them. Thank you in advance for your time.

Sincerely yours,

Amos J. Thurman

AMOS J. THURMAN

1110½ Hay Street, Fayetteville, NC 28305 • preppub@aol.com • (910) 483-6611

OBJECTIVE   To offer my problem-solving and decision-making skills to an organization in need of a positive and energetic professional who has excelled in managing financial, human, and physical resources for maximum productivity.

EXPERIENCE   **HUMAN RESOURCES RECRUITER.** Mega Force Staffing, Inc., San Antonio, TX (2003-present). Direct a 115-person staff which supports 3,000 "salesmen" involved in personnel recruiting throughout 17 states in the U.S.; control a $2.5 million budget and formulate policies and procedures.
- Directed an update and merger of one million automated records that resulted in error-free record keeping. Led a conference which developed solutions for personnel problems.
- Supervise the contractual relationship between Mega Force Staffing and its corporate clients in 17 states; continuously troubleshoot problems related to client relationships, contract negotiations, and accounts receivable.

PERSONNEL MANAGER. United Technologies, West Chester, PA (2000-02). Managed a personnel administration center which serviced more than 700 executives and 8,000 employees; scheduled/coordinated advanced training programs and presided over executive promotion selections.
- Developed and implemented a plan to cut a 2,000-person recruiting force by 500 people; saved $2 million while boosting productivity.
- Designed a professional development course which led to better-trained sales personnel and vastly increased sales productivity.

REGIONAL PERSONNEL ADMINISTRATOR. Manpower, Inc., Canton, OH (1996-99). Administered a 14-state territory covered by 1,800 personnel recruiters.
- Guided the organization to unprecedented production results.
- Developed a quality assurance plan that led to 100% completion of goals.

SALES AND RECRUITING COORDINATOR. Kelly Staffing, Inc., New York, NY (1994-96). Led a diverse staff of 28 employees including advertising, logistics, public relations, sales promotion, and educational professionals who supported 132 recruiters; managed a $700,000 budget and internal control systems.
- Conceived of and implemented an innovative personnel rotation plan that reduced employee turnover 25% and improved production 15%.
- Led the organization to be recognized as "the best" among eight similar organizations.

Highlights of other experience: Excelled in jobs in the aviation field.
- As a **Training Chief**, directed instructor pilots and created courses of instruction.
- As an **Airport Manager** for two years, achieved a perfect safety record: there were no ground or air accidents.

EDUCATION   B.S. degree in **Business Administration**, Ithaca College, Ithaca, NY, 1991.
Completed advanced training in personnel management and administration.
Have begun course work in an MBA program.

PERSONAL   Enjoy putting projects together and seeing successful results. Often described as "a perfectionist." Can provide excellent professional and personal references.

Date

Exact Name of Person
Title or Position
Name of Company
Address (no., street)
Address (city, state, zip)

HUMAN RESOURCES CONSULTANT

for a private staffing firm

Dear Exact Name of Person: (or Dear Sir or Madam if answering a blind ad)

I would appreciate an opportunity to talk with you soon about how I could contribute to your organization through my versatile skills related to human resources management.

Recruited for my current position as Human Resources Consultant and Account Executive for Employment Opportunities, Inc. in Allentown, PA, I am known as a concerned and fair leader who can be counted on to exceed organizational goals. I excel in building morale and team spirit by setting the standard for my subordinates and peers and by displaying the highest caliber of personal and professional ethics. A well-organized individual, I can manage multiple complex tasks simultaneously.

I believe I have excelled professionally because of the valuable skills in teamwork which I gained as an athlete in high school, college, and after college. I was fortunate to receive numerous sports honors while in high school and college, and I became a free agent draft pick of the Pittsburgh Steelers. It is my belief that sports is a great training ground for leaders because the athlete learns how to persist despite seemingly insurmountable obstacles. Because of my involvement in sports, I offer unlimited confidence in my ability to deal with others in an effective manner.

I hope you will welcome my call soon to arrange a brief meeting at your convenience to discuss your current and future needs and how I might serve them. Thank you in advance for your time.

Sincerely yours,

Lyle O. Vernon

Alternate last paragraph:
I hope you will call or write me soon to suggest a time convenient for us to meet and discuss your current and future needs and how I might serve them. Thank you in advance for your time.

LYLE O. VERNON

1110½ Hay Street, Fayetteville, NC 28305   •   preppub@aol.com   •   (910) 483-6611

OBJECTIVE To benefit an organization that can use a versatile professional with a strong background of knowledge and experience in human resources and personnel recruiting/administration along with proven skills in sales, marketing, and business/operations management.

EDUCATION **B.A. degree in Sociology,** Widener University, Chester, PA 1992.
Studied **Computer Technology**, Butler County Community College, Butler, PA.
Was elected Student Body President.

SPORTS HONORS
- Free Agent Draft Pick, Pittsburgh Steelers (N.F.L.), 1993.
- Pre-Season All A.C.C., All-Conference Selection, 1992.
- All-Conference, All-City-County Player of the Year, J.C. Coleman Player of the Year, Team MVP, Shrine Bowl, All-East High School All-American, Team Captain.
- Named Best Field Athlete in *Track;* Best Defensive Player in *Basketball;* and Best Offensive Player in *Football,* was Co-Captain and Co-MVP Football and Basketball.

EXPERIENCE **HUMAN RESOURCES CONSULTANT & ACCOUNT EXECUTIVE.** Employment Opportunities, Inc., Allentown, PA (2003-present). Work with human resources executives and personnel managers throughout Pennsylvania to meet their needs for temporary and permanent employees.
- For one major account, played a key role in revising the employee handbook; for another major account, assisted in the formulation of a testing/screening module.
- Handle administrative matters related to Workman's Compensation, payroll corrections, employee wage increases, and employee terminations/disciplinary actions.
- Perform pre-employment drug screening, background and reference checks.
- Was recruited for this position in Allentown after excelling in a supervisory role in Scranton; supervise 350 temporary employees (90% of Hispanic origin).

TERRITORY MANAGER. Kraft Foods Company, Reading, PA (1995-02). Began with Kraft Foods as a Sales Representative I; was rapidly promoted to Sales Representative II, and then was selected as Territory Manager.
- Serviced wholesale and retail accounts, both chains and independents, in our territory.
- Developed a weekly strategy and trained merchandisers on implementation methods after making key management decisions including targeting areas for greatest production yields. In 1998, was named to a Direct Sales President's Club, a sales honor reserved for top sales producers.
- In a national corporate competition, led my team to win thousands of dollars in prizes as we finished in first, second, and third place nationally three years in a row based on sales volume as well as numerous technical measures related to inventory control, shelf space increases, and customer service. Trained/managed employees promoting Kraft products on displays and through sampling at retail, special events, and trade shows.

CREDIT MANAGER. United National Bank, Chester, PA (1993-95). Trained and supervised a staff of five employees in the Credit Application Department.

Other experience: After college, worked from 1992-93 in an administrative role in a freight distribution business; tracked lost freight and accounted for warehouse discrepancies.

PERSONAL Can provide exceptional professional references. Received Key to City of Chester in 1994!

Date

Exact Name of Person
Exact Title
Exact Name of Company
Address
City, State, Zip

HUMAN RESOURCES COORDINATOR
for the Department of Natural Resources

Dear Exact Name of Person: (or Dear Sir or Madam if answering a blind ad)

I would appreciate an opportunity to talk with you soon about how I could contribute to your organization through my experience and effectiveness in coordinating human resources. With the enclosed resume, I would like to make you aware of my background in personnel and administrative management as well as the contributions I could make to your organization.

In my current position as a Human Resources Coordinator for the Department of Natural Resources, I have been credited with bringing about improvements in numerous operational areas. I have been involved in managing finances for more than 350 employees on staff while acting as an advisor for personnel pay, travel and recruitment issues. In a previous position with San Diego State University's Personnel Department, I was involved in a wide range of personnel and human resources activities. Because of my desire to contribute to the community, I have also volunteered for several years as a Personnel Assistant with a local support services organization.

Throughout my career I have been evaluated as an articulate and intelligent individual who possesses the ability to remain in control and handle any amount of pressure or stress. If you can use an experienced management professional known for honesty and dedication to excellence, I hope you will contact me to suggest a time when we might meet to discuss your needs. I can assure you in advance that I could rapidly become an asset to your organization.

Sincerely,

Angela K. Messex

ANGELA K. MESSEX

1110½ Hay Street, Fayetteville, NC 28305 • preppub@aol.com • (910) 483-6611

OBJECTIVE To contribute to a company that can use an individual with outstanding human resources skills, training, and education.

EDUCATION **B. A. in Human Resources Management,** Pepperdine University, Claremont, CA, 2002. Completed two-year **Personnel Assistant** program at San Diego State University, San Diego, CA, 1999.

EXPERIENCE **HUMAN RESOURCES COORDINATOR.** Department of Natural Resources, Claremont, CA (2003-present). Provide administrative support to the Department of Natural Resources personnel assigned to the Claremont area. Manage finances for more than 350 employees.
- Act as the advisor for personnel pay, travel, and recruitment issues.
- Publish orders and hold responsibility for $100,000 travel budget.
- Manage the financial, administrative, and travel records of over 160 personnel members.
- On formal performance evaluations, was evaluated as "a hard charger who is willing to do whatever it takes to get the job done."
- Routinely wrote and delivered briefings and speeches praised for their concise style.
- Utilize computers regularly, and have developed specialized expertise with Excel while using that program to manage the temporary duty budget. Became skilled in database management.
- Maintain daily statistical records for annual reports. Continuously seek new methods of improving internal efficiency while maintaining administrative and personnel files.

PERSONNEL ASSISTANT (VOLUNTEER—PART-TIME). Radell's Community Support Services, Claremont, CA (1997-present). In this volunteer job which I perform on a full-time basis, work in numerous phases of human resources administration.

RECEPTIONIST/PHOTOLITHOGRAPHIC TEAM LEADER. San Diego Herald, San Diego, CA (1997-2002). Managed personnel files while also writing and presenting briefings to supervisors and newspaper editors for short and long-range training calendars.
- As a Photolithograhic Team Leader, managed two people and performed daily photolithographer operations using plate, camera, layout, and photomechanical procedures; was responsible for equipment in excess of $350,000.

ADMINISTRATIVE ASSISTANT. San Diego State University—Personnel Office, San Diego, CA (1996-1997). Supported five administrative employees in the Personnel Office supporting 500 students; was involved in the full range of personnel administration activities.
- Researched, prepared, and processed registration packets and financial aid information packets. Typed correspondence used notes, drafts, verbal instructions, or other courses to prepare documents.
- Prepared suspense control documents and maintained suspense files.
- In an ongoing process once a month, acted as supervisor in charge of training and managing all administrative duties; counseled students on how to handle personal and career matters.
- Acted as Customer Service Representative.

COMPUTERS Highly proficient in utilizing a variety of software and operating systems.

PERSONAL Outstanding personal and professional references upon request. Strong work ethic.

CAREER CHANGE

Date

Exact Name of Person
Exact Title
Exact Name of Company
Address
City, State, Zip

Dear Exact Name of Person: (or Dear Sir or Madam if answering a blind ad)

HUMAN RESOURCES COUNSELOR & CASE WORKER
This individual has a strong desire to transition into the academic community.

With the enclosed resume, I would like to make you aware of my interest in exploring positions within student affairs, academic affairs, and student life at your institution. I am a highly educated individual with a track record of strong results related to building rapport with people of all ages and socioeconomic levels.

From my enclosed resume you will see that I have earned three degrees: a B.A. in Sociology from the University of Phoenix, and an M.A. in Sociology and a Master of Divinity in Theology from the University of Arizona. I have succeeded professionally as a chaplain through University of Arizona Divinity School and as a case worker with the Department of Social Services.

You will notice on my resume that, while earning my M.A. in Sociology, I performed extensive analysis and interviewing in order to learn about students' experiences in adjusting to the large university setting. My findings and analysis served in part as the inspiration for a course at University of Arizona that is helping students adapt to life at the school. I co-authored "First Experiences of the Bureaucratic Kind: Freshman Experience with Campus Bureaucracy," published in *The Journal of Higher Education*.

While involved in field experiences through the University of Arizona Divinity School, I had many opportunities to refine my human resources skills. I was evaluated as "a caring individual who people learn to trust" and I was commended for my ability to "initiate new ideas and carry through with those ideas." I am known as a compassionate individual who genuinely cares about people, and I am also respected as an excellent organizer.

Although I am held in the highest regard in my current position can provide excellent references at the appropriate time, I have decided that I wish to use my social service skills to aid students.

If you can use an intelligent individual who excels in building effective relations and helping others reach personal and professional goals, I hope you will call or write me soon to suggest a time when we might have a brief discussion of how I could contribute to your organization.

Sincerely,

Jonathan B. Golding

JONATHAN B. GOLDING

1110½ Hay Street, Fayetteville, NC 28305 • preppub@aol.com • (910) 483-6611

OBJECTIVE To offer my reputation as a creative, compassionate individual with excellent counseling and listening skills. I offer strong analytical and fact-finding abilities along with a talent for helping and motivating young adults and ministering to people of all ages.

PUBLICATIONS Co-authored "First Encounters of the Bureaucratic Kind: Freshman Experience with Campus Bureaucracy," published in *The Journal of Higher Education,* 1996.

EDUCATION **Master of Divinity in Theology,** University of Arizona, Tucson, AZ, 2003.
- Maintained a 3.1 GPA while excelling in two part-time paid positions related to my field.

M.A., Sociology, University of Arizona, Tucson, AZ 1998.
- Achieved a 3.8 GPA while simultaneously working as a Graduate Research Assistant.
- Interviewed administrators and freshman about students' experiences in adjusting to the large university setting; my findings and analysis served in part as the inspiration for a course at U of A that is helping students adapt to life at school.

B.A., Sociology, University of Phoenix, Phoenix, AZ, 1996.
Completed special training which included Red Cross Shelter Operations and Disaster Relief Caseworker course and Clinical Pastoral Education.

EXPERIENCE *Am held in high regard; have been hired and rehired on three separate occasions by the Maricopa County Department of Social Services, Tucson, AZ, in the process of earning three degrees:*
HUMAN RESOURCES COUNSELOR & CASE WORKER II. (1996-present). Have become highly skilled in handling multiple tasks and dealing with individuals of all socioeconomic levels while counseling people and coordinating public assistance caseloads of up to 400 cases within regulated guidelines.
- Am adept at "tracking down" the right department or person within bureaucracies who can solve the client's needs; highly proficient in performing computer research, locate and "track down" a highly mobile clientele while performing liaison with employers, government agencies, and other organizations to obtain data and records.
- Observe strict attention to detail because federal audits require that paperwork be perfect; am skilled in interpreting and applying state and federal guidelines which must be stringently adhered to in matters of budgeting; process financial information while budgeting monthly income and calculating benefit amounts and Medicaid deductibles.
- Recognized for **outstanding service** in 2002.

Gained experience in counseling and research while financing my education:
STUDENT CHAPLAIN and **ASSISTANT MINISTER.** University of Arizona Divinity School Field Education, Tucson, AZ (2002-03). Held two separate positions:
- Carried out activities which included preaching, developing and leading a Bible study class for older adults, leading a youth group during retreat, and visiting hospital patients.

GRADUATE RESEARCH ASSISTANT. University of Arizona, Tucson, AZ (1999-03). As the principal research assistant for a project sponsored by the American Association of Retired Persons, examined friendship patterns, habits, and lifestyle changes of older adults (55 to 85) through random telephone calls.

PERSONAL Offer excellent counseling, communication, and analytical skills. Am proficient with computers and knowledgeable of Microsoft Word and Windows. Excellent references.

Date

Exact Name of Person
Title or Position
Name of Company
Address (no., street)
Address (city, state, zip)

HUMAN RESOURCES DEPARTMENT MANAGER for AT&T

Dear Exact Name of Person: (or Dear Sir or Madam if answering a blind ad)

I would appreciate an opportunity to talk with you soon about how I could contribute to your organization through my background of outstanding performance in functional areas including personnel, human resources, security, logistics, and operations management.

In my current position with AT&T, I manage a personnel recruiting program for management trainees while managing a staff of 32 people. I have developed a highly effective counseling program which has improved employee morale while decreasing turnover. In a previous position with Beatrice Foods, I was recruited to serve as Reengineering Manager when the company needed an astute human resources manager to provide leadership in reducing its 600-person work force in half.

Known as an articulate and intelligent individual with a concerned and compassionate style of leadership, I have advanced ahead of my peers in a track record of accomplishments in the human resources field. Throughout my career I have consistently been recognized as a superb planner with a talent for seeing to the details that allow the organization to meet both short-term and long-range goals and objectives.

I believe you would find me to be an enthusiastic and energetic individual who works well under stress and severe time constraints.

I hope you will welcome my call soon to arrange a brief meeting at your convenience to discuss your current and future needs and how I might serve them. Thank you in advance for your time.

Sincerely yours,

Raymond W. Early

Alternate last paragraph:
I hope you will call or write me soon to suggest a time convenient for us to meet and discuss your current and future needs and how I might serve them. Thank you in advance for your time.

RAYMOND W. EARLY

1110½ Hay Street, Fayetteville, NC 28305　•　preppub@aol.com　•　(910) 483-6611

OBJECTIVE　　To contribute through my reputation as an articulate and intelligent professional who offers the ability to solve problems as well as with a background as a talented administrator.

EXPERIENCE　　**HUMAN RESOURCES DEPARTMENT MANAGER.** AT&T, Santa Clara, CA (2003-present). Using my communication skills and background of success, interview and prescreen applicants for possible employment. Oversee the personnel department of 32 people.
- Initiated a new employee benefits package which was credited with reducing employee turnover. Evaluate employee performance and recommend promotions.
- Known for my emphasis on training and safety, ensure that every contact with less experienced personnel is used as a chance to provide training.
- Developed and now manage a highly effective counseling program.

REENGINEERING MANAGER. Beatrice Foods, Sacramento, CA (2001-02). Because of my reputation as an outstanding planner and strategist, was recruited to manage the complex details of a corporate reorganization which reduced a 600-person work force to 300 people and eliminated unnecessary equipment valued in excess of $5 million.
- In a job normally held by a more experienced person, reduced the disruptive aspects of a major restructuring/downsizing and significantly improved the quality of maintenance and logistics operations.

ASSISTANT PERSONNEL MANAGER. U.S. Chamber of Commerce, Washington, DC (2000). Managed eight departments which developed plans and coordinated operational and maintenance support for a 550-person organization.
- Became adept at coordinating human resources for maximum efficiency and planned an association reorganization evaluated as "brilliant and comprehensive."

ASSOCIATE MANAGER. General Motors, Detroit, MI (1998-99). Excelled in a position which required the ability to handle diversity and change while attending to complex details during the development and execution of a $10 million annual operating budget and the coordination of all aspects of logistical support for a 1,600-person organization.
- Ensured compliance with EEO and Affirmative Action guidelines.
- Created the model plan used for logistics operations throughout the region.

STRATEGIC PLANNING MANAGER. Lion Manufacturing Co., Detroit MI (1996-97). Developed the guidelines to be used in the reduction of personnel due to downsizing. Assisted dismissed employees in acquiring positions elsewhere.

RECRUITER. Kelly Staffing, Inc., Chicago, IL (1994-95). Implemented recruiting strategies which resulted in recruiting approximately 5,000 qualified young adults annually. Ensured the quality and quantity of personnel to meet increased personnel needs of major customers.

GENERAL MANAGER. U.S. Army, Ft. Meade, MD (1990-93). Streamlined and improved all measurable areas of support and performance while directing all aspects of training, performance, maintenance, and logistics at the headquarters of a 1,200-person organization.

EDUCATION　　Completing a master's degree in **Human Services**, Santa Clara University, Santa Clara, CA.
B.A., Psychology, Portland State University, Portland, OR, 1991.

PERSONAL　　Known for my honesty and integrity. Methodical planner with a knack for meeting deadlines.

Date

Exact Name of Person
Exact Title
Exact Name of Company
Address
City, State, Zip

HUMAN RESOURCES DEVELOPMENT MASTER'S DEGREE CANDIDATE
currently working as an Instructor/Writer at a major medical center

Dear Exact Name of Person: (or Dear Sir or Madam if answering a blind ad)

With the enclosed resume, I would like to make you aware of my extensive background related to human resources and acquaint you with my interest in seeking employment with your organization.

Human Resources Education
As you will see from my enclosed resume, I gained extensive experience related to human resources while performing with distinction in the medical field. I earned, with honors, two M.A. degrees—in Human Resources Development and Management.

Personnel Training and Employee Development Experience
Presently excelling in a job which requires strong teaching, research, and writing skills, I provide academic and performance counseling for students in an executive development course for medical supervisors. In addition to instructing and counseling students, I write and revise lesson plans, update materials and equipment, and recruit subject matter experts to help develop and instruct sections of the course. Prior to this assignment, I worked in medical centers as a Medical Aide, which required extensive public contact as well as excellent communication skills, tact, and patience.

Outstanding personal reputation and language skills
I have consistently been cited for my ability and willingness to give my time to mentor, train, and instruct others and for my effectiveness in working with people from varied backgrounds. I am fluent in Spanish. A member of the Society of Human Resource Managers, I am a versatile and highly self-motivated individual known for my ability to adapt to challenges, stress, and deadlines.

If you can use an articulate and self-motivated leader with experience related to human resources management as well as training program development and management, please contact me soon to suggest a time when we might have a brief discussion of how I could contribute to your organization. I will provide excellent professional and personal references at the appropriate time.

Sincerely,

Neville L. Montrose

NEVILLE L. MONTROSE

1110½ Hay Street, Fayetteville, NC 28305 • preppub@aol.com • (910) 483-6611

OBJECTIVE To offer a broad base of experience in human resource management as well as employee training, development, and instruction to an organization that can use a versatile professional with outstanding organizational, management, communication, and problem-solving skills.

AFFILIATION Member of the **Society of Human Resource Managers.**

EDUCATION & TRAINING

M.A., Human Resources Development, California State University, Los Angeles, CA, 2003; 3.65 GPA.

M.A., Management, California State University, Los Angeles, CA, 2002; 3.65 GPA.
- *Thesis:* Evaluated the human resource program of Northern Arizona University; focused research on cost effectiveness of the program and how well it prepared students for "the real world".

B.S., Nursing Studies, Northern Arizona University, Flagstaff, AZ, 1994; 3.6 GPA.

SPECIAL SKILLS

Computers: Familiar with Microsoft Office Suite.
Languages: Speak, read, write, and understand Spanish.
Security clearance: Top Secret security clearance.
Medical: National Registry Emergency Medical Technicians, EMT Basic and Paramedic. Licensed in pediatric, advanced cardiac, advanced trauma life support, and EMT
- Current EMT-B, EMT-P, BCLS, ACLS, PALS, and PHTLS; trained in ATLS.

EXPERIENCE

INSTRUCTOR/WRITER. Los Angeles Medical Training Center, Los Angeles, CA (2002-present). Provide a wide range of academic counseling and instruction along with technical consulting and support related to research, organization, and writing materials for a course for medical supervisors.
- Act as **Primary Instructor** for subjects which include the administrative records and reports and maintenance functions as well as medical subjects and surgical procedures.
- Receive praise from students, peers, and subordinates for superior teaching skills as well as for my leadership style.

MEDICAL AIDE. Bayside Medical Offices, La Jolla, CA (2000-01). Working with four physicians, controlled inventories of supplies in order to provide treatment and care to patients; refined instructional and human resources management skills while working with nurses and dealing with patients in this busy medical setting. Assisted with treatment, and frequently was praised by patients for my skill and tact while treating them.
- Supported nurses by voluntarily taking over some of their duties when we were understaffed or very busy.
- Acted as a mentor for new personnel to train them on office requirements.
- Became adept at quickly establishing and setting up medical care facilities and controlling inventories of equipment and supplies in order to provide proper treatment.

MEDICAL AIDE. Beale Medical Center, Memphis, TN (1994-99). Gained and refined skills in providing routine and emergency medical treatment, assisting with nursing care, and maintaining medical records and files.

Highlights of earlier experience: Worked as an EMT for an ambulance company in Arizona.

PERSONAL Excellent references on request.

Date

Exact Name of Person
Exact Title
Exact Name of Company
Address
City, State, Zip

HUMAN RESOURCES DIRECTOR

for Hechts, a prominent retailer

Dear Exact Name of Person: (or Dear Sir or Madam if answering a blind ad)

I would appreciate an opportunity to talk with you soon about how I could contribute to your organization through my experience and effectiveness in managing human, material, and fiscal resources.

With the enclosed resume, I would like to make you aware of my background with its emphasis on personnel and administrative management as well as through the contributions I can make in automation technology. In my current position as Personnel Manager at Hechts in Atlanta, I have been credited with bringing about improvements in numerous operational areas. In my previous position as Human Resources Director, I established management techniques and programs which were adopted for use in Mega Force recruiting offices throughout the country.

In a previous job with K-Mart, I ensured personnel availability for more than 100 stores. With the majority of my experience centered in administration and personnel, I have developed versatile knowledge of functional areas including supply and logistics, automation, and assets management as well as in advertising, public affairs, and program development and management.

Throughout my career I have been evaluated as an articulate and intelligent individual who possesses the ability to remain in control and handle any amount of pressure or stress. If you can use an experienced management professional known for honesty and dedication to excellence, I hope you will contact me to suggest a time when we might meet to discuss your needs. I can assure you in advance that I could rapidly become an asset to your organization.

Sincerely,

Harold E. Raynes

HAROLD E. RAYNES ("Harry")

1110½ Hay Street, Fayetteville, NC 28305 • preppub@aol.com • (910) 483-6611

OBJECTIVE	To contribute through managerial experience refined in a distinguished career in human resources; recognized for sound decision-making skills as well as for effectiveness in maximizing human, material, and fiscal resources.
EDUCATION & TRAINING	**B.S., Business Administration**, University of Mobile, Mobile, AL, 1994. **A.A., Business Administration**, Calhoun Community College, Decatur, AL, 1990. Completed advanced training programs emphasizing staff development and management.
COMPUTERS	Proficient with Windows, Microsoft Excel, Word, and PowerPoint.
EXPERIENCE	**HUMAN RESOURCES DIRECTOR.** Hechts, Atlanta, GA (2003-present). Oversee a nine-person staff as the developer of personnel plans and programs.

- Manage functions including promotions, performance reports, and personnel availability.
- Developed employee training programs and revitalized employee recognition programs.

HUMAN RESOURCES DIRECTOR. Mega Force Staffing Services, Inc., Atlanta, GA (2002-2003). Cited for developing improvements in every aspect of operations, directed a staff of 30 in personnel recruiting while ensuring the quality of advertising, public affairs, budgeting and accounting, supply, administration, and educational programs.

- Designed a standardized interview script used in recruitment. Accounted for $2 million worth of equipment.
- Applied my technical knowledge of both hardware and software while managing a complete automation project to include developing and conducting individual and collective training for 250 geographically scattered people.
- Provided "flawless" management of a $3.5 million budget. Established management techniques and programs adopted by my counterparts from coast to coast.

DIRECTOR OF TRAINING AND PLANS. Motorola, Inc., Tallahassee, FL (1999-02). After a year as the Assistant Director, was promoted to oversee the integration of all aspects of training for the company's recruiting operations and to develop doctrine for sales training and production management subject matter; managed a $1.6 million operating budget.

- Planned and directed the organization's largest and most successful training event ever.

OPERATIONS MANAGER. Kelly Staffing Service, Montgomery, GA (1996-98). Provided expertise in such diverse areas as analyzing statistical data, advising and briefing senior executives, planning and carrying out policy decisions, and supervising a staff of guidance counselors for a region with 37 recruiting offices scattered throughout 37,586 square miles.

PERSONNEL AND ADMINISTRATIVE OPERATIONS MANAGER. K-Mart, Inc., Mobile, AL (1993-95). Exceeded standards for timely and accurate processing of personnel actions while supervising six people preparing performance reports for employees at all levels, promotions, and ensuring personnel availability for more than 100 stores.

GENERAL MANAGER. Walgreens, Huntsville, AL (1990-92). Managed a 214-person organization with and $17 million worth of property and equipment while ensuring availability of adequate stock and personnel.

PERSONAL	Have frequently been described as "unflappable" and as an individual who can be counted on under pressure, change, and stress. Can provide outstanding references upon request.

Date

Exact Name of Person
Title or Position
Name of Company
Address (no., street)
Address (city, state, zip)

HUMAN RESOURCES MANAGER

in a medical environment

Dear Exact Name of Person: (or Dear Sir or Madam if answering a blind ad)

I would appreciate an opportunity to talk with you soon about how I could contribute to your organization through my proven management, strategic planning, and communication skills.

As you will see from my enclosed resume, I have earned a reputation as an astute problem solver and "opportunity finder" while excelling in challenging jobs in the medical field. Most recently I was selected for a "hot seat" job which involved me in designing and implementing systems used to provide medical and logistical support for Southwestern General Hospital. In a previous job at Children's Hospital in Boston, I had the position of Executive Manager, and I worked with executives in rebuilding the hospital's medical infrastructure.

I pride myself on my ability to walk into a new organization and find new ways to improve productivity and minimize costs. I have become known for my strong belief in "leadership by example" and for my selflessness in putting first the needs of others and the organization's goals, utilizing the Total Quality Management (TQM) system. With a proven ability to work well with others, I excelled in positions at several major medical hospitals where I was responsible for managing hundreds of people and multimillion-dollar assets.

I hope you will call or write me soon to suggest a time convenient for us to meet and discuss your current and future needs and how I might serve them. Thank you in advance for your time.

Sincerely yours,

Oscar M. Helmes

OSCAR M. HELMES

1110½ Hay Street, Fayetteville, NC 28305 • preppub@aol.com • (910) 483-6611

OBJECTIVE To contribute to an organization that can use an experienced manager, motivator, and problem solver who offers exceptional planning, public relations, and communication skills along with versatile knowledge related to human relations, medical services, and logistical operations.

EDUCATION Earned **Master of Arts (M.A.) degree**, **Human Resources Management**, University of Pennsylvania, Philadelphia, PA, 1996.
Received **Bachelor of Science (B.S.) degree**, Home Economics (Dietetics), Gettysburg College, Gettysburg, PA, 1992.

EXPERIENCE **HUMAN RESOURCES MANAGER.** Southwestern General Hospital, Los Alamos, NM (2002-present). Was handpicked for this top-level planning job which involves developing strategic medical plans along with the operational details of those plans, for overall reorganization of services provided at Southwestern General. This includes updating recruitment practices, personnel policy, and the employee benefits plan.
- Direct strategic planning related to the medical services provided.
- Ensure availability of qualified personnel to ensure a smooth and profitable operation.

LOGISTICS OPERATIONS MANAGER. General Mills, St. Paul, MN (2000-02). Designed and implemented logistical systems and procedures for this major food manufacturer.
- Automated the inventory control computer system, resulting in improved availability of supplies, which was regarded as "instrumental in increasing overall productivity."

EXECUTIVE MANAGER. Children's Hospital, Boston, MA (1998-00). Supervised six managers and 24 other personnel while overseeing provision of medical, maintenance, and supply, and transportation services. Was in charge of the personnel department.
- Updated personnel policies, improving employee morale and reducing turnover.
- Designed their first formal employee orientation program, which ensured all employees received up-to-date information concerning policies, rules, and benefits. Evaluated the employee benefits package and recommended changes which resulted in a cost savings to Children's Hospital.
- Reduced worker's compensation payments through new safety programs.

HEALTH SERVICES PLANNING COORDINATOR. Women's Clinic, Philadelphia, PA (1996-97). Was selected to direct the reorganization of services, to include selection of personnel, benefits plan, and suppliers.
- Praised for improving the availability of services as well as profitability.

HUMAN RESOURCES MANAGER. Gettysburg Medical Center, Gettysburg, PA (1994-96). Directed the Support Services and Personnel departments in developing new personnel policies and benefit plans. Planned and directed personnel training and staff development, including budgets, training needs analysis, short- and long-term training plains, leadership development, on-the-job training, testing and evaluation, and employee orientation.
- Supervised 800 personnel working in this 500-bed hospital with a pharmacy, laboratory, optometry clinic, psychiatric clinic, occupational and physical therapy clinics, as well as in social work, dietary services, and patient administration.

PERSONAL Received numerous commendations and awards recognizing my superior management ability. Am a selfless person who can put first the needs of others and the organization's goals.

Date

Exact Name of Person
Title or Position
Name of Company
Address (no., street)
Address (city, state, zip)

HUMAN RESOURCES MANAGER
for Reliant Energy

Dear Exact Name of Person: (or Dear Sir or Madam if answering a blind ad)

I would appreciate an opportunity to talk with you soon about how I could contribute to your organization through my versatile experience and education as well as through my background of superior performance in positions requiring integrity and a strong character. With a reputation as a talented communicator, administrator, and planner of large-scale operations, I offer experience in such diverse areas as collecting and analyzing statistics, preparing and presenting concise and thorough briefings and reports, and training and counseling employees to achieve outstanding results.

As you will see from my resume, I offer an M.A. degree in Human Resources Development. Throughout my working experience, I have been chosen for positions where I was called on to guide, counsel, and lead employees in a wide range of training and operations activities.

I have consistently been singled out as an exceptionally skilled writer and briefer who can present complex concepts in an easily understood manner. Known for my keen intellect, common sense, and ability to think on my feet, I have been effective in dealing with people ranging from the general public, to people making decisions on college and vocational choices, to technical and administrative personnel.

An aggressive, energetic, and enthusiastic professional, I am also known for my adaptability and sound judgment. I have always excelled in positions which require high levels of integrity, good character, and leadership talents. I am experienced in supervising vocational counselors and providing counseling.

I hope you will welcome my call soon to arrange a brief meeting at your convenience to discuss your current and future needs and how I might serve them. Thank you in advance for your time.

Sincerely yours,

Ernest R. Ebbings

ERNEST R. EBBINGS

1110½ Hay Street, Fayetteville, NC 28305 • preppub@aol.com • (910) 483-6611

OBJECTIVE I want to contribute to an organization that can use a versatile professional who offers proven abilities related to personnel administration, counseling, and operations management along with strong analytical, communication, and public relations skills.

EDUCATION & TRAINING **M.A., Human Resources Development** with minor concentration in Public Administration, University of Colorado, Pueblo campus, CO, 2001.
B.S., Psychology, North Central College, Naperville, IL, 1992.
- Graduated *magna cum laude* with a 3.86 GPA.

A.A., General Studies, North Central College, Naperville, IL, 1990.
Completed advanced training in operations, management, and supervision, human resources, counseling, and interviewing techniques.

COMPUTERS Knowledgeable of computer software including Word, Excel, Access, and WordPerfect.

EXPERIENCE **HUMAN RESOURCES MANAGER.** Reliant Energy, Pasadena, CA (2002-present). Was recruited for this position which involves supervising 15 employees gathering and analyzing information for government reports and internal use. Oversee a budget of $1.5 million.
- Developed training programs for all departments which resulted in increased productivity.
- Supervised renovation of employee and executive dining rooms.
- Reorganized the benefits and compensation packages for employees which resulted in increased employee morale as well as financial savings for the company.
- Earned praise from upper management for a new employee manual which I designed and wrote.

SENIOR DATA ANALYST. Citigroup, Inc., Pueblo, CO (1996-02). Because of my excellent investigative skills and "common sense approach," was handpicked for this job supervising 12 specialists in collecting and analyzing marketing data related to these areas:

personnel security   property accountability
administration   personnel training and counseling
budget preparation   long-range planning

- Contributed to major changes in a wide variety of job specialties which included administration, maintenance, and operations.

MARKETING CONSULTANT. Sara Lee Foods, Muskegon, MI (1993-95). In a consulting position normally held by someone of more experience, provided weekly written and oral briefings containing my analysis of the marketplace; as a general manager, supervised and trained 28 employees.
- Established standard operating procedures (SOPs) for a 1,400-person organization while guiding 195 employees in achieving the highest test scores in the parent organization in every area of job performance and knowledge tested.

Highlights of earlier experience: In an advertising agency, gained experience in the areas of employee program development and administration, marketing, and analysis while earning a reputation for "setting the performance standard."

PERSONAL Certified as a Notary Public. Member of the Shriners, Veterans of Foreign Wars, and American Legion. Recognized for personal integrity and high moral standards, offer refined problem-solving skills/techniques. Excellent references on request.

Date

Exact Name of Person
Exact Title
Exact Name of Company
Address
City, State, Zip

HUMAN RESOURCES VICE PRESIDENT

for the Fortune 500 company General Technologies

Dear Exact Name of Person: (or Dear Sir or Madam if answering a blind ad)

With the enclosed resume, I would like to express my interest in exploring employment opportunities with your organization.

As you will see from my resume, I offer a distinguished record of accomplishments built while managing human resources support for a large organization with diverse employee populations. While advancing with General Technologies, I have consistently earned recognition as a management professional who can be counted on to achieve excellent results while exceeding expected standards. Currently as Human Resources Vice President for a 3,000-person division of General Technologies, I was handpicked to oversee a seven-person staff of mid-level managers and provide oversight for an $18 budget.

I am considered one of General Technologies's top performers and am recognized as a leader in efforts which resulted in the division's exceeding every goal and standard of performance, training, and job skills/knowledge. I have been singled out for praise from senior officials and chosen for assignments where I have been recognized as a critical player in improving morale and employee performance. I excel in motivating and guiding others to develop their own leadership style, and I am confident that among my greatest strengths is my ability to encourage others to exceed individual and corporate goals.

Respected for my analytical skills and sound judgment, I am known for my ability to deal with people in a respectful, calm, and decisive style. If you can use a versatile and mature management professional, I hope you will contact me soon to suggest a time we might meet to discuss how I could contribute to your organization. I can provide excellent professional and personal references at the appropriate time. Thank you for your time and consideration.

Sincerely,

James N. Britt

JAMES NATHAN BRITT ("Jim")

1110½ Hay Street, Fayetteville, NC 28305 • preppub@aol.com • (910) 483-6611

OBJECTIVE To contribute to an organization that can use a concerned and detail-oriented professional with extensive experience in management who is known for exceptionally strong communication, motivational, instructional, and supervisory skills.

EDUCATION & TRAINING Earned a **B.A.** in **Business Administration**, Drew University, Madison, NJ, 1992.
Excelled in General Technologies' advanced leadership and technical training.

EXPERIENCE *Have advanced at General Technologies while building a reputation as a talented motivator, leader, and team builder:*

2002-present: HUMAN RESOURCES VICE PRESIDENT. Trenton, NJ. Selected ahead of my peers for this managerial role, oversee a staff of seven mid-level managers who provide human resources support for the 3,000 employees at this division of United Technologies.

- Plan and administer an $18 million budget.
- Am recognized as the leader in efforts which resulted in the division's exceeding every standard of performance, training, and job skills/knowledge.
- Coordinated projects which "significantly upgraded" productivity and profitability.
- Mentored subordinates who earned prestigious honors including divisional "Employee of the Month" awards.
- Am respected as a counselor and motivator who truly cares about the professional and personal development as well as the concerns of each and every person I supervise.

1998-01: TRAINING, ADMINISTRATION, AND HUMAN RESOURCES MANAGER. Columbus, OH. Earned praise from senior officials for my emphasis on team building while managing training and daily performance of 80 personnel with an additional 40 subordinates assigned during special projects; controlled a $4 million inventory.

- Developed an employee training program which resulted in a 9% increase in productivity levels over the course of less than two years.
- Initiated automation for inventory control, which improved availability of supplies.
- Mentored a training program for supervisors, which earned praise from executives for focusing on technical/professional knowledge and individual development.
- Described on official evaluations as "one who puts concern for employees ahead of his own personal interests," my confidence and enthusiasm were noted as a catalyst in building morale and molding junior personnel into effective leaders.

1994-97: OPERATIONS MANAGER. Tulsa, OK. Handpicked as acting senior personnel advisor, supervised four people while scheduling, planning, and coordinating a special project.

- Developed standard operating procedures for this position in the management of the project.
- Coordinated maintenance and operation of $150,000 in automation equipment used in this project.
- Was sought out for my advice and guidance as well as my willingness to contribute time to motivate and mentor junior personnel.
- Earned promotion based on performance as the Assistant Operations Manager and supervisor of up to 20 people — streamlined operating procedures and consistently exceeded expected standards despite limited personnel levels and budget constraints.

Highlights of earlier experience: Advanced rapidly into managerial and supervisory roles.

PERSONAL Skilled communicator and motivator. Proficient with Microsoft Word, Excel, and PowerPoint.

Date

Exact Name of Person
Exact Title
Exact Name of Company
Address
City, State, Zip

HUMAN SERVICES DEPARTMENT MANAGER
for the Alcoa corporation

Dear Exact Name of Person: (or Dear Sir or Madam if answering a blind ad)

With the enclosed resume, I would like to express my interest in exploring employment opportunities with your organization.

My reputation as a talented motivator, team builder, and innovator has been shown throughout my career in human resources. In my current position as Human Services Department Manager with Alcoa in Syracuse, NY, I supervise six mid-level managers while controlling a multimillion-dollar budget. I led my employees to receive the Alcoa award for "Best Division" given to recognize teamwork as well as distinguished individual performance. On a formal performance evaluation, I was commended for "setting the standard for innovative program development and implementation."

In a previous position with Coca-Cola as Labor Relations Manager, I was the pivotal coordinator between labor and management. In another position, as Employee Relations Specialist with International Paper, I oversaw all employee benefits plans and training programs. I also implemented automation of personnel records, ensuring accuracy in reporting data.

While earning a name as an individual who has a knack for creatively applying any computer software knowledge to enhance efficiency, I have become known as a talented leader and developer of others. I have been described as a leader who "fosters a work environment that results in significant innovation and high morale."

If you would like to discuss the possibility of my joining your organization, I hope you will contact me. I can provide excellent professional and personal references at the appropriate time. Thank you for your time and consideration.

Sincerely,

Derek C. Merrick

DEREK C. MERRICK

1110½ Hay Street, Fayetteville, NC 28305 • preppub@aol.com • (910) 483-6611

OBJECTIVE To benefit an organization that can use a respected strategic thinker with a proven ability to build teams, motivate others, and implement new concepts while demonstrating my expertise in human resources management.

EDUCATION & TRAINING

M.S., Human Resources Administration, Marywood University, Scranton, PA, 1992.
B.S., Communications, Marywood University, 1990.

EXPERIENCE

HUMAN SERVICES DEPARTMENT MANAGER. Alcoa, Syracuse, NY (2002-present). Was handpicked for this position over more experienced people. Oversee administrative and personnel support services for this major manufacturer.

- Supervise six mid-level managers while controlling a multimillion-dollar budget.
- Initiated revision of the employee benefits plan which was credited with improving morale and decreasing turnover. On a formal performance evaluation, was commended for "setting the standard for innovative program development and implementation."
- Led my employees to receive the Alcoa award for "Best Division" given to recognize teamwork as well as distinguished individual performance.

PERSONNEL MANAGER. PepsiCo, New Rochelle, NY (1999-01). Supervised 16 people while overseeing recruitment and interviewing; hiring, terminating, and promotions; and benefit plans, employee training programs, and labor relations.

- Completely revamped the employee medical plan, which resulted in extensive cost savings. Was commended as an outstanding communicator and team builder; was praised for "developing a superbly trained staff characterized by exceptionally high morale and 99% retention."
- Was described as "fostering a work environment that resulted in a significant improvement in productivity."
- Was praised as an "expert liaison between management and labor."

LABOR RELATIONS MANAGER. Coca-Cola, Inc., Paterson, NJ (1996-98). Was the pivotal coordinator between labor and management. Held regular conferences with union representatives to ensure continued high productivity. Monitored plant and office physical conditions as well as company policies and benefits for all employees. Kept current with state, federal, and OSHA regulations.

- Credited with skillfully avoiding a threatened labor problem.

EMPLOYEE RELATIONS SPECIALIST. International Paper, Seattle, WA (1994-96). Reviewed and revised employee benefits plans, training programs, and ensured compliance with EEO and Affirmative Action. Implemented automation of personnel records to ensure accuracy of reporting data.

- Was credited with improving employee productivity through revitalization of the employee incentive plan. Initiated and designed a new employee orientation presentation.
- Supervised renovation of employee and executive dining rooms.
- Responsible for ensuring employee manual was up-to-date.

Highlights of other experience: Served in various positions in the field of human resources, to include Personnel Assistant, Personnel Clerk, and Benefits Administrator.

PERSONAL Am an accomplished communicator and achiever. Am known as a "people person." Enjoy performing in community theater in my spare time. Excellent references on request.

Date

Exact Name of Person
Title or Position
Name of Company
Address (no., street)
Address (city, state, zip)

HUMAN SERVICES PROGRAM DIRECTOR
for the Eckerds organization

Dear Exact Name of Person: (or Dear Sir or Madam if answering a blind ad)

I would appreciate an opportunity to talk with you soon about how I could contribute to your organization through my versatile management skills, diversified experience in program development and human services administration, as well as through my exemplary personal qualities and strong leadership ability.

As you will see from my resume, I was selected for my most recent position over more senior executives because of my reputation as an astute strategic planner, creative program developer, and resourceful operations manager. In this job I have applied my expert knowledge of several popular software programs to prepare audiovisual presentations and literature related to a wide range of programs which I developed.

After earning my Master's degree and Bachelor's degree (summa cum laude), I excelled in several positions that involved quantitative decision making and microcomputer applications. I have enjoyed using my creativity and initiative in applying advanced technical concepts in the human services field. For example, in my current job I developed a new database using Access which helped line managers identify their employees' training needs.

When you look at my resume, you will see that I am a skilled planner, budgeter, financial administrator, and instructor. I believe I offer a unique combination of creativity and technical knowhow that could be of use to your organization in today's competitive marketplace. I offer a proven ability to develop the human services programs needed within the organization, and I also have a high degree of comfort in utilizing tools of modern technology in order to efficiently implement and coordinate those programs.

You will, I am certain, find me to be a warm and caring individual who subscribes to high personal and professional standards of honesty, loyalty, and integrity. I can provide exceptional references upon your request.

I hope you will welcome my call soon to arrange a brief meeting at your convenience to discuss your current and future needs and how I might serve them. Thank you in advance for your time.

Sincerely yours,

Roberto J. Lopez

ROBERTO J. LOPEZ

1110½ Hay Street, Fayetteville, NC 28305 • preppub@aol.com • (910) 483-6611

OBJECTIVE To contribute to an organization that can use a skilled administrator who offers proven abilities related to operations management, program development, personnel supervision, computer operation, and financial planning and budgeting.

COMPUTER EXPERTISE **Software:** Highly proficient with Microsoft Word, WordPerfect, Access, and PowerPoint.
Operating systems: Adept at using Windows.

EDUCATION & TRAINING Earned **M.A., Human Resources Administration**, Loyola College, Baltimore, MD, 1993.
Graduated **summa cum laude** with a **B.A.** degree in **Human Resources Management,** Coppin State College, Baltimore, MD, 1991; elected to the Delta Epsilon Chi Honor Society.

EXPERIENCE **ADMINISTRATOR/PROGRAM MANAGER.** Eckerds, Chicago, IL (2002-present). Was commended for the "inspirational leadership" I provide in supervising the continuous professional development of a small staff while simultaneously planning, budgeting for, implementing, evaluating, and refining a wide range of personnel programs for 1,600 people.
- Apply my expertise with word processing and graphics software to prepare brochures, audiovisual presentations, and informational literature.
- Plan and coordinate public relations programs.
- Was credited with achieving accident-free operations with an average of 98% attendance.
- Developed a new database using Access which helped line managers identify their employees' training needs.

HUMAN SERVICES PROGRAM DIRECTOR. Campbell Soup Co., Edinboro, PA (2000-02). Performed extensive public speaking while planning, budgeting for, and supervising the implementation of diversified human services programs that included personnel, employee benefits, training, logistics, and labor relations.
- Vigilantly enforced rigid safety standards in a hazardous industrial work environment.
- Became highly skilled in budgetary planning and financial administration.
- On my own initiative, undertook a project which involved preparing a survey which pinpointed the strengths and weaknesses of a new health program; my initiative allowed executives to take actions to remedy program shortfalls.

ASSISTANT PERSONNEL MANAGER. Monarch Foods, Elgin, IL (1998-00). As the "right arm" and trusted confidante for the chief executive officer, planned educational programs; supervised a staff involved in recruiting, interviewing, and hiring of personnel.
- Developed programs cited as "the most successful ever" within this organization.

INSTRUCTOR/TRAINING PROGRAM MANAGER and PROPERTY MANAGER. U.S. Army, Ft. Meade, MD (1995-97). At one of the Army's major training institutions, administered numerous training programs while controlling assets of half a million dollars.
Highlights of comments from formal performance evaluations:
From formal written evaluations, here are excerpts which reveal my personal qualities:
- "He is an original thinker with imaginative reasoning."
- "He has excellent personal qualities, a great sense of humor, and possesses an abundance of wit and charm."
- "He is always cheerful, always positive, and always there."
- "Maturity, trust, worthiness, and compassion are his hallmarks."

PERSONAL Outstanding personal and professional references on request.

Date

Exact Name of Person
Title or Position
Name of Company
Address (no., street)
Address (city, state, zip)

LABOR RELATIONS MEDIATOR
for Boeing Aircraft

Dear Exact Name of Person: (or Dear Sir or Madam if answering a blind ad)

I would appreciate an opportunity to talk with you soon about how I could apply my extensive experience in personnel administration as well as my abilities related to budgeting, educational program instruction and administration, and personnel recruiting to your organization.

While employed by Boeing Aircraft, Seattle, WA, I have advanced in a "track record" of accomplishments. In my most recent job as a Labor Relations Mediator, I supervise a 30-person staff and investigate and resolve employee and union complaints/grievances. I have become widely recognized as the "resident expert" on company and government regulations. Previously, as Personnel Manager, I created several programs which improved productivity. My successful projects included developing and implementing an orientation program, an "open forum" workshop, drug and alcohol abuse prevention plans, and a program allowing managers and supervisors an opportunity to speak out on manpower planning and other personnel actions. I also was praised for the revised absenteeism policy which greatly improved turnover and productivity. Then, as Personnel Department Administrator, I initiated a program for receiving input from managers and supervisors on their views of manpower planning and other personnel matters.

In prior employment as Personnel Administrator and Professor at Towson University, Towson, MD, I directed nine employees in a 250-student university Business Administration department where I controlled budgeting, interviewed and recruited prospective students, and developed procedures and plans to ensure the continued success of the program.

I offer a bachelor's degree and graduate study in Personnel Administration, proven experience, and a reputation as a fair but demanding leader which I am certain would allow me to make valuable contributions to your organization.

I hope you will welcome my call soon to arrange a brief meeting at your convenience to discuss your current and future needs and how I might serve them. Thank you in advance for your time.

Sincerely yours,

Linus Armour

LINUS F. ARMOUR

1110½ Hay Street, Fayetteville, NC 28305   •   preppub@aol.com   •   (910) 483-6611

___

OBJECTIVE	To contribute to an organization through my exceptional abilities in personnel administration as well as my communication, motivational, problem-solving, and decision-making abilities.
EXPERIENCE	*Advanced in a "track record" of accomplishments, Boeing Aircraft, Seattle, WA:*

2002-present: LABOR RELATIONS MEDIATOR. Supervise a 30-person staff and investigate and resolve employee and union complaints/grievances.
- Have become widely recognized as the "resident expert" on company and government regulations.
- Keep subordinate company managers aware of problem areas and solutions.
- Conducted a study on the effects of drug/alcohol abuse on performance.

1997-01: PERSONNEL DEPARTMENT ADMINISTRATOR. Supervised three mid-level manager and 24 employees; coordinated and revised operational procedures.
- Developed the organization's drug and alcohol abuse prevention plans.
- Initiated a program for receiving input from managers and supervisors on their views of manpower planning and personnel matters.

1994-96: PERSONNEL MANAGER. Oversaw the Benefits Administrator; directed a 40-person staff.
- Established a revised policy on absenteeism which greatly improved turnover and productivity.
- Supervised three alcohol and drug abuse counselors.
- Increased productivity 10% and reduced costs 15%.
- Developed an automated database on statistics required to be maintained by the government.
- Initiated a series of semiannual workshops allowing employees to meet with senior management to discuss matters of general interest.

ASSISTANT PROFESSOR. The Citadel, Charleston, SC (1992-94). Counseled and instructed 800 military science students including handling recruiting, advertising, and budgeting.

PERSONNEL ADMINISTRATOR and **PROFESSOR.** Towson University, Towson, MD (1990-1992). Worked part-time; directed a nine-person staff in a university Business Administration department with 250 students: developed and controlled a $47,000 budget, interviewed prospective students, and formulated departmental procedures; taught two classes, Marketing and Economics.
- Initiated recruiting procedures which led to a 30% increase in enrollment.
- Achieved the highest after-graduation employment rate among 23 universities—90% of my students were employed within two months after graduation.

Highlights of other experience: Excelled in positions including Personnel Advisor, General Manager, and Equal Opportunity Advisor.

EDUCATION and TRAINING	B.S. in **Personnel Administration**, Towson University, Towson, MD, 1990. Studied **Personnel Administration** in a graduate program, Michigan State University, East Lansing, MI.
PERSONAL	Am known as a persistent and dedicated professional. Offer a broad background in personnel administration and human resources. Excellent references on request.

Real-Resumes Series edited by Anne McKinney

CAREER CHANGE

Date

Exact Name of Person
Title or Position
Name of Company
Address (no., street)
Address (city, state, zip)

LOGISTICAL SUPPORT MANAGER

with the Ford Motor Company. This individual has "instant credibility" in his pursuit of a human resources position since he has committed his leisure time to earning a degree in the subject.

Dear Exact Name of Person: (or Dear Sir or Madam if answering a blind ad)

I would appreciate an opportunity to talk with you soon about how I could contribute to your organization through my leadership and supervisory experience gained while employed by Ford Motors, Detroit, MI.

During my experience at Ford, I developed a reputation as a leader and professional who could be counted on to get the job done. Since then I have continued to build on this reputation and have excelled in team-building and improving performance. At Ford, I have received special training in race relations and diversity management.

My work at Ford ignited a strong professional interest in the human resources field, and I have utilized my leisure time to complete a master's degree in Human Resources Administration. I am now exploring opportunities in the human resources field.

I hope you will welcome my call soon to arrange a brief meeting at your convenience to discuss your current and future needs and how I might serve them.

Sincerely yours,

Lucas E. Abraham III

Alternate last paragraph:
I hope you will call or write me soon to suggest a time convenient for us to meet and discuss your current and future needs and how I might serve them.

LUCAS E. ABRAHAM III

1110½ Hay Street, Fayetteville, NC 28305   •   preppub@aol.com   •   (910) 483-6611

OBJECTIVE   To offer the leadership and supervisory skills I have refined through overseeing the performance of diverse teams of employees while gaining a reputation for my ability to make decisions and work independently.

EDUCATION   As an **Honors Student** at Michigan State University, East Lansing, MI, completed a **Master of Arts degree in Human Resources Administration, 2003.**
B.S., Business Administration, Michigan State University, East Lansing, MI, 1993.
- Specialized course work included the following:

Human resource management	Organizational behavior	Marketing
International business management	General psychology	Business law
Sociology of deviant behavior	Business communication	Management
Management information systems	Desktop computers	Accounting

EXPERIENCE   *Advanced in supervisory and logistics management roles, Ford Motors, Detroit, MI:*
LOGISTICAL SUPPORT MANAGER. (2002-present). Directed the acquisition, receipt, storage, use, and transportation of more than 100 types of technologically advanced communications/electronics items and repair parts for a test center.
- Prepared milestones and coordinated with contractors, and transportation personnel to ensure uninterrupted services and meet deadlines.

SENIOR SUPPLY OPERATIONS MANAGER. (2000-02). Trained and supervised five employees finding ways to reduce excess inventory and costs in the headquarters.
- Established demand criteria, thereby greatly reducing inventory carrying and storage costs by $300,000. Automated recordkeeping operations from a manual system.
- Managed more than 40 separate contracts including maintenance contracts in excess of $650 million and a property book valued at over $10 million.
- Assisted in the development of computer programs classifying equipment.

MATERIAL MANAGEMENT SUPERVISOR. (1996-99). Received a bonus for my performance as the advisor on supply operations and procedures for 13 executives; supervised a staff of seven specialists.
- Handled a wide range of managerial duties including coordinating logistics activities with other divisions.
- Singled out to manage a special project, determined requirements and coordinated air transportation for sensitive material being shipped to another division.
- Analyzed statistical data/reports to ensure compliance with standards and regulations.

PURCHASING AGENT. Sensory Aids Service, Veteran's Affairs Medical Center, Augusta, ME (1993-1996). Made purchasing decisions with minimal to no supervision while working with suppliers all over the U.S. of sensory items ranging from wheelchairs to artificial eyes; communicate extensively with veterans on a daily basis.
- Displayed outstanding coordination skills with suppliers, patients, and hospital personnel to ensure that supplies, equipment, and repairs were provided for disabled veterans.

Highlights of previous experience: Earned a reputation as a gifted counselor and motivator while excelling in other management positions. Maintained excellent employee relations.

PERSONAL   Strengthened my ability to deal with diverse groups of people through my management experience. Can provide excellent references upon request.

Date

Exact Name of Person
Title or Position
Name of Company
Address (no., street)
Address (city, state, zip)

MEDICAL OPERATIONS MANAGER

for the Davis Medical Staffing Agency

Dear Exact Name of Person: (or Dear Sir or Madam if answering a blind ad)

I would appreciate an opportunity to talk with you soon about how I could contribute to your organization through my versatile management experience and proven ability to adapt to tough new challenges.

While currently managing 12 employees involved in processing temporary employment applications at Davis Medical Staffing Agency, Roanoke, VA, I increased by 300% the recruiting of Physician Assistants. I also creatively designed a system to reduce processing time for applications.

In previous positions, I have excelled in managing dozens of people involved in human resources administration. As Personnel Manager at Compaq Computers, we reduced the processing time for employee terminations by 8%, and production of personnel awards improved by 37%. We also developed a new awards "starter kit" for supervisors and updated personnel handbooks.

In several jobs I have successfully managed complex service operations. At Intel, I designed an automated inventory system which greatly reduced downtime.

In every organization in which I have worked, I have made significant contributions to internal management, customer service, and employee productivity. You would find me to be a dynamic leader with a keen intellect who is continuously identifying new opportunities to reduce costs, improve profitability, or develop new services. I am confident that I could combine my creativity and experience to make valuable contributions to your organization, too.

I hope you will welcome my call soon when I try to arrange a brief meeting to discuss your current and future needs and how I might serve them. Thank you in advance for your time.

Sincerely yours,

Adrian B. Harold

Alternate last paragraph:
I hope you will call or write me soon to suggest a time convenient for us to meet and discuss your current and future needs and how I might serve them. Thank you in advance for your time.

ADRIAN B. HAROLD

1110½ Hay Street, Fayetteville, NC 28305 • preppub@aol.com • (910) 483-6611

OBJECTIVE To benefit an organization that can use a dynamic leader who has excelled in managing people, service operations, and finances through applying my keen intellect, superior writing and speaking skills, as well as my ability to creatively and cost-effectively solve problems.

EDUCATION & TRAINING

M.B.A. degree (3.6 GPA), St. Edwards University, Austin, TX, 1992.
B.S. degree (3.1 GPA), Midland College, Midland, TX, 1988; was a scholarship recipient.
Excelled academically in rigorous executive development training programs related to human resources administration, service operations management, and strategic planning.

EXPERIENCE

MEDICAL OPERATIONS MANAGER. Davis Medical Staffing Agency, Roanoke, VA (2003-present). Manage 12 employees involved in processing employment applications; oversee testing administration and monitor the selection of qualified applicants while consistently meeting or exceeding all recruiting goals.
- Through innovative marketing, increased by 300% the recruiting of physician assistants.
- Implemented a new "qualification system" that reduced costs of applicant screening.
- On my own initiative, creatively designed a system to reduce processing time for applications for employment.

PUBLIC RELATIONS MANAGER. Smith Corporation, Chester, VA (2000-02). Planned, organized, and coordinated press releases, public awareness campaigns, employee newsletters, and advertising to assure a good public image for this manufacturing company.
- Supervised 10 employees.

SUPPORT SERVICES MANAGER. Lane Company, Lynchburg, VA (1997-99). Supervised employee benefits, personnel, and labor relations managers. Scheduled monthly meetings for performance reviews of those departments.
- Developed a new plan for recruitment; was considered the subject matter expert on government policies pertaining to employment, such as Affirmative Action and EEO.

OPERATIONS MANAGER. Intel, Canton, OH (1995-97). Supervised 20 employees involved in managing maintenance, personnel, and supplies and equipment. Became known for my innovative employee programs to boost morale and increase productivity.
- Designed an automated inventory system credited with greatly reducing downtime.

PERSONNEL MANAGER. Compaq Computers, Jersey City, NJ (1993-94). Oversaw 30 employees involved in providing personnel administration services for this major computer manufacturer.
- Modified internal procedures with the result that the response time to correspondence was cut from one week to three days; the processing time for employee terminations was cut by 8%; and the production of personnel awards improved by 37%.
- Updated personnel handbooks; developed a new awards "starter kit" for supervisors.

ADMINISTRATIVE SERVICES MANAGER. Wal-Mart, Austin, TX (1991-92). Supervised 22 employees involved in managing services and equipment, including word/message processing, records/forms inventory control, printing and reproduction, mail distribution, preparation/publishing of correspondence, weekly bulletins, and staff directories.

PERSONAL Received several awards recognizing my exceptional leadership and management ability. Offer a proven ability to organize, motivate, and lead people. Excellent references.

Date

Exact Name of Person
Title or Position
Name of Company
Address (no., street)
Address (city, state, zip)

OPERATIONS SUPERVISOR
for E.I. du Pont de Nemours

Dear Exact Name of Person: (or Dear Sir or Madam, if answering a blind ad)

I would appreciate an opportunity to talk with you soon about how I could contribute to your organization through my experience in the field of personnel training and operations management.

In my current position at E.I. du Pont, I supervise 12 employees who gather, verify, and formally report data pertaining to employee turnover, retention, and absenteeism as well as productivity. I developed a new dbase application that automated what had been a tedious manual process, and we produced an automated personnel reporting system which resulted in the production of highly reliable data for use by management.

While at General Mills as Automated Systems Manager, I provided written guidance and technical training to users of a newly introduced computer system and managed a budget of $1.5 million for software testing. In a prior position at Tech Data as Personnel Manager, I supervised four people involved in personnel administration activities including employee promotions, terminations; accident reporting; and labor relations. I developed a statistical reporting system which provided a viable management tool for staff personnel in reducing absenteeism and improving the productivity rate.

As an experienced motivator and manager, I have excelled in training, developing, and supervising employees. In every job I have held, teaching and training others has been a vital part of my job, and I have conducted training for groups of up to 150 people.

I hope you will write or call me soon to suggest a time when we might meet to discuss your needs and goals and how I might serve them. Thank you in advance for your time.

Sincerely,

Dean C. Kenyon

DEAN C. KENYON

1110½ Hay Street, Fayetteville, NC 28305   •   preppub@aol.com   •   (910) 483-6611

OBJECTIVE   To contribute to an organization that can use a versatile professional with extensive experience in human resources along with proven management and problem-solving abilities.

COMPUTERS   Expert with software including WordPerfect, Word, PowerPoint, Excel, and dBase.

EXPERIENCE   **OPERATIONS SUPERVISOR.** E.I. du Pont de Nemours, Annapolis, MD (2002-present). Supervise 12 employees in a branch which gathers, verifies, and formally reports data pertaining to employee turnover and absenteeism as well as productivity and supply.
- Developed a new dBase application that automated what had been a tedious manual process; produced a statistical reporting system which resulted in the production of highly reliable data while training employees to use specialized software and to maintain an automated data base.
- Conduct classes for groups ranging from 50 to 150 people.
- Received a prestigious commendation for my leadership in working with 10 programmers over a 90-day period to develop a new automated program that improved personnel data reporting.

AUTOMATED SYSTEMS MANAGER. General Mills, Minneapolis, MN (1997-02). Was handpicked for this job providing written guidance and technical training to users of a newly introduced computer system; conducted classes for up to 50 people.
- Supervised 10 people while overseeing the efficient distribution of computers to 1,100 people involved in personnel management activities supporting 200,000 employees.
- Conducted on-site training for computer users while working closely with personnel from the manufacturer.
- Managed an operating budget of $1.5 million for software testing and travel/lodging.
- Coordinated extensively in troubleshooting and resolving software and other problems.

PERSONNEL MANAGER. Tech Data, Baltimore, MD (1995-97). Supervised four people involved in personnel administration activities including employee promotions, terminations; accident reporting; and labor relations and grievances.
- Developed a statistical reporting system which provided a viable management tool for staff personnel.
- Designed a dBase system to monitor the status of all recommendations for promotions and awards which greatly increased efficiency and boosted employee satisfaction.

QUALITY CONTROL MANAGEMENT CONSULTANT. General Motors, Detroit, MI (1991-94). Served as a member of a high-level quality assurance team which visited sites throughout the U.S. to evaluate compliance with data processing policies/procedures.

Highlights of military experience: TRAINING OFFICER. U.S. Army, England (1986-91). Served as Training Officer for the largest personnel system data base (SIDPERS) in the world; conducted critical on-site evaluations of personnel administration operations.

EDUCATION   **Associate's** degree in **Business Administration**, Central Texas College, Germany, 1990. Extensive college-level courses related to personnel administration and management.

PERSONAL   Can provide excellent references upon request.

Date

Exact Name of Person (if known)
Title or Position
Name of Company
Address (no., street)
Address (city, state, zip)

ORGANIZATIONAL DEVELOPMENT CONSULTANT
for a division of Pillsbury

Dear Exact Name of Person (or Dear Sir or Madam if answering a blind ad):

I would appreciate an opportunity to talk with you about how my background related to personnel administration and financial services could benefit your organization.

As you will see from my resume, I offer a proven ability to strengthen the human resources area of any size organization. Most recently, I have excelled in a "hot-seat" job which involves working extensively with upper management at Pillsbury. I am involved in developing strategic plans related to "downsizing" at five entities while developing and establishing a new organization to consolidate them into one restructured operation. In a previous position as Personnel Manager with a Fortune 500 Company, I managed a $600 million project which involved setting up new offices in London, Bangkok, Tel Aviv, and New York. In another job with a 20-year old company with 500 employees, I designed formal personnel policies and initiated programs related to safety, security, and training.

My expertise in the area of finance complements my background in the human resources area. In a job with Stewart's Financial Services as a Financial Planner and Sales Manager, I transformed one of the company's worst-performing offices into one of the company's top sales producers among its 112 offices. While motivating and leading a sales team, I also prepared financial profiles for individuals; planned savings and retirement packages; designed corporate pension/profit-sharing plans; and developed health and disability programs.

You would find me to be an energetic and hardworking professional who strives on solving problems in our fast-changing economy.

I hope you will welcome my call soon to arrange a brief meeting at your convenience to discuss your current and future needs and how I might serve them. Thank you in advance for your time.

Sincerely yours,

Bruce N. Avila

Alternate last paragraph:
I hope you will call or write me soon to suggest a time convenient for us to meet and discuss your current and future needs and how I might serve them. Thank you in advance for your time.

BRUCE N. AVILA

1110½ Hay Street, Fayetteville, NC 28305 • preppub@aol.com • (910) 483-6611

OBJECTIVE To benefit an organization that can use a dynamic motivator and astute problem solver with an exceptionally strong background in personnel administration and finance, including experience in managing organizational change, developing strategic plans, and reorganizing human resources for greater productivity/efficiency.

EXPERIENCE **ORGANIZATIONAL DEVELOPMENT CONSULTANT.** Baker Corporation (a new division of Pillsbury, Inc.), Minneapolis, MN (2002-present). Was handpicked for this job because of my expertise in organizational effectiveness and my reputation as a creative problem solver; work with a select group of strategists to develop and implement plans for establishing a new organization mandated by upper management which will consolidate five separate operating entities into one restructured, centralized operation.

- Oversee a staff of nine professionals while preparing detailed plans and budgets related to the redesign, consolidation, or elimination of more than 100 units.
- Make detailed financial projections related to personnel and equipment costs.
- Contribute vital input to upper management which authorized creation of this new organization. Have proven my ability to create leaner organizations redesigned to achieve goals with greater flexibility and at lower cost.

FINANCIAL PLANNER and **SALES MANAGER**. Stewart's Financial Services, Duluth, MN (1998-02). While hiring/training a staff of nine sales professionals, transformed — in only 18 months — one of the company's lowest producing sales offices into one of Stewart's top performers among its 112 offices nationwide.

- As a Financial Consultant worked with corporations and businesses in developing:
    Individual financial profiles
    Savings, security, and retirement packages
    Corporate pension/profit-sharing plans and retirement programs
    Health insurance and disability programs
- Earned membership in the "Key Club" as a key sales producer.

HUMAN RESOURCES DIRECTOR. L. J. Monroe & Son, Spokane, WA (1996-97). Developed and implemented formal personnel and human resources policies for a 20-year-old company with 500 employees and $80 million in annual sales.

- Initiated personnel programs related to safety, security, and training.

PERSONNEL MANAGER. IBM, Seattle, WA (1992-95). For this Fortune 500 company, designed manpower needs and oversaw personnel staffing/administration for a $600 million start-up project involving 2,500 employees.

- Established offices in London, Bangkok, Tel Aviv, and New York.
- Handled grievances, layoffs, transfers, terminations, and recruitment.

Highlights of other experience:

- As Director of Personnel for a 700-employee company, reduced employee turnover costs while recruiting employees, supervising training, and editing publications.

EDUCATION **B.S., Business Administration**, Central Washington University, Ellensburg, WA, 1990.

PERSONAL Am an energetic positive thinker who thrives on solving tough problems. Am familiar with computer software including Excel, PowerPoint, Word, Access, and word processing programs. Excel in managing multiple complex projects. Excellent references on request.

Date

Exact Name of Person
Exact Title
Exact Name of Company
Address
City, State, Zip

PERSONNEL ADMINISTRATION MANAGER at Wal-Mart

Dear Exact Name of Person: (or Dear Sir or Madam if answering a blind ad)

With the enclosed resume, I would like to make you aware of my interest in exploring employment opportunities with your organization and acquaint you with my distinguished track record of achievements as a human resource manager.

As you will see from my resume, I have excelled in positions requiring top-notch management, communication, and organizational skills. While gaining experience with numerous popular software programs including Microsoft Word, Excel, and others, I refined my knowledge of human resources and personnel administration. In my most recent position, I directed personnel services with a staff of 54 employees involved in handling personnel administration for thousands of people. Praised for my leadership ability and strong personal initiative, I recently established "from scratch" a new Personnel Administration Center for a superstore and led my staff to receive nine commendable ratings on quality control inspections.

In previous jobs, I trained and supervised employees in all aspects of personnel administration. On several occasions I was selected for "hot-seat" jobs which required a proven leader with strong problem-solving abilities.

Although my employer thinks highly of my performance, I am in the process of permanently relocating to Columbus, Georgia, and I am interested in exploring career opportunities with organizations in that area.

If you can use a hard worker with a proven ability to manage multiple priorities and produce outstanding bottom-line results under tight deadlines, I hope you will contact me to suggest a time when we might meet to discuss your needs. Thank you in advance for your time.

Sincerely,

Faith R. Denton

FAITH R. DENTON

1110½ Hay Street, Fayetteville, NC 28305 • preppub@aol.com • (910) 483-6611

OBJECTIVE   To benefit an organization that can use a skilled administrative manager with exceptional communication and organizational skills who offers a background in personnel supervision, training, and administration, operations management, and office administration.

COMPUTERS   Familiar with many of the most popular computer operating systems and software including: Windows, Microsoft Word, Excel, and PowerPoint, WordPerfect, and others.

EXPERIENCE   *Advanced to positions of increasing responsibility while serving at Wal-Mart (2000-present):*

2002-present: **PERSONNEL ADMINISTRATION MANAGER.** Decatur, GA. Oversee administrative support activities, directing a personnel department of 54 employees in the development and implementation of a wide variety of personnel programs.

- Manage the orientation of new employees, submission of evaluations and awards, and preparation of personnel reports; serve as liaison between personnel, finance, and corporate headquarters.
- In a new "superstore," established a Personnel Administration Center (PAC) "from scratch," ensuring that the center effectively met the organization's needs.
- Control a budget of $500,000; received commendable ratings on audits.
- Was cited in an official evaluation for possessing "unparalleled leadership abilities" and for using my vast expertise to overcome obstacles that would stop others.
- As a trainer, was described as "a true teacher of subordinates," who created a positive atmosphere where personnel can actively participate in the learning process.

2000: **PERSONNEL SUPERVISOR.** Peoria, IL. Supervised four personnel clerks while overseeing support services for approximately 1,000 personnel; designed a new application form and updated the company employee manual.

- Initiated an in-depth training program and oversaw quality assurance of all reports; reduced operational and financial errors by 40%. Praised for bringing about a 100% improvement of the personnel services for the organization.

Other experience:

PERSONNEL SUPERVISOR. Sprint, Port Huron, MI (1995-99). Managed personnel functions; oversaw preparation of employee evaluations and accountability of personnel records as well as personnel activitiesww such as promotions, terminations, and transfers.

- Supervised and trained nine employees in all aspects of personnel administration; was credited with increasing the division's proficiency. Reorganized the Personnel Accountability System, dramatically improving accountability and service.

PROCESSING SUPERVISOR. Home Depot, Midland, MI (1990-95). Started as a Processing Clerk and advanced to this position, supervising as many as 10 personnel processing 40-80 applicants daily; ensured compliance with all state and federal regulations regarding hiring by keeping up-to-date on changes.

- Ensured that all personnel documents were prepared while maintaining an error rate of less than 0.01%. Implemented computer training of section personnel to prepare the office for the installation of a new operating system for managing data input of records.

EDUCATION   Completed 98 semester hours of college course work towards a Bachelor's degree, University of Maryland, College Park, MD, 1990-present; am completing degree in my spare time.

PERSONAL   Excellent personal and professional references are available upon request.

Date

Exact Name of Person
Exact Title
Exact Name of Company
Address
City, State, Zip

PERSONNEL ADMINISTRATION SUPERVISOR for Westinghouse

Dear Exact Name of Person: (or Dear Sir or Madam if answering a blind ad)

With the enclosed resume, I would like to make you aware of my experience in office administration and customer service as well as in the management of services related to human resources and personnel administration.

As you will see from my resume, I have been promoted ahead of my peers at Westinghouse because of my strong personal initiative, analytical skills, and problem-solving ability. In my current job as Personnel Administration Supervisor, I have managed personnel and administrative support for 2,500 people. On my own initiative, I developed a performance feedback tracking log which boosted morale, and I was selected to write a proposal for improving the interviewing process for use in the entire company. I am proud of the role I have played in enriching the lives of employees through my dedicated efforts and behind-the-scenes organizational skills.

In all of my jobs I have expertly utilized a computer with numerous software applications in order to maintain databases, write reports, compile statistics, and track data. I am highly computer literate and offer an ability to rapidly master new programs.

In my previous job I was described as "the most motivated customer-oriented personnel assistant I have met in 8 years." I pride myself on my strong customer service orientation, and I believe my professional customer service attitude is inspired by my sincere desire to help others. I have discovered that my attention to detail and organizational skills have helped me be of service to numerous people on many occasions. For example, I once created a Newcomer's Welcome Package. I have found that customers and employees are much happier with the organizations they work for and buy from if the organizations provide correct information on a timely basis.

I would like to become a part of an organization that can use a hard-working and disciplined young professional who aims for excellence in all I do. If you can use my considerable skills and talents, please contact me to suggest a time when we might meet to discuss your needs and how I might serve them. Thank you in advance for your time.

Yours sincerely,

Celia M. Ginsburg

CELIA M. GINSBURG

1110½ Hay Street, Fayetteville, NC 28305 • preppub@aol.com • (910) 483-6611

OBJECTIVE   To benefit an organization that can use an experienced professional who offers outstanding customer service skills and the ability to handle multiple priorities along with experience related to human resources, personnel administration, and operations management.

EDUCATION   Earned **Bachelor's degree** in **Business Management**, Columbus State University, GA, 1994.

Received **Associate's degree** in **Personnel Administration**, Morris Brown College, Atlanta, GA, 3.5 GPA, 1992.

Excelled in extensive training sponsored by Westinghouse related to computer operations, personnel administration, customer service, files maintenance, publications, and other areas.

EXPERIENCE   *Have excelled in my career with Westinghouse, Columbus, GA (1994-present):*

2003-present: PERSONNEL ADMINISTRATION SUPERVISOR. Manage three people while directing personnel and administrative support for 2,500 personnel at this division; oversee the control and processing of human resources activities such as promotions, dismissals, training programs, benefits plans, employee orientation, budget, and employee recognition plans.

- Have been commended in writing for my attention to detail in updating more than 3,000 personnel records, with no errors.
- Upon taking over this position, quickly eliminated all overdue and late paperwork and ensured the production of daily and weekly reports on time and without error.
- On my own initiative, developed a performance feedback appraisal tracking log which boosted morale and allowed all personnel to begin receiving their evaluations on time.
- Because of my reputation as an outstanding thinker and writer, was handpicked to write a proposal for improving the interviewing process at Westinghouse.
- Was praised in a formal performance evaluation for my contributions; for example, developed a comprehensive checklist which streamlined in-processing of new personnel.

2000-02: PERSONNEL ASSISTANT. Became skilled in utilizing the Microsoft Office software while updating personnel files, preparing weekly and daily reports, and providing administrative support to 3,000 people; supervised and trained five people.

- Refined my verbal communication skills while briefing groups of up to 200 personnel to explain technical matters related to benefits, programs, and other personnel matters.
- On my own initiative, created a Newcomer's Welcome Package. Was described in writing as "the most motivated customer-oriented personnel assistant I have met in 8 years."
- Singled out for my creativity and organizational pride, coordinated morale-boosting events such as a Christmas door decorating contest, summer picnics, and Christmas parties and also held the office of secretary for a booster club.

1996-00: PERSONNEL SPECIALIST. Functioned as the Primary Customer Account Representative while providing administrative and personnel support for 500 individuals.

- Played a key role in conducting a survey on morale which gained 96% employee participation and which led to quality improvements in programs and procedures.
- Expertly trained more than 50 supervisory personnel from 20 Westinghouse divisions.
- On my own initiative, reorganized the management system pertaining to the personnel performance and evaluations program, which increased productivity by 20%.

Other experience (1994-96): Rapidly distinguished myself as a self-starter in my first job.

PERSONAL   Outstanding references. Known as a personable professional who gets things done.

CAREER CHANGE

Date

Exact Name of Person
Title or Position
Name of Company
Address (no., street)
Address (city, state, zip)

PERSONNEL ADMINISTRATOR & REGIONAL MAINTENANCE OPERATIONS MANAGER

This individual is seeking to emphasize her involvement in personnel administration more than her operations management skills.

Dear Exact Name of Person: (or Dear Sir or Madam if answering a blind ad)

I would appreciate an opportunity to talk with you soon about how I could contribute to your organization through my experience in human resources management as well as through my outstanding problem-solving, analytical, and decision-making abilities.

As you will see from my resume, I offer a "track record" of advancement in managing both human and material resources. I am an exceptionally fast learner with a wide range of experience.

I have trained and managed departments with as many as 143 employees, planned and controlled annual budgets of as much as $800,000, and directed operations with $7 million in equipment. Always alert to opportunities for increasing "bottom-line" results for my employer, I have consistently found ways to streamline procedures and improve employee job knowledge.

Although highly valued by my current employer, I have decided to leave the operations and logistics field in order to seek employment in the field of personnel administration in which I earned a master's degree. In previous positions, I discovered my greatest satisfaction came from my ability to establish and maintain good employee relations.

I hope you will welcome my call soon to arrange a brief meeting at your convenience to discuss your current and future needs and how I might serve them. Thank you in advance for your time.

Sincerely yours,

Ella G. Thrush

Alternate last paragraph:
I hope you will call or write soon to suggest a time convenient for us to meet and discuss your current and future needs and how I might serve them. Thank you in advance for your time.

ELLA G. THRUSH

1110½ Hay Street, Fayetteville, NC 28305 • preppub@aol.com • (910) 483-6611

OBJECTIVE To apply my outstanding personnel administration and human resources management expertise to an organization in need of a professional with strong analytical, decision-making, and problem-solving abilities and leadership skills.

EDUCATION & TRAINING

Master's degree in Personnel Administration, Western Illinois University, Des Plaines, IL, 2003.

B.A., Political Science, Western Michigan University, MI, 1986.

Excelled in almost 2,000 hours of advanced training for logistics operations executives.

EXPERIENCE

PERSONNEL ADMINISTRATOR & REGIONAL MAINTENANCE OPERATIONS MANAGER. Computer Resources, Des Plaines, IL (2003-present). Direct training and performance of 143 employees at this central distribution center while controlling more than $12 million in equipment and managing an $800,000 annual budget.

- Manage seven maintenance sites supporting 780 widely dispersed customers.
- Maintain a consistent record of exceeding the goal of 95% efficiency and availability despite severe personnel shortages as high as 30% in some departments.
- Established an automated database to ensure prompt shipments.
- Completed M.A. in Personnel Administration in my spare time while excelling in my full-time job.

GENERAL MANAGER. Hewlett Packard, Schenectady, NY (2000-02). Oversaw operations and personnel for this major manufacturer; successfully led employees to outstanding performance in productivity. Initiated renovation of company's employee dining facilities.

LOGISTICS CONSULTANT. Gateways Computers, Columbia, MO (1998-99). Brought about improvements in procedures for storing, maintaining, and transporting inventory.

Advanced in this "track record" with Dell Computers, Austin, TX:

1996-97: HUMAN RESOURCES AND ADMINISTRATIVE MANAGER. Directed the performance of a staff involved in providing administrative/personnel support for this 1,700-person organization.

- Advised senior executives on staffing and personnel policies. Achieved "outstanding" ratings in major evaluations of training programs and personnel systems.

1995-96: SPECIAL PROJECT MANAGER. Prepared and controlled a $233,000 annual budget, more than $7 million worth of equipment, and the performance of 134 employees.

- Managed a successful special project: made plans, coordinated logistical support, and moved 92 employees 3,000 miles to the Colorado division.
- Automated the company's budget and accounting record keeping.

1992-94: DEPARTMENT MANAGER. Was handpicked to direct the support services department, overseeing the benefits administer and personnel department.

- Guided employees to a 5% increase in job knowledge test scores, improving productivity.

1990-91: DEPARTMENT SUPERVISOR. Supervised 37 employees and managed functional areas ranging from supply and maintenance to personnel administration.

- Was cited for "outstanding management" of automated systems security procedures.

LANGUAGES Speak German and French proficiently.

Date

Exact Name of Person
Title or Position
Name of Company
Address (number and street)
Address (city, state, and zip)

PERSONNEL & TRAINING SUPERVISOR
for International Paper

Dear Exact Name of Person: (or Sir or Madam if answering a blind ad)

Can you use an astute professional with proven skills related to human resources management?

In my current position as Personnel and Training Supervisor for International Paper, I have initiated and implemented improvements which dramatically improved productivity. I guide employees' professional development and have led employees to exceed employer standards for performance and job knowledge. I also direct all phases of a comprehensive training program.

During previous employment, I have excelled in positions as Technical Writer and Employee Relations Specialist where I played a key role in compiling the materials used for training new personnel.

As you see on my resume, I earned my B.A. degree in Business Administration. I am fluent in Spanish and have broad knowledge of the personnel field.

If you can use a versatile and resourceful motivator with proven management abilities, excellent communication and public relations skills, I would enjoy meeting you in person to discuss your needs. I hope you will call or write me soon to suggest a time when we might meet. Thank you in advance for your time.

Sincerely,

Arlene N. Anderson

ARLENE NANCY ANDERSON

1110½ Hay Street, Fayetteville, NC 28305 • preppub@aol.com • (910) 483-6611

OBJECTIVE I want to contribute through my education in business administration, my outstanding skills as a planner and organizer, my talents as a decision maker, and my ability to train, motivate, and supervise others.

EDUCATION **B.A., Business Administration** with a concentration in **Management**, University of Northern Iowa, Cedar Falls, IA, 1992.

LANGUAGE Fluent in Spanish--speaking, reading, and writing.

EXPERIENCE **PERSONNEL & TRAINING SUPERVISOR.** International Paper Co., Columbia, IL (2003-present). After excelling in an entry-level position, was promoted to oversee 14 employees working in three different areas; managed ongoing and special training while controlling a $1.5 million budget.
- Reported to executives on personnel training and on any problems/situations that could impact organizational efficiency.
- Guided employee professional development and led employees in exceeding employer standards for performance and job knowledge.
- Recognized as the subject matter expert on government policies such as Affirmative Action and the EEO Act.
- Planned and directed personnel administration including employee promotions, transfers, terminations accident reporting, labor relations and grievances, and office administration.

Previously excelled in this progression with Proctor & Gamble, Cincinnati, OH:
2000-02: TECHNICAL WRITER. Was selected ahead of more experienced personnel to head a team of specialists who wrote, edited, and processed reports which were sent to various government agencies.
- Played a key role in compiling the materials now used for training new personnel.

1997-99: EMPLOYEE RELATIONS SPECIALIST. Prepared monthly statistical reports for executives and briefed them on personnel strength and projected shortages, turnover, and absenteeism. Established a new employee orientation presentation.
- Was promoted to Technical Writer on the basis of my organizational and planning skills, writing ability, and reputation for sound judgment.

Military experience:
INTELLIGENCE ANALYST. U.S. Army, San Antonio, TX (1993-96). Became skilled in applying my analytical and decision-making abilities to provide communications specialists with information.
- Refined my written communication skills preparing technical analytical reports for government agencies.

SPECIAL SKILLS
- Familiar with Word, Excel, WordPerfect, and PowerPoint.
- Excel as a team builder and leader.

COMPUTERS Highly proficient with software including Windows, Word, PowerPoint, Access, Excel.

PERSONAL Can provide excellent personal and professional references upon request. Held a Top Secret security clearance while serving in the U.S. Army. Known for integrity and reliability.

Date

Exact Name of Person
Title or Position
Name of Company
Address (no., street)
Address (city, state, zip)

PERSONNEL ASSISTANT
in an academic environment at the University of Idaho with prior experience in the temporary placement personnel staffing industry

Dear Exact Name of Person: (or Dear Sir or Madam if answering a blind ad)

With the enclosed resume, I would like to make you aware of my interest in exploring employment opportunities with your organization and acquaint you with my track record of achievements related to human resources and personnel.

As you will see from my resume, I have excelled in positions requiring top-notch management, communication, and organizational skills. As Personnel Assistant at the University of Idaho, I have refined my knowledge of human resources and personnel administration. I act as the university's liaison with the Job Training Service Center and prepare vacancy announcements for faculty and staff positions.

In previous jobs, I trained and supervised employees in all aspects of personnel administration. I have excelled as a Recruitment and Placement Specialist for Mega Force and as a Personnel Placement Specialist for Kelly Temporary Services. Because of my boundless energy and relentless enthusiasm for tackling new projects, I have always been singled out to take responsibility for new projects which require a strong leader with a highly resourceful nature. I have earned a reputation as someone who can get the job done, no matter what.

If you can use a hard worker with a proven ability to manage multiple priorities and produce outstanding bottom-line results under tight deadlines, I hope you will contact me to suggest a time when we might meet to discuss your needs. Thank you in advance for your time.

Sincerely,

Ellen C. Albright

ELLEN C. ALBRIGHT

1110½ Hay Street, Fayetteville, NC 28305 • preppub@aol.com • (910) 483-6611

OBJECTIVE To benefit an organization through my experience related to personnel management along with my specialist skills in office management and reputation as an effective communicator.

EXPERIENCE **PERSONNEL ASSISTANT.** University of Idaho, Moscow, ID (2003-present). Have been promoted to act as the Administrative Assistant/Secretary to the university Personnel Director; assure that personnel policies and procedures are implemented and that the most qualified individuals are selected for the work force.
- Prepare vacancy announcements for faculty and staff positions; review applications and ensure they are complete and that the prospective employees meet all qualifications; forward applications to appropriate department heads for their consideration.
- Handle a wide range of activities which call for heavy public contact: answer phones and route calls, schedule appointments as well as meetings and workshops for the director and office staff, and make travel arrangements for office personnel.
- Make arrangements for monthly new employee orientation sessions.
- Act as the university liaison with the Job Training Service Center: locate openings in campus offices, establish orientation programs, and work closely with counselors.
- Apply my word processing skills while preparing numerous internal reports and records including such items as budgets, the university directory, billing, and application logs.
- Maintain personnel files which includes setting up files, removing outdated files and information, reorganizing filing systems as needed, and ensuring confidentiality.

CLERK/TYPIST. University of Idaho, Moscow, ID (2000-02). Managed day-to-day clerical operations in the university's admissions office including maintaining records and answering correspondence. Contributed to smooth operations through my helpful, cheerful attitude.

Gained experience in personnel management and exposure to the business community in management and support jobs in the temporary placement industry:
RECRUITMENT AND PLACEMENT SPECIALIST. Mega Force Staffing Service, Seattle, WA (1998-00). Processed applications for personnel seeking temporary employment while providing information and typing related correspondence.
- Processed requests from employers with vacancies. Analyzed documentation to ensure applicants were qualified and available. Verified applicant data.
- Was singled out to conduct employee orientation programs because of my outstanding communication skills and ability to relate to others.

PERSONNEL PLACEMENT SPECIALIST. Kelly Temporary Service, Tacoma, WA (1995-97). Interviewed applicants for clerical and general office jobs and placed them in temporary assignments while also supervising in-house employees.
- Sharpened my sales ability by "selling" our service to new accounts.

EDUCATION B.A. in **Business Administration**, Marquette University, Milwaukee, WI, 1994.
- A Dean's List student, also active in the Student Government Association, Entrepreneur Club, and named to the scholarship selection committee.

AFFILIATIONS Served as the vice president for community development, Seattle Jaycees.
A member of the American Business Women's Association, was named to "Outstanding Young Women in America" and nominated for "Who's Who in Young American Women."

PERSONAL Have a knack for conducting successful interviews and placing people at ease.

CAREER CHANGE

Date

Exact Name of Person
Title or Position
Name of Company
Address (no., street)
Address (city, state, zip)

PERSONNEL ASSISTANT at Tech Data. This individual is exploring career opportunities outside her current industry.

Dear Exact Name of Person: (or Dear Sir or Madam if answering a blind ad)

I would appreciate an opportunity to talk with you soon about how I could benefit your organization through my experience in office administration, personnel management, and proven time management abilities.

Throughout my experience at Tech Data, San Antonio, TX, I have been selected for ever-increasing levels of responsibility in recognition of my ability to think logically, prioritize, and follow through until a job is accomplished. Known for my highly resourceful nature, I have often been handpicked for special projects which require creativity and initative. In one project, after extensive analysis, I made recommendations which led to the revision of the wage and salary schedules at Tech Data and resulted in significant cost savings. On another occasion, I streamlined procedures for processing new employees into their proper training classes. I have been told that my actions have contributed to reduced employee turnover and increased employee morale.

In addition to my practical experience in office administration and personnel management, I offer dedication, maturity, and a cheerful attitude which could be valuable assets to your business.

Although I am highly regarded by my current employer and can provide outstanding references, I am selectively exploring opportunities in other organizations. As you will see from my resume, I have used my spare time to pursue my Bachelor's degree in Personnel Management, and I will soon be completing my degree with a 3.75 GPA.

I hope you will call or write soon to suggest a time convenient for us to meet and discuss your current and future needs and how I might serve them. Thank you in advance for your time.

Sincerely yours,

Jeremiah D. Sudbury

JEREMIAH D. SUDBURY

1110½ Hay Street, Fayetteville, NC 28305 • preppub@aol.com • (910) 483-6611

OBJECTIVE To contribute my experience related to office administration to an organization that can use a professional known for outstanding abilities in managing time, prioritizing work flow, ensuring quality service, and motivating employees to guarantee smooth operations.

EQUIPMENT EXPERTISE
- Am experienced in operating a wide variety of computer systems.
- Use software including PowerPoint, Excel, Word, and Access.

EXPERIENCE *Advanced on a fast track of promotion with Tech Data, San Antonio, TX:*
2003-present: PERSONNEL ASSISTANT. Established filing and correspondence systems used to maintain a variety of personnel records for employees and ensure all documentation is prepared and filed according to guidelines; prepare reports on personnel matters for senior officials.
- Research records to determine personnel in need of specialized training programs and to identify class vacancies.
- After extensive analysis, made recommendations which led to the revision of the wage and salary schedules in order to reflect the current economic situation; this resulted in cost savings for Tech Data.
- Streamlined procedures for processing new employees into their proper training classes.
- Plan and manage an annual performance evaluation program.
- Was singled out by executives and senior managers for my knowledge of procedures and for my ability to make suggestions which improved audit results.
- Reduced employee turnover through improving personnel relations and boosting morale; have developed a spirit of teamwork.

2000-02: TRAINING SPECIALIST. Managed the administration of the assignment process for management and executive development training courses. Refined my research and problem-solving abilities while handling the details of providing accurate and timely services on a large scale.
- Achieved and maintained a 97% productivity rate.

1998-00: PERSONNEL CLERK. Collected data on personnel performance evaluations to determine eligibility for promotion, analyzed material, and entered data into computer; maintained personnel files.
- Made arrangements for regularly scheduled employee orientation presentations.
- Ensured Personnel Manager was kept up to date on EEO and Affirmative Action changes.
- Reviewed and prepared reports for approval by higher headquarters personnel.

Highlights of prior U.S. Army service include:
ADMINISTRATIVE SPECIALIST. Ft. Carson, CO (1995-97). Was commended with an "Impact Award" for bringing personnel administration center's report turn-in rate from around 70% to 98%.
- Gained extensive experience in working with the public in a department emphasizing customer contact and providing quality customer services.

RECORDS CLERK. Ft. Polk, LA (1992-95). Refined my organizational skills and ability to attend to details while processing information and maintaining automated records.

EDUCATION Currently completing courses toward B.A. in Personnel Management at Central Texas College; pursue my education in my spare time at nights and on weekends. 3.7 GPA.

CAREER CHANGE

Date

Exact Name of Person
Exact Title
Exact Name of Company
Address
City, State, Zip

PERSONNEL DIRECTOR
for a major
chemical company

Dear Exact Name of Person: (or Dear Sir or Madam if answering a blind ad)

With the enclosed resume, I would like to express my interest in exploring employment opportunities with your organization.

As you will see from my resume, I offer a reputation as a results-oriented professional who has consistently achieved advancement ahead of my peers. I am highly respected and have been strongly encouraged to remain at Dow Chemical. However, I have made the decision to seek opportunities in another industry.

Currently overseeing a 12-person staff at Dow as Personnel Director, I control a $500,000 annual operating budget and provide guidance on areas where training is needed. In a previous assignment as a Personnel Coordinator at Coca Cola, I was cited as the key factor in the success of efforts to solve personnel issues rooted in morale and training deficiencies. I also directed the employee orientation program for all departments, which was credited with improving productivity and reducing turnover.

Throughout my career I have been singled out for praise from senior officials in recognition of my success at resolving problems and developing workable solutions, organizing activities for maximum productivity, and communicating ideas and information. I have also produced excellent results as a Training Manager and Administrative Support Manager.

I have earned respect for my sound judgment and ability to gain the cooperation and best efforts of others. If you can use a mature human resources professional with a high level of initiative who thrives on meeting deadlines and challenges, I hope you will keep me in mind for future opportunities in which I would be able to contribute to your organization. I can provide excellent professional and personal references at the appropriate time. Thank you for your time and consideration.

Sincerely,

Moishe E. Steinberg

MOISHE E. STEINBERG ("Mo")

1110½ Hay Street, Fayetteville, NC 28305 • preppub@aol.com • (910) 483-6611

OBJECTIVE To benefit an organization that can use a dynamic leader, communicator, and manager with exceptionally strong abilities related to managing projects, finances, and people.

EXPERIENCE **PERSONNEL DIRECTOR.** Dow Chemical Co., Mansfield, OH (2003-present). Supervise a staff of 12 people providing administrative personnel support for more than 500 employees including ensuring payrolls were met and promotions and awards presented in a timely manner.
- Control a $500,000 annual budget.
- Improved productivity ratings to 97% from a low 60% within three months.
- Refined my skills in attending to details while overseeing large projects.
- Oversee employee benefit reports and records, safety, sexual harassment claims, and OSHA and EEO compliance.
- Rewrote the attendance policy and created a schedule in which people could flex their time, which has saved the company $.5 million annually and greatly reduced turnover.
- Created an employee orientation program to ensure all employees were up to date on company policies, regulations, and benefits.

PERSONNEL COORDINATOR. Coca Cola Company, Pensacola, FL (2001-2002). Oversaw preparation of required reports and other paperwork related to personnel administration.
- Provided training classes for all levels of the organization.
- Produced the company newsletter.
- Counseled supervisors in resolving employee grievances.
- Organized United Way and Junior Achievement campaigns.
- Directed the employee orientation program for all departments, which was credited as resulting in increased productivity.

TRAINING MANAGER. Pfizer, Inc., Savannah, GA (1998-01). Coordinated training operations for more than 26,000 employees.
- Implemented safety program changes which reduced injuries 30%.
- Prepared materials in a clear, concise manner for technical manuals.

LOGISTICS MANAGER. K-Mart, Allentown, PA (1995-97). Supervised 30 employees while providing maintenance and supply support for a 2,000-person organization, controlling multimillion-dollar inventories, and planning/administering a $500,000 annual budget.
- Received praise for leading the department to official recognition as "one of the two best" in the company.
- Achieved a 20% budget increase while other departments suffered 20-30% cuts.

ADMINISTRATIVE SUPPORT MANAGER. Systel Corp., Memphis, TN (1992-94). Provided training and administrative support to a 600-person division while supervising 22 employees and controlling an $80,000 budget.
- Developed skills in managing, training, and counseling employees.

EDUCATION **B.S., Personnel Management,** University of Kansas, Lawrence, KS, 1992.

COMPUTERS Proficient with computer software including Access, Excel, and PowerPoint.

PERSONAL Have been noted for my superior communication skills and as a motivator. Will relocate.

Date

Exact Name of Person
Exact Title
Exact Name of Company
Address
City, State, Zip

PERSONNEL COORDINATOR,
temporary service agency

Dear Exact Name of Person: (or Dear Sir or Madam if answering a blind ad)

With the enclosed resume, I would like to make you aware of my experience in office administration and customer service as well as in the management of services related to human resources and personnel administration.

In my current job as Personnel Coordinator, I manage 25 professionals who perform recruiting, hiring, and contract negotiations with client organizations who utilize Manpower Temporaries to find employees. Known for my tact and discretion, I maintain personnel files and prepare reports on turnover, absenteeism, and productivity. I am proud of the role I have played in enriching numerous organizations through the quality employees which Manpower has provided, and numerous clients have praised my dedicated efforts and organizational skills.

In all of my jobs I have expertly utilized a computer with numerous software applications in order to maintain databases, write reports, compile statistics, and track data. I am highly computer literate and offer an ability to rapidly master new programs.

In my previous job at Star Companies, I excelled in a "track record" of advancement to increasing responsibilities within a diversified corporate environment. I pride myself on my strong customer service orientation, and I believe my professional customer service attitude is inspired by my sincere desire to help others. I have discovered that my attention to detail and organizational skills have helped me be of service to numerous people on many occasions.

I would like to become a part of an organization that can use a hard-working and disciplined young professional who aims for excellence in all I do. If you can use my considerable skills and talents, please contact me to suggest a time when we might meet to discuss your needs and how I might serve them. Thank you in advance for your time.

Yours sincerely,

Barbara L. Polaski

BARBARA L. POLASKI

1110½ Hay Street, Fayetteville, NC 28305 • preppub@aol.com • (910) 483-6611

OBJECTIVE To contribute to an organization through my background in customer service, human resources and employee selection, and office administration.

EXPERIENCE **PERSONNEL COORDINATOR.** Manpower Temporaries, Bloomington, IN (2003-present). Was aggressively recruited for this position by the regional vice president of Manpower Temporaries, who is a church acquaintance. Without prior industry experience, am excelling in managing 25 employees who conduct interviewing, hiring, counseling, and contract negotiations with clients.
- Personally negotiate contracts with clients and maintain client/employee relations.
- Maintain personnel files and prepare reports on turnover, absenteeism, and productivity.
- Process all aspects of worker's compensation, unemployment claims, and wage verification.
- Discreetly handle confidential information.

Excelled in a "track record" of advancement to increasing responsibilities within a diversified corporate environment, Star Companies, Chicago, IL.
2002-03: ADMINISTRATIVE ASSISTANT. Performed administrative tasks for the General Manager, Leasing Director, and Marketing Director of the mall at Deerfield Green, a $40 million multiuse development that is part of The Star Companies' real estate portfolio.
- Recorded monthly sales reports for three retail properties.
- Prepared contract lease proposals, lease agreements, commencement of term agreements, and termination agreements.
- Handled basic office accounting including petty cash reconciliation, coding invoices for payment, and collection/processing of rents.
- Coordinated maintenance staff and assigned duties.

2001-02: EXECUTIVE SECRETARY. Performed administrative tasks for the Executive Vice President/Asset Management Division, Chief Engineer, and Office Manager.
- Coordinated meetings; scheduled interviews; screened incoming calls.
- Typed documents of a confidential nature.
- Organized and maintained property management files.
- On a monthly basis, updated and distributed interoffice directories.

2000: SECRETARY. Was promoted rapidly after excelling in performing secretarial tasks for two retail leasing agents, Retail Development Division; prepared contract lease proposals, lease agreements, and lease summaries while also setting up and maintaining tenant files.

Other experience: SECRETARY and **CREDIT CLERK.** Deerfield National Bank, Deerfield, IL (1995-99). Performed secretarial tasks for three commercial loan officers, Commercial Lending Division; prepared loan documents and mortgage packages while handling customer requests for services including wire transfers, draws on notes, and depository functions.
- As a Credit Clerk, prepared internal credit checks for loan officers and maintained credit information in credit files; provided credit references on customer accounts by phone and through written correspondence.

OFFICE SKILLS Type 65 wpm; operate dictaphone, adding machine, and calculator.
Knowledgeable of software including Word, Excel, Access, and QuickBooks.

PERSONAL Am a hardworking, self-motivated professional who strives for excellence.

CAREER CHANGE

Date

Exact Name of Person
Exact Title
Exact Name of Company
Address
City, State, Zip

PERSONNEL DRUG TESTING ADMINISTRATOR
SBC Communications

Dear Exact Name of Person: (or Dear Sir or Madam if answering a blind ad)

With the enclosed resume, I would like to express my interest in exploring employment opportunities with your organization.

As you will see from my resume, I offer a reputation as a results-oriented professional who has consistently achieved advancement ahead of my peers. I am highly respected and have been strongly encouraged to remain at SBC Communications. However, I have made the decision to seek opportunities in another industry.

Currently handling all drug screenings for SBC personnel nationwide as Personnel Drug Testing Administrator, I verify that personnel have taken the prescribed tests and make appropriate recommendations to medical staff or human resources department.

In a previous position as Assistant Personnel Manager at American International Group, I was cited as the key factor in the success of efforts to solve personnel issues rooted in morale and training deficiencies. Earlier, as Employee Benefits Supervisor, I also directed the employee orientation program for all departments, which was credited with improving productivity and reducing turnover.

Throughout my career I have been singled out for praise from senior officials in recognition of my success at resolving problems and developing workable solutions, organizing activities for maximum productivity, and communicating ideas and information.

I have earned respect for my sound judgment, ability to gain the cooperation and best efforts of others, and talent for guiding and motivating personnel to excel. If you can use a human resources professional with a high level of initiative who thrives on meeting deadlines and challenges, I hope you will keep me in mind for future opportunities in which I would be able to contribute to your organization. I will provide excellent professional and personal references at the appropriate time. Thank you for your time and consideration.

Sincerely,

Harold E. Yardell

HAROLD E. YARDELL ("Hal")

1110½ Hay Street, Fayetteville, NC 28305 • preppub@aol.com • (910) 483-6611

OBJECTIVE To offer expertise in human and resources management to an organization that can use a skilled professional with a proven background of success in the areas of personnel and property accountability as well as budgeting, office management, and data processing operations.

EDUCATION **B.A.** in **Business Administration** Passaic County Community College, Paterson, NJ, 1992. Completed intensive training programs in Human Resources Management and Business Administration at SBC Corp.

EXPERIENCE **PERSONNEL DRUG TESTING ADMINISTRATOR.** SBC Communications, Lakewood, NJ (2002-present). Handle all drug screenings for SBC personnel nationwide, including coordinating with drug testing agencies to schedule testing and verifying that personnel have taken the proper prescribed tests.

- Ensure proper documentation is received with specimens that may appear to be inaccurate; perform final analysis for drug screenings.
- Determine inconsistencies between proclaimed drug intake and formal drug screening reports to make recommendations to medical staff or human resources department.
- Perform a variety of administrative functions including data entry to create or update medical files, file and post medical records, and correspond through e-mail.

Was consistently selected for positions normally held by more senior professionals during my employment at American International Group, Manchester, NH.
1999-01: ASSISTANT PERSONNEL MANAGER. Handpicked by the Personnel Manager, turned a department known for low morale and serious personnel problems into a team which became a model of efficiency and productivity with the capability of exceeding expected standards.

- Led a 35-person section with the assignment of preparing a wide range of documentation and reports in a timely manner, exceeding the department's goals for on-time rates and accuracy by 1.9%. Ensured timely preparation of personnel records and documentation.

1996-98: PERSONNEL SUPERVISOR. Earned the praise of senior executives for my success in supervising a 210-person shift at one of the company's key plants.

- Received a Letter of Appreciation from the Personnel Manager for my efforts which resulted in improving the opportunities and quality of the work environment for American International employees.
- Trained, counseled, and supervised the performance of employees while providing an example for cooperation and teamwork within a diverse work force.
- Gained experience in contract negotiations while negotiating with the labor relations representative.

1993-95: EMPLOYEE BENEFITS SUPERVISOR. Supervised a 15-person staff; determined benefits plan for company employees. Responsible for designing an audiovisual employee orientation which was credited with improving productivity and decreasing turnover
- Prepared and presented briefings to high-level executives.

LANGUAGES Working knowledge of Spanish and Italian.

PERSONAL Am accustomed to working long hours under tight time constraints. Offer a reputation as a good listener who is especially adept at bringing out the best in others. Am available for relocation worldwide according to employer needs. Excellent references on request.

Date

Exact Name of Person
Exact Title
Exact Name of Company
Address
City, State, Zip

PERSONNEL MANAGER
for Borden Foods

Dear Exact Name of Person (or Dear Sir or Madam if answering a blind ad):

With the enclosed resume, I would like to make you aware of my interest in exploring employment opportunities with your organization and introduce you to my background related to the field of human resources.

Currently completing an M.A. in Human Resources Management at Colgate University, I was selected for the position of Personnel Manager at Borden Foods over more experienced candidates because of my excellent school record. In this position, I oversee the personnel department with a staff of 30 and a budget of $14 million. On a formal evaluation, I was described as "an incisive, imaginative leader." I also initiated the design of a new computer program which maintains an accurate and timely record of all personnel data.

While at Kraft Foods, I was promoted to Assistant Personnel Manager due to my excellent performance as Personnel Clerk. As Assistant Personnel Manager, I ensured availability of qualified personnel, kept records on turnover rates, absenteeism, and worker's compensation payments. I also initiated preparation of a new, updated employee manual to ensure employees were informed about company policies and available benefits, which was credited with reducing turnover and improving morale.

If you are in need of an experienced professional who offers outstanding oral and written communication skills, I would appreciate your contacting me. I can provide outstanding references at the appropriate time.

Yours sincerely,

Nikki M. Thomas

NIKKI M. THOMAS

1110½ Hay Street, Fayetteville, NC 28305 • preppub@aol.com • (910) 483-6611

OBJECTIVE   To benefit an organization that can use an accomplished young professional who has gained extensive expertise related to skills in managing multiple tasks while providing effective human, fiscal and resource management.

EDUCATION & TRAINING   Completing **M.A., Human Resources Management,** Colgate University, Hamilton, NY.
Earned **B.S., Humanities,** Pace University, New York, NY, 1996.

EXPERIENCE   **PERSONNEL MANAGER.** Borden Foods, Inc., Hamilton, NY (2003-present). Was selected for this position over more experienced persons because of my excellent school record. Supervise the personnel department with a staff of 30 and a budget of $14 million.
- On a formal evaluation, was described a *"an incisive, imaginative leader."*
- Manage functions including promotions, employee evaluations, and status of personnel availability.
- Develop employee training programs and keep the employee manual up to date.
- Established excellent labor relations for which I was rewarded by upper management with a commendation. Initiated design of a new computer program which maintains an accurate and timely record of all personnel data.

Advanced on the fast track with Kraft Foods due to my ability to learn quickly and achieve excellent results:
ASSISTANT PERSONNEL MANAGER. Kraft Foods, Garden City, NY (2001-2003). Because of my excellent performance in the position of Personnel Clerk, was promoted to Assistant Personnel Manager. Ensured availability of qualified personnel and kept records on turnover rates and absenteeism data.
- Initiated preparation of a new, updated employee manual to ensure employees were informed about company policies and available benefits, which was credited with reducing turnover and improving employee morale.
- Kept the Personnel Manager aware of any changes in EEO and Affirmative Action guidelines. Reduced worker's compensation payments through an emphasis on safety and aggressive case management.

PERSONNEL CLERK. Kraft Foods, Garden City, NY (1999-01). Gained valuable knowledge about the personnel department and its functions. Kept records of worker's compensation payments; typed recommendations for promotions, terminations, employee evaluations, and other paperwork as requested.
- Promoted to Assistant Personnel Manager because of strong communication skills.

SECRETARY. Merrill Lynch, New York, NY (1996-98). In this busy financial institution, performed clerical duties for the brokers. Acquired valuable knowledge of the financial field. Was known for my cheery disposition and willingness to take on any duty.

ASSISTANT TO INSTRUCTOR. Pace University, New York, NY (1994-96). While attending college full time, assisted a professor in the human relations department with office duties.

FULL-TIME STUDENT. Pace University, New York, NY (1992-1996). Earned a B.S. in Humanities, which inspired my interest in human relations and the field of human resources.

PERSONAL   Highly motivated individual who can provide outstanding references. Outstanding communicator. Can provide excellent references upon request.

Date

Exact Name of Person
Exact Title
Exact Name of Company
Address
City, State, Zip

PERSONNEL MANAGER AND RETENTION SPECIALIST
with Johnson & Johnson

Dear Exact Name of Person: (or Dear Sir or Madam if answering a blind ad)

With the enclosed resume, I would like to make you aware of my track record of accomplishments and of the outstanding managerial, training, supervisory, and planning skills I have polished while at Johnson & Johnson.

As you will see from my resume, I am presently working as a Personnel Manager and Retention Specialist for Johnson & Johnson, Fresno, CA. In approximately eight years with this organization, I have led the way to improvements in all measurable areas of operations. Personnel retention rates remain at approximately 125%, and 55% of company personnel have attended advanced professional training.

I have consistently earned the respect and loyalty of my subordinates for my fair and firm manner and problem-solving skills. In the position of Employee Relations Manager, I was credited with a 25% increase in productivity as a direct result of my efforts in automating the office. Earlier as Assistant Program Supervisor and then as Training Program Supervisor, I was frequently sought out by name for my resourcefulness and knowledge.

If you can use an articulate, results-oriented professional with a reputation for high personal standards of integrity and loyalty, I hope you will welcome my call soon when I try to arrange a brief meeting to discuss your goals and how my background might serve your needs. I can provide outstanding references at the appropriate time.

Sincerely,

Andrew C. Artemis

Alternate Last Paragraph:
I hope you will write or call me soon to suggest a time when we might meet to discuss your needs and goals and how my background might serve them. I can provide outstanding references at the appropriate time.

ANDREW C. ARTEMIS

1110½ Hay Street, Fayetteville, NC 28305 • preppub@aol.com • (910) 483-6611

OBJECTIVE To offer a track record of outstanding achievements in the management of human resources, training and mentoring of personnel, and supervision of employees in fast-paced settings under high levels of pressure and tight deadlines.

EDUCATION **Bachelor's degree in Human Resources**, University of San Diego, CA, 1994.
Received extensive training at Johnson & Johnson with an emphasis on leadership, supervision, and management as well as personnel recruiting and Equal Opportunity Program management.

EXPERIENCE *Have excelled in the following record of promotion as an advisor and manager for administrative, training, and operational activities, Johnson & Johnson, Fresno, CA:*

2003-present: PERSONNEL MANAGER & RETENTION SPECIALIST. Act as the senior advisor on personnel and administrative matters for top management while overseeing and coordinating all aspects of both internal training and professional school attendance.
- Was credited with developing an informative company manual outlining company policies, rules, and benefits.
- Led the way to outstanding achievements: 125% retention of qualified personnel; 55% of company personnel have attended advanced professional training; and have achieved a 97% productivity rating.
- Ensure compliance with OSHA, EEO, and Affirmative Action guidelines and requirements.
- Proposed and supervised renovations in both employee and executive dining facilities.

2001-03: EMPLOYEE RELATIONS MANAGER. Received commendable ratings for my planning and management of the Equal Opportunity Program.
- Was sought out for my resourcefulness and fairness when receiving complaints and ensuring solutions which reduced discrimination and sexual harassment.
- Prepared and produced statistical reports; inspected subordinate branch programs and made recommendations on changes which would improve their effectiveness.
- Brought about a 25% increase in productivity by automating office functions.

1998-00: TRAINING PROGRAM SUPERVISOR. Officially cited for "positive attitude and tactful critiques" which led to superior results, frequently requested by name to assist in improving training which ensured the availability of trained personnel.
- Earned the respect of my superiors, peers, and subordinates for my commitment, integrity, and control displayed while developing well-trained and highly skilled young professionals.
- Established training programs in each area of production and set up schedules.

1995-97: ASSISTANT PROGRAM SUPERVISOR. Expertly handled multiple functional areas including training as well as advising a senior supervisor on any problems with scheduling or providing instruction.
- Scheduled locations for each department's training session and oversaw actual instruction to assess value and participation.
- Promoted ahead of my peers on the basis of my effectiveness in this position.

PERSONAL Offer a reputation as an articulate professional with high personal standards of loyalty and integrity. Am proficient with many popular computer operating systems and software including Windows, Microsoft Word, Excel, Access, PowerPoint, and Corel.

Date

Exact Name of Person
Title or Position
Name of Company
Address (no., street)
Address (city, state, zip)

PERSONNEL MANAGER
at Monarch Foods

Dear Exact Name of Person: (or Dear Sir or Madam if answering a blind ad)

Can you use an energetic, enthusiastic professional who offers "top-notch" talents as an innovative problem solver and decision maker along with proven expertise as a manager of people, assets, and financial resources?

I have officially been described as an "exceptional performer" and "articulate and persuasive communicator who excels in motivating employees to outstanding results." I offer a solid track record of accomplishments and a history of being able to step into any situation and find a way to build morale and instill team spirit.

I have consistently earned leadership roles and been selected ahead of my peers in tough competitions — ranging from being selected as captain of my high school football team, to winning one of 75 full academic scholarships from among 3,500 students. This trend has continued during my career as I have been chosen for numerous positions ahead of more experienced executives.

Known for my resourceful and entrepreneurial nature, I was recently handpicked to lead a new venture in which we downsized a clumsy organization which had grown too large into a small, more flexible company which now provides excellent customer service. I possess a proven combination of "common sense," drive to succeed, technical knowledge, and expertise in managing human, fiscal, and material resources that would make me valuable to you.

I hope you will welcome my call soon to arrange a brief meeting at your convenience to discuss your current and future needs and how I might serve them. Thank you in advance for your time.

Sincerely yours,

Colin T. Kinston

Alternate last paragraph:
I hope you will call or write soon to suggest a time convenient for us to meet and discuss your current and future needs and how I might serve them. Thank you in advance for your time.

COLIN T. KINSTON

1110½ Hay Street, Fayetteville, NC 28305   •   preppub@aol.com   •   (910) 483-6611

OBJECTIVE   To offer my analytical, planning, decision-making, and problem-solving skills to an organization that can use a dynamic and resourceful leader who excels in motivating people and in turning new ideas into operating realities.

EXPERIENCE   **PERSONNEL MANAGER.** Monarch Foods, Dearborn, MI (2003-present). Was handpicked for this job managing a 12-person staff with an essentially entrepreneurial role: developed and implemented plans to establish a new "super company" of 500 people which is a highly streamlined version of the 1,600-person division that the team "inactivated" and "downsized."
- Earned praise for my expertise in organizational development through my success in implementation of this assignment.
- Manage functions including promotions and personnel availability.

GENERAL MANAGER. Borden Foods, Ann Arbor, MI (2000-02). Managed 16 mid-level managers and 75 employees while controlling a $16 million budget; planned special projects and training activities, and continuously advised/briefed senior executives.
- Restructured 25% of the organization's personnel resources and 60% of material resources in such a way that customer support was strengthened and costs reduced.
- Directed employee training and orientation programs for all departments, which was credited as resulting in increased productivity. Revised the wage and salary schedules to reflect the current economic situation, which resulted in a cost savings for Monarch.

OPERATIONS MANAGER. Merck Corporation, Indianapolis, IN (1998-00). Refined my expertise in planning and coordinating large-scale projects while directing the organization's relocation to Illinois; maintained perfect accountability of $30 million in assets.
- Developed training programs for the management team which resulted in a more consistent management style. Managed 54 employees and 12 mid-level managers.

MAINTENANCE PRODUCTION MANAGER. Sikorsky Corp., Santa Clara, CA (1994-97). Managed 47 employees providing logistical support for 256 aircraft in 8 locations and performing maintenance on two UH-1H helicopters; conducted flight tests.
- Was handpicked over seven senior managers to set up and oversee a team of aircraft specialists. Rewrote the organization's standard operating procedures; implemented many ideas that improved internal efficiency and maintenance quality.

PRODUCT DEVELOPMENT CONSULTANT. Lockheed-Martin, Los Angeles, CA (1991-93). Tested modifications to aircraft and their electronic systems and advised research and development engineers on modifications; conducted experimental test flights as a test pilot.
- Managed a $20 million research and development budget and a program providing security for sensitive and high-tech materials and equipment.

Military experience: ASSISTANT AIRFIELD MANAGER. U.S. Army, Ft. Carson, CO (1987-91). Was evaluated as an "intelligent and innovative problem solver" while supervising nine employees in a 24-hour-a-day refueling center; acted as VIP pilot.

EDUCATION   **M.B.A.**, San Jose State University, San Jose, CA, 1994.
B.S. in Psychology, The University of Arizona, Phoenix, AZ, 1986.

PERSONAL   Am completing an intensive German-language study program. Am a self-motivated high achiever who works well with people. Outstanding references upon request.

Date

Exact Name of Person
Exact Title
Exact Name of Company
Address (no., street)
Address (city, state, zip)

PERSONNEL POLICY DEVELOPMENT MANAGER
for Georgia Pacific Corporation

Dear Exact Name of Person: (or Dear Sir or Madam if answering a blind ad)

Enclosed you will find a copy of my resume. I am very interested in the position of Personnel Director which you advertised in *The Spokane Gazette*. I am an accomplished performer who excels in motivating employees. Your job listing states that you need an articulate professional who can deal with senior executives in a start-up position. I am a dynamic self-starter who can step into a position of this type and exceed your expectations.

Currently at Georgia Pacific Corp., Boise, ID, I have excelled in leadership positions. I am involved in researching and developing personnel policies for a 39,000-person organization. I regularly communicate suggestions and remedies to top-level senior executives and am confident that I possess the demeanor that would allow me to work closely with your top executives. A recent formal performance evaluation praised me as "an expert analyst of complex issues" and cited my ability to dissect problems and develop cost-effective, practical solutions.

Since earning my B.A. degree in Human Resources from the University of Iowa, I have proven my ability to step into new organizations and rapidly become a contributing member. In my first job out of college, I was promoted to manage a Personnel Administration Center for Walgreens. Subsequently I served as Personnel Supervisor for the John Deere company, where the employee benefits program was my responsibility.

I welcome the opportunity to talk to you soon and hope that it will be possible to arrange a brief meeting at your convenience to discuss the current and future needs of your organization and how I might serve them. Thank you in advance for your time.

Sincerely,

Alice N. Rasputin

ALICE N. RASPUTIN

1110½ Hay Street, Fayetteville, NC 28305 • preppub@aol.com • (910) 483-6611

OBJECTIVE   To offer my reputation as a dynamic leader and exceptional performer who is recognized as a top-notch planner and project manager with the maturity, professional demeanor, and communication skills required of developing executives.

EXPERIENCE   **PERSONNEL POLICY DEVELOPMENT MANAGER.** Georgia Pacific Corp., Boise, ID (2003-present). Assess and monitor personnel availability and productivity; supervise six administrative specialists while playing a key role in personnel policy development for a 39,000-person organization.

- Prepare monthly confidential reports for the chief executive and the senior personnel officer, reporting on the status of each department and making recommendations on how to bring any undermanned department up to strength.
- Decreased the number of absentees by initiating an employee flex-time program which in turn increased productivity.
- Officially cited as an "expert analyst of complex issues," have consistently been described as able to dissect problems and develop cost-effective, practical solutions.
- Excelled in a sensitive and demanding position usually reserved for more senior managers. Am known as a professional who thrives under stress and is always in control.

PERSONNEL SUPERVISOR. John Deere, Inc., Waterloo, IA (2000-02). Managed all aspects of personnel accountability; supervised four specialists, including the employee benefits administrator.

- Ensured critical positions were staffed with the most qualified managers available and that human resources were equitably assigned among all departments.
- Excelled in conducting training which resulted in more productive employees.
- Organized the United Way and Junior Achievement campaigns.
- Was singled out by the chief executive to apply my research and analytical abilities and decisiveness to take charge of several special projects with short turnaround times.

PERSONNEL AND ADMINISTRATION CENTER MANAGER. Walgreens, Cedar Rapids, IA (1995-99). Supervised four employees in the personnel administrative management office.

- Achieved an exceptional 95% accuracy and timeliness rate.
- Developed a checklist for ensuring all personnel actions were completed and also monitored the Affirmative Action and EEO compliance.
- Was cited as being tenacious in lobbying higher headquarters and obtaining the personnel to fill critical jobs while other branches were seeing manpower shortages.
- Applied outstanding communication skills teaching writing, proofreading official documents, and assisting anyone needing guidance in preparing written communications.

EDUCATION   **B.A. degree in Human Resources**, University of Iowa, Iowa City, IA, 1994; minor concentration in Economics.

- Was a Dean's List scholar ranked 32nd in a class of 965 highly talented and dedicated future business leaders.
- Was handpicked for three of the most prestigious summer jobs available to a business or economics major in the Department of Human Resources.
- Received the Hewitt Award, the highest distinction for excellence in economics.
- Earned more individual titles in two years than any other graduate in the school's history competing at the national level in impromptu and extemporaneous speech.

PERSONAL   Excellent references upon request. Will relocate according to employer need.

Date

Exact Name of Person
Title or Position
Name of Company
Address (number and street)
Address (city, state, and ZIP)

PERSONNEL RECRUITER AND TRAINING MANAGER
for a staffing service

Dear Exact Name of Person: (or Dear Sir or Madam if answering a blind ad)

I would appreciate an opportunity to talk with you soon about how I could contribute to your organization through my well-developed managerial skills as well as through my background which has emphasized expertise in recruiting, training, counseling, and leading others.

You will see from my enclosed resume that I offer a track record of accomplishments. I feel that this background has given me the opportunity to hone natural abilities as a leader. I am very comfortable and effective as a public speaker and instructor with a strong base of experience in developing and overseeing results-oriented training programs.

I have regularly been selected to take on challenging jobs and consistently achieved outstanding results. In my most recent job at Mega Forces Staffing Services in Chicago, IL, I excelled in recruiting record numbers of applicants for temporary positions. I guided the program to recognition as the best of 73 nationwide branches for successfully placing qualified personnel.

With a reputation as a talented, intelligent, and articulate professional, I am confident that I offer a combination of natural abilities and experience certain to make me a valuable asset to any organization.

I hope you will welcome my call soon to arrange a brief meeting at your convenience to discuss your current and future needs and how I might serve them. Thank you in advance for your time.

Sincerely yours,

Alden G. Condor

Alternate last paragraph:
I hope you will call or write me soon to suggest a time convenient for us to meet and discuss your current and future needs and how I might serve them. Thank you in advance for your time.

ALDEN G. CONDOR

1110½ Hay Street, Fayetteville, NC 28305 • preppub@aol.com • (910) 483-6611

OBJECTIVE To offer strong abilities in the areas of personnel recruiting and management as well as an extensive background in ensuring the optimum utilization of human and fiscal resources.

EXPERIENCE **PERSONNEL RECRUITER & TRAINING MANAGER.** Mega Forces Staffing Services, Chicago, IL (2002-present). Consistently achieve record numbers of applicants while recruiting persons for temporary positions. Prepare job descriptions and announcements; screen and interview prospective employees.
- Significantly increased applicants by 100% to 200% each year!
- Guided the program to recognition as the best of 73 among all nationwide branches in terms of successfully placing qualified personnel.
- Earned a commendation from headquarters for superior performance in a highly visible job which required a great deal of public contact with civic, professional, and educational members of the public from throughout the area.
- Designed a new application form which, due to its versatility, decreased the amount of paperwork to be handled and filed.

PERSONNEL MANAGER. McVee Foods, Pontiac, MI (2000-02). Handpicked from a group of 10 highly qualified and talented managers, was chosen to direct personnel and financial management for a 1,205-person organization.
- Achieved the highest-possible ratings in each of six major audits as well as exceptional results in all areas of individual and group training evaluated.
- Supervised 12 employees, including employee relations and benefits specialists.
- Designed a training program for personnel in preparation for introduction of a new product which required specialized skills.
- Rewrote the policy regarding attendance and created a flex-time schedule for employees.

TRAINING MANAGER. New York Life Insurance, Garden City, NY (1997-99). Oversaw a 15-person staff of supervisors while involved in planning and directing training activities for an 850-person organization.
- Coordinated all training materials sent to agents in other branches.
- Developed and implemented a quality assurance program for the parent organization.

EMPLOYEE RELATIONS SPECIALIST. Prudential Insurance, Macon, GA (1993-96). Oversaw the preparation of personnel records; maintained data on safety, EEO and Affirmative Action compliance, and kept up to date on OSHA and federal guidelines.
- Initiated an audiovisual presentation to keep employees informed of company policies, rules, and benefits.

PERSONNEL CLERK. McGuffey's Department Store, Augusta, ME (1991-93). Prepared personnel records; typed recommendations for wage increases and promotions. Answered multi-line phones.
- Implemented improvements to in-house training for junior managers and supervisors.

EDUCATION **B.S., Human Resources**, The University of Maine, Orono, 1990.
- Held membership and elected offices in student organizations including: historian for Kappa Alpha Psi National Fraternity, vice president of Alpha Phi Omega Fraternity.

PERSONAL Am known for my physical and mental toughness. Have a talent for counseling, teaching, and training others to superior results. Recognized as a sound thinker with good judgment.

Date

Exact Name of Person
Title or Position
Name of Company
Address (number and street)
Address (city, state, and ZIP)

PERSONNEL RECRUITER
for the Department of Transportation

Dear Exact Name of Person: (or Dear Sir or Madam if answering a blind ad)

I would appreciate an opportunity to talk with you soon about how I could contribute to your organization through my versatile skills and knowledge as well as through my positive attitude and strong background in leading and motivating others to achieve superior results and high productivity.

As a Personnel Recruiter, I have earned promotion to become a senior recruiting professional and Office Operations Manager for the Department of Transportation in Washington, DC. My five-person team was recognized as the best of seven in the department in 2003 for exceeding sales goals. Prior to my selection for this high-visibility role, I refined my technical skills and mechanical aptitude working in the areas of industrial maintenance, power generation, and industrial gas manufacturing. One of my strengths is my ability to relate well to people at all levels, from so-called "blue-collar" employees to highly educated professionals.

A quick learner who easily masters new procedures and methods, I am adept at presenting a solid professional image in my dealings with the public, members of the business community, and employees at all levels. I am also a highly competitive individual who is known for my resourcefulness in finding new ways to contribute to the "bottom line."

I hope you will welcome my call soon to arrange a brief meeting at your convenience to discuss your current and future needs and how I might serve them. Thank you in advance for your time.

Sincerely yours,

Glen K. Erwin II

Alternate last paragraph:
I hope you will call or write me soon to suggest a time convenient for us to meet and discuss your current and future needs and how I might serve them. Thank you in advance for your time.

GLEN K. ERWIN II

1110½ Hay Street, Fayetteville, NC 28305 • preppub@aol.com • (910) 483-6611

OBJECTIVE   To offer my background in personnel recruiting to an organization that can use a dynamic communicator with exceptional sales skills.

EXPERIENCE   *Advanced to a senior managerial level through my expertise in sales and knowledge of how to motivate employees to maximum efforts, the Department of Transportation, Washington, DC (2000-present):*

2002-present: SENIOR PERSONNEL RECRUITER and **OFFICE OPERATIONS MANAGER.** Recognized as one of the very best among a group of 45 nationwide recruiters, supervise four sales professionals; work with young adults to ensure their familiarity with the advantages of a government career.

- Identify, interview, test, and counsel prospects while earning a reputation as a positive thinker who is totally focused on reaching goals.
- Officially described as a "solid leader," guided the office to recognition as "Office of the Month" twice in 2002 and three times in 2003 as well as the best of seven in 2003.
- Singled out for my sound judgment and ability to work under pressure, was a major contributor to the region's selection as "Zone of the Year."
- Present a positive image of U.S. Government service as liaison with local businesses for a variety of activities including a choral group, parades, fairs, and charity fund raisers.

2000-02: PERSONNEL RECRUITER. Was promoted on the basis of my performance while preparing paperwork for prospective recruits, maintaining files, scheduling and monitoring vocational aptitude tests, and recruiting new personnel.

- Made significant contributions to the branch efforts which led to recognition as "National Department of the Year" for 2002 after setting numerous monthly and quarterly records.
- Acted as a positive force in the community through my participation in civic events.

Refined technical and mechanical skills in highly specialized fields, U.S. Navy:
WORK CENTER SUPERVISOR. Savannah, GA (1996-00). Advanced to a supervisory role overseeing 10 cryogenic technicians maintaining readiness for an oxygen/nitrogen liquid generating plant, high and low-pressure air compressors, dryers, refrigeration units, and high-pressure gaseous systems within the work center.

- Received an achievement medal in recognition of my superior performance during such projects as assisting contractor personnel in the complete change-out of four high-pressure air compressors which increased the reliability of critical equipment.
- Was officially cited for my top-notch performance, superb leadership, and quality organizational and planning skills.
- Placed in charge of the Aviators Breathing Oxygen (ABO) program, made emergency repairs to a critical oxygen sampling device and restored it within 24 hours.

MACHINIST'S MATE. Long Beach, CA (1992-95). As assistant work center supervisor, supply specialist, and damage control specialist, handled the demands of operating/maintaining a main steam turbine engine and auxiliary machinery.

- Was officially described as the best machinist's mate in the division.
- Excelled as engine room supervisor, a role normally reserved for more senior personnel.
- Played a key role which led to high ratings in an external evaluation of engine room and casualty control operations given by professionals known for their high standards.

PERSONAL   Am highly skilled in determining what motivates people and in using that knowledge to get the most out of my employees. Can work well and productively with anyone.

Date

Exact Name of Person
Title or Position
Name of Company
Address (number and street)
Address (city, state, and zip)

PERSONNEL RECRUITER
for Sara Lee Products Company

Dear Exact Name of Person: (or Sir or Madam if answering a blind ad)

I would appreciate an opportunity to talk with you soon about how I could contribute to your organization through my knowledge related to human resources management and personnel recruiting.

You will see from my resume that as a Personnel Recruiter for Sara Lee Products, I have consistently exceeded my goals. I received a "Gold Seal Award" which is given only to personnel who are the highest achievers. Known as a persuasive speaker and good listener who can be counted on for honesty and personal integrity, I have earned the trust and respect of all with whom I come into contact.

Prior to my selection for this position, I worked as Personnel Supervisor at Monarch Foods in Spokane, WA, where I became known as an articulate and assertive leader with a talent for bringing out the best in my co-workers.

I hope you will welcome my call soon to arrange a brief meeting to discuss your current and future needs and how I might serve them. Thank you in advance for your time.

Sincerely,

Ivan S. Horowitz

Alternate last paragraph:
I hope you will call or write me soon to suggest a time convenient for us to meet and discuss your current and future needs and how I might serve them. Thank you in advance for your time.

IVAN S. HOROWITZ

1110½ Hay Street, Fayetteville, NC 28305 • preppub@aol.com • (910) 483-6611

OBJECTIVE To offer a background of outstanding results in recruiting qualified personnel and in maximizing human resources through my talent for developing solid working relationships, my skill in selling ideas, and my knack for relating to others.

TRAINING Excelled in a 2,000-hour comprehensive national apprentice program for professionals in the career counseling and personnel recruiting field; this six-month program at Johns Hopkins University was sponsored by the Sara Lee Company.

Completed additional training programs and courses including a "Persuasive Communication" course in sales and recruiting and a workshop emphasizing the following:
- communication skills
- cultural awareness
- grievance and redress procedures
- sexual harassment
- employee rights, responsibilities, accountability, and privileges

EXPERIENCE **PERSONNEL RECRUITER.** Sara Lee Products, Canton, OH (2002-present). Utilize my skills as a good listener and persuasive speaker while achieving outstanding results and consistently exceeding sales quotas as a representative of Sara Lee Products to prospective employees.
- Earned respect for my outstanding ability to quickly build rapport with everyone with whom I come into contact. Demonstrate my knowledge and dedication while representing the advantages of a career with our company.
- Recruited more than 30 people during my first two years in this position.
- Was commended for my contributions to the success of this recruiting program.
- Achieved 113% of my personal goal by the end of my first year at Sara Lee.
- Received a special "Gold Seal Award" for a record number of recruits in October 2002.
- Was cited for excellent leadership skills and willingness to serve as a mentor for peers.

PERSONNEL SUPERVISOR. Monarch Foods, Spokane, WA (2000-02). Advanced on a "fast track" while earning a reputation as an assertive, articulate, and technically proficient leader.
- Officially described as "extremely knowledgeable, industrious, and resourceful," provided oversight of the Employee Benefits Manager and Labor Relations Manager.
- Implemented a thorough new training program for one group of specialists and oversaw training which allowed personnel to qualify for promotion.
- Was cited for my outstanding contributions in providing administrative and operational support for more than 100 people.
- Earned praise for my positive attitude and pride and was described as someone who raised the morale and team spirit of my peers.
- Developed training programs for managers and employees.
- Volunteered during numerous community relations projects.
- Represented the senior executive at monthly staff meetings.
- Was credited as the individual responsible for a "no discrepancies found" rating during a change-of-management inventory.
- Screened applications, interviewed qualified applicants, and provided those newly hired with company written materials, such as the employee manual.
- Completed a Total Quality Leadership training program, 2000.
- Earned a Letter of Commendation for finding staff for a seriously understaffed engineering department which allowed them to earn their two-year recertification.

PERSONAL Known as a highly resourceful individual who thrives on developing creative solutions to problems. Familiar with various computer software including Word. Excellent references.

Real-Resumes Series edited by Anne McKinney

CAREER CHANGE

Date

Exact Name of Person
Exact Title
Exact Name of Company
Address
City, State, Zip

PERSONNEL RECRUITER & SALES REPRESENTATIVE at Hewlett Packard. This individual seeks to transition into the university environment.

Dear Exact Name of Person: (or Dear Sir or Madam if answering a blind ad)

Can you use an enthusiastic and energetic professional who offers exceptional communication and motivational skills along with a reputation for versatility and adaptability? I am responding to your recent advertisement for a Student Recruiting Specialist at the University of North Carolina.

As you will see from my resume, I was selected to receive special training and then assigned as a personnel recruiter. In this job I "sell" the idea of a career at Hewlett Packard to qualified young people. Through this position I have refined my public speaking and communication skills while interacting with educators, community leaders, and other large audiences and marketing the company to them as well as during one-on-one contacts. I am known as a skilled communicator who is able to speak confidently and persuasively to any size audience including with my subordinates, peers, and supervisors.

With a strong belief that communication skills are the key to success in nearly any job or work environment, I believe I could become a valuable asset to your organization through these skills as well as through my other knowledge and abilities. I am a hardworking and congenial individual who truly enjoys helping my organization prosper. I take pride in my ability to motivate others through my example and help them develop their skills to a higher level while inspiring a spirit of teamwork.

Although I have enjoyed my work at Hewlett Packard, I am attracted to your ad because I am a great fan of the University of North Carolina at Chapel Hill. It would be an honor to be involved in recruiting the nation's "best and brightest" students for UNC.

If you can use an experienced and mature leader who has long been recognized as a reliable and honest individual with uncompromising personal standards, I hope you will contact me soon to suggest a time when we might meet to discuss your needs. I can assure you that I could quickly become an asset to your organization.

Sincerely,

Victor A. Leland

VICTOR A. LELAND
1110½ Hay Street, Fayetteville, NC 28305   •   preppub@aol.com   •   (910) 483-6611

OBJECTIVE   To contribute to an organization that can use a versatile and adaptable professional who offers excellent communication and sales skills as well as a reputation for being effective in motivating and training others while setting the example of professionalism and dedication.

EDUCATION & TRAINING   **B.A. in Personnel Administration**, St. Olaf College, Northfield, MN, 1990.
Excelled in approximately 290 hours of company-sponsored training in programs which emphasized personnel recruiting, retention, and sales techniques as well as professional leadership and supervisory courses.

EXPERIENCE   *Have excelled in the following history of advancement while building a reputation as a skilled communicator and detail-oriented professional who excels in motivating others to achieve top-notch results, Hewlett Packard, Duluth, MN:*

2002-present: PERSONNEL RECRUITER & SALES REPRESENTATIVE. Am refining sales and communication skills organizing and making daily presentations to large audiences as well as one-on-one to individuals in order to "sell" qualified young people on the advantages of a career at Hewlett Packard.

- Deal on a regular basis with educators and community leaders while refining marketing, sales, and interpersonal communication skills.
- When the company merged with Compaq, played a key role in restructuring activities.
- Proficient in PowerPoint and Excel, have learned to use computers while preparing sales presentations and developing effective sales tools and visual aids. Developed a highly effective Internet presence which has significantly aided in corporate recruiting.

2000-02: TRAINING DEPARTMENT CLERK. Handled a wide range of training activities as a clerk and special assistant to the Training Department Chief.

- Initiated an audiovisual employee orientation presentation for all new employees.
- Was credited with playing an instrumental role in the department's recognition as the "Best" at Hewlett Packard.
- Emphasized safety with the result that the plant achieved a "zero accident" rate.
- Wrote job descriptions for 100 employees. Provided on-the-job training for 30 people.
- Was credited with reducing the absenteeism rate by instituting a new incentive plan.
- Was known for my ability to meet challenges head on and operate under deadlines.

Highlights of military experience:
TRAINING SPECIALIST. U.S. Army, Ft. Dix, NJ (1996-99). Supervised and trained personnel including participants in an OJT program while focusing on carrying out inspections in order to enforce sanitation and food preparation procedures and guidelines.

- Oversaw the operation and maintenance for $200,000 worth of equipment.
- Earned praise from my superiors for my expertise in overseeing the preparation and serving of meals for 250 people during one three-month exercise which was conducted in a harsh and hostile environment.

FOOD SERVICE SPECIALIST. U.S. Army, Germany (1992-95). Supervised and trained 14 subordinates in a dining facility while maintaining control of $30,000 worth of equipment.

- Contributed through my dedication and hard work while playing a vital role in the organization's recognition as "Best Dining Facility" of its size in the Army.

PERSONAL   Am known as an outstanding communicator and motivator. Excellent references upon request.

Date

Exact Name of Person
Title or Position
Name of Company
Address (no., street)
Address (city, state, zip)

PERSONNEL RECRUITING MANAGER
for Prudential Insurance Company

Dear Exact Name of Person: (or Dear Sir or Madam if answering a blind ad)

I would appreciate an opportunity to talk with you soon about how my experience, skills, and abilities could be of benefit to your organization.

In my current position as Personnel Recruiting Manager at Prudential Insurance, Inc, in Atlanta, GA, I was chosen to provide leadership and guidance to a geographically dispersed sales force. I exceeded corporate goals in all measured areas while planning, overseeing and conducting personnel recruiting activities. In the most recent fiscal year, I led my staff to reach 117% of the organization's sales goals.

Prior to that, I served as a Personnel Manager for Goody's Markets, where I improved numerous functional areas including training and administrative support. I was recognized as the subject matter expert on government policies pertaining to employment such as Affirmative Action and the EEO Act.

As Training Manager at K-Mart Corp. in Minneapolis, MN, I earned a reputation as a consummate professional who could be counted on to ensure that no details were overlooked while ensuring the quality of training on a large scale.

I hope you will welcome my call soon to arrange a brief meeting at your convenience to discuss your current and future needs and how I might serve them. Thank you in advance for your time.

Sincerely yours,

Cecil E. Hellinger

Alternate last paragraph:
I hope you will call or write soon to suggest a time convenient for us to meet and discuss your current and future needs and how I might serve them. Thank you in advance for your time.

CECIL E. HELLINGER

1110½ Hay Street, Fayetteville, NC 28305 • preppub@aol.com • (910) 483-6611

OBJECTIVE   To contribute to an organization in need of a mature, energetic manager of human and material resources offering outstanding abilities related to prioritizing activities, setting goals, motivating and developing subordinates, and implementing complex activities.

EDUCATION   **Master of Business Administration** degree, Augsberg College, Minneapolis, MN, 2000.
B.A., History, Vincennes University, Vincennes, IN, 1990.

EXPERIENCE   **PERSONNEL RECRUITING MANAGER.** Prudential Insurance, Inc., Atlanta, GA (2003-present). Chosen to provide leadership and guidance to a geographically dispersed sales force, exceeded corporate goals in all measured areas while planning, overseeing, and conducting personnel recruiting activities.

- Quickly learned the intricacies of recruiting, and improved an already successful sales force. Reached 117% of the organization's fiscal 2003 sales goals.
- Presented a positive image of Prudential, which resulted in an increased number of qualified recruits.

PERSONNEL MANAGER. Goody's Markets, Hot Springs, AR (2001-02). Improved numerous functional areas including training, job performance, and administrative support, to include employee benefits.

- Directed a staff which maintained personnel records along with the administrative support at the organization's headquarters. Recognized as the subject matter expert on government policies pertaining to employment, such as Affirmative Action and EEO.
- Through personal involvement, was credited with retaining 100% of the company's skilled and qualified personnel when their original period of employment was completed.
- Restructured the supervisory training program: as a result, employee turnover was greatly reduced and productivity increased.

TRAINING MANAGER. K-Mart Corp., Minneapolis, MN (1998-00). Displayed a talent for handling complex, simultaneous programs while scheduling and coordinating a wide range of training courses and practical exercises, resolving problems, and preparing progress reports.

- Earned a reputation as a consummate professional who could be counted on to ensure that no details were overlooked while ensuring the quality of training.
- Applied analytical and written communication abilities to produce concise, comprehensive executive correspondence, course materials, and standard operating procedures.

Advanced as a military officer known for superior management expertise and a dynamic style of leadership, U.S. Army:
LOGISTICS MANAGER. Ft. Stewart, GA, and Saudi Arabia (1994-97). Relocated a 1,000-person organization involved in a major training exercise to the Middle East in a smooth and efficient transition while guaranteeing the availability of all supplies and equipment.

- Was credited with defusing a potentially serious problem related to the loss of property.

LOGISTICS SUPPORT MANAGER. Germany (1990-93). Advanced from a First-Line Supervisor's job (1991-92), to become the Assistant to the General Manager (1993), and then was selected for this role coordinating logistical support for subordinate units of the parent organization and monitoring logistical operations within the headquarters.

PERSONAL   Read, write, and speak German and lived in Germany for approximately three years. Consistently cited for my integrity and honesty.

Date

Exact Name of Person
Exact Title
Exact Name of Company
Address
City, State, Zip

PERSONNEL RECRUITING SPECIALIST
for Proctor & Gamble

Dear Exact Name of Person: (or Dear Sir or Madam if answering a blind ad)

With the enclosed resume, I would like to express my interest in exploring employment opportunities with your organization.

In my present job as Personnel Recruiting Specialist at Proctor & Gamble, I am applying my expertise in sales and recruiting to advertise the advantages of a career with Proctor & Gamble. Described as a "top producer," I consistently earn recognition throughout the company for my example of professionalism and integrity.

In a previous job at Monarch Foods as Training Supervisor, I supervised and trained employees and prepared specialized on-the-job training which was credited with increasing the productivity rate. I updated the employee manual and played a major role in preparing a new employee orientation presentation. Prior to that at Monsanto Chemical, I provided administrative support as the Assistant Personnel Manager. I initiated a new computer program for maintaining personnel records which greatly reduced the time required to retrieve information.

If you can use a mature professional who is highly self-motivated and thrives on meeting challenges head on, I hope you will contact me soon to suggest a time we might meet to discuss how I could contribute to your organization. I will provide excellent professional and personal references at the appropriate time. Thank you for your time and consideration.

Sincerely,

Warren G. Browning

WARREN G. BROWNING

1110½ Hay Street, Fayetteville, NC 28305 • preppub@aol.com • (910) 483-6611

OBJECTIVE To contribute to an organization that can use a well-rounded professional offering proven effectiveness in sales and personnel recruiting to an organization in need of an articulate and persuasive manager and supervisor.

EDUCATION & TRAINING **B.A., Personnel Administration**, Franklin University, Columbus, OH, 1994.
Received extensive company-sponsored training in leadership and sales training, human relations, diversity planning, benefits administration, and counseling.

SKILLS Skilled in supervising others; proficient in recruiting and sales.

EXPERIENCE **PERSONNEL RECRUITING SPECIALIST.** Proctor & Gamble, Cincinnati, OH (2003-present). Represented the company and the advantages of a career at Proctor & Gamble to qualified young people, their parents and educators, and community members.
- Described as a "top producer," consistently earn recognition throughout the company for my example of professionalism, integrity, and high standards.
- Prospect for qualified applicants, then personally screen and interview them.
- Earned respect for my enthusiastic, self-confident manner and ability to relate to people of all ages and educational levels.
- Excel at identifying and solving problems through a positive attitude and work ethic.

TRAINING SUPERVISOR. Monarch Foods, Topeka, KS (1998-02). Officially described as "blending management skills with technical expertise," supervised and trained employees; prepared specialized on-the-job training programs which were credited with increasing the productivity rate.
- Supervised seven instructors, demonstrating methods of instruction, and supplied them with training materials.
- Updated the current employee manual to ensure correct information on company policies, rules, and benefits were clearly communicated to all employees.
- Played a major role in preparing a new employee orientation presentation.
- Supervised the administration of testing to ensure quality instruction.
- Planned and managed an annual performance evaluation program.
- Developed subordinate personnel who went on to become effective leaders by emphasizing personal accountability, decision making, and self-improvement.

ASSISTANT PERSONNEL MANAGER. Monsanto Chemical, St. Louis, MO (1994-1997). Provided administrative support for the Personnel Department; prepared reports on absenteeism rates, productivity, and absenteeism.
- Rewrote the policy regarding attendance, and created a schedule in which people could flex their time.
- Kept the Personnel Manager up to date on any changes in government requirements, such as OSHA, Affirmative Action, and EEO.
- Initiated a new computer program for maintaining personnel records which greatly reduced the time required to retrieve information.
- Responsible for organizing the United Way campaign.

PERSONAL Am known as a "go-getter" who always gets the job done. Single, am available for travel and relocation. Excellent references provided upon request.

CAREER CHANGE

Date

Exact Name of Person
Exact Title
Exact Name of Company
Address
City, State, Zip

PERSONNEL RECRUITING SUPERVISOR

for Haldane Staffing Services. This individual seeks to transition out of the recruiting and placement business into a customer service position in another industry.

Dear Exact Name of Person: (or Dear Sir or Madam if answering a blind ad)

With the enclosed resume, I would like to make you aware of my background as a reliable, outgoing customer service and sales professional and to acquaint you with the exceptional communication and organizational skills which I could put to work for your company.

As you will see from my resume, I am excelling as a Personnel Recruiting Supervisor for one of the nation's largest personnel placement companies. While working in this fast-paced environment, I excel in all aspects of human resources management, placing an average of 15-20 applicants per week. While handling multiple simultaneous tasks and constantly shifting priorities, I guide our placement candidates through every stage of the hiring process, conducting an average of ten employment interviews daily, supervising completion of applicant paperwork, and matching applicant skills to open positions with our client companies. I also interact with representatives from client companies, taking job orders for temporary positions and negotiating the terms and conditions of our agreement.

Although I am highly regarded by my current employer and can provide excellent personal and professional references at the appropriate time, I am currently interested in pursuing career opportunities in the customer service field. If you can use an articulate, hardworking professional with the proven ability to excel in a variety of challenging environments, I hope you will write or call me soon to suggest a time when we might meet to discuss your needs and goals and how my background might serve them. I can provide outstanding references at the appropriate time.

Sincerely,

Allison T. McGinty

ALLISON T. McGINTY

1110½ Hay Street, Fayetteville, NC 28305 • preppub@aol.com • (910) 483-6611

OBJECTIVE   To benefit an organization that can use an articulate, self-motivated professional with exceptional communication and organizational skills who offers a background of excellence in a variety of challenging customer service, sales, and human resources environments.

EXPERIENCE   **PERSONNEL RECRUITING SUPERVISOR.** Haldane Staffing Services, Newark, NJ (2002-present). Started with Haldane as a temporary placement candidate and was selected on the basis of my exemplary performance to assume an important role in the local office of one of the largest personnel placement agencies in the country.

- Interview at least ten applicants for temporary placement daily, determining their suitability for open and advertised positions with our client companies.
- Interact with local employers, take job orders for personnel positions, and negotiate the terms and conditions under which we would provide employees.
- Supervise completion of paperwork for new applicants, including I-9s, W-4s, drug screens, and other tax and release forms.
- Match new and existing applicants to open job orders to ensure that the client companies' positions are filled as quickly as possible.
- Successfully place a minimum of 15-20 temporary applicants per week.
- Guide new applicants through the entire hiring process, from completing paperwork, to initial interview, to placement with one of our client companies.
- Write, edit, and submit advertising copy for classified listings of open positions; follow up to ensure that the ad was printed accurately and ran on the correct day.
- Handle all accounts payable for the office, including payments for utilities, advertising expenses, office supplies, maintenance and repair contracts, etc.
- Oversee inventory control and ordering for all office supplies, including all necessary applicant employment forms and other printed materials.

CUSTOMER SERVICE REPRESENTATIVE and **RECEPTIONIST.** Prudential Insurance (through Haldane Staffing Services), Newark, NJ (1998-2001). Provided assistance to policyholders of this large national insurance company; transferred callers that could only be assisted by a licensed agent to the appropriate person.

- Answered customer inquiries regarding deductible amounts, as well as on whether claims had been filed against a policy and other matters concerning recent accidents.
- Assisted customers with completing paperwork such as claims forms.

Highlights of earlier experience:
RECEPTIONIST. Smith & Jones Attorneys. Provided a full range of administrative and clerical support for this busy law firm; answered multi-line phones, took messages, and greeted customers.

- Received telephone dictation from potential clients concerning their legal situation and presented them to one of the attorneys to determine if the case would be worth pursuing.

EDUCATION   Completed 20 hours of college course work in Office Automation Technology at Passaic County Community College, Paterson, NJ, 1995.

COMPUTERS   Familiar with Windows and Word, Excel, and Access as well as proprietary systems and software designed for use in the personnel/placement industries.

PERSONAL   Excellent personal and professional references are available upon request. Outgoing individual known for my tact and diplomacy when dealing with others.

Date

Exact Name of Person
Title or Position
Name of Company
Address (no., street)
Address (city, state, zip)

PERSONNEL RECRUITMENT MANAGER & REGIONAL SALES MANAGER
with Costco Wholesale

Dear Exact Name of Person: (or Dear Sir or Madam if answering a blind ad)

Can you use a self-starter and creative thinker with outstanding verbal communication and sales abilities who excels in motivating others to work together for achieving group and individual goals?

As you will see from my resume, at present I am the Personnel Recruitment Manager and Regional Sales Manager for Costco Wholesale. In this capacity I manage a sales force distributed among five offices, provide guidance to sales managers, advise a chief executive, develop sales incentive programs, and supervise job performance. One of my major accomplishments was developing an incentive program which has already led to a 10% increase in sales.

In a prior position, I served as Training Team Manager at General Mills, Minneapolis, MN. I planned and directed personnel administration, and I earned recognition for my resourcefulness and leadership skills in providing training for 2,000 employees.

Earlier experiences included managing logistics support, maintenance, and training operations centers with as many as 215 employees. This career progression has given me a chance to prove my adaptability as well as my ability to handle a number of tasks simultaneously.

I hope you will welcome my call soon to arrange a brief meeting at your convenience to discuss your current and future needs and how I might serve them. Thank you in advance for your time.

Sincerely yours,

Reginald O. Bonner

REGINALD O. BONNER
1110½ Hay Street, Fayetteville, NC 28305 • preppub@aol.com • (910) 483-6611

OBJECTIVE To benefit an organization that can use an articulate and persuasive professional who offers a reputation for outstanding communication and team building skills as well as leadership abilities.

EDUCATION, TRAINING **B.S., Business Administration**, Colorado State University, Fort Collins, CO, 1992.
Excelled in advanced training programs for recruiters and sales managers.

EXPERIENCE **PERSONNEL RECRUITMENT MANAGER & REGIONAL SALES MANAGER**. Costco Wholesale, Chicago, IL (2002-present). Manage a sales force which covers the Iowa and Illinois territory from five separate area offices; serve as the advisor to a chief executive on all activities related to the methods used and results of employee actions in locating and recruiting qualified people for careers at Costco.
- Created and oversaw a sales incentive award program which resulted in a 10% increase in sales.
- Developed systems used by sales managers to increase their sales by allowing them to obtain information needed to make accurate and timely decisions.
- Prepare sales management plans and analyze the results. Supervise guidance counselor operations.
- Attend two-day sales training programs on a regular monthly basis: these programs emphasize all aspects of sales from prospecting, to building rapport, to closing the sale.
- Proficiently utilize software including Word, Excel, WordPerfect, and PowerPoint.

TRAINING TEAM MANAGER. General Mills, Minneapolis, MN (2000-02). Earned recognition for my management and leadership skills as the director of a 10-person staff which provided training for 2,000 employees.
- Designed and implemented courses for each department specialty.
- Planned and directed personnel administration including employee promotions, transfers, terminations, accident reporting, labor relations, and grievances.
- Analyzed needs and long- and short-term training plans.

Advanced in maintenance and supply management roles, U.S. Army, Ft. Ord, CA:
VEHICLE MAINTENANCE FACILITY MANAGER. (1997-99). Directed operations in a facility which maintained/repaired multimillion-dollar vehicles and support equipment.
- Ensured that backup documentation was complete and up-to-date at all times.

SUPPLY CENTER OPERATIONS MANAGER. (1994-96). Managed a repair parts resupply facility providing parts and direct support repair services to 162 companies.
- Directed regular "wall-to-wall" inventories of $2 million worth of supplies and equipment.
- "Turned around" a facility with major backlogs of parts needing repair and, despite serious personnel shortages, significantly reduced repair time.

TRAINING MANAGER. (1993). As "second-in-command" of a 215-person headquarters, oversaw training, maintenance activities, supply, and day-to-day job performance.
- Improved the maintenance equipment readiness rate to 95%, well above standards, which led to "commendable" ratings in major inspections of training and maintenance.

AFFILIATION Hold membership in the American Marketing Association.

PERSONAL Enjoy working with young people in sports and youth organizations.

CAREER CHANGE

Date

Exact Name of Person
Title or Position
Name of Company
Address (no., street)
Address (city, state, zip)

PERSONNEL RECRUITMENT SUPERVISOR

with Electronics Staffing Services. This individual seeks a career change from personnel recruiting into a new area (possibly sales) in which he can apply his strong sales skills.

Dear Exact Name of Person: (or Dear Sir or Madam if answering a blind ad)

I would appreciate an opportunity to talk with you soon about how I could contribute to your organization through my versatile skills in sales and marketing, management and administration, personnel training and development, as well as in conducting investigations and solving a wide range of problems.

As you will see from my resume, my current position is Personnel Recruitment Supervisor at Electronics Staffing Services, Pasadena, CA, where I was quickly identified as a dynamic manager and motivator. I supervise six sales/recruiting offices and five separate offices which process new employees in the western region. I act as the "right arm" of the chief executive officer and oversee the skillful utilization of a computer bank matching employees with jobs.

In a previous position as Sales Manager in the northeast, I transformed recruiting employees cited as "losers" into the #1 sales team in the parent organization. In a prior position with a company in the health care field, I excelled as Sales Manager for Health Staffing Services in Spokane, WA.

With a belief that communication skills are the key to success in most jobs, I am confident I could become a valuable asset to your organization in a number of areas. I am a hardworking and congenial individual who truly enjoys helping my organization prosper and who takes pride in my ability to develop the skills of less experienced colleagues.

I hope you will call or write me soon to suggest a time convenient for us to meet and discuss your current and future needs and how I might serve them. Thank you in advance for your time.

Sincerely yours,

Oscar P. Martinez

OSCAR P. MARTINEZ

1110½ Hay Street, Fayetteville, NC 28305 • preppub@aol.com • (910) 483-6611

OBJECTIVE To contribute to an organization that can use a dynamic manager who has excelled in a "track record" of challenging assignments through applying my skills in training and motivating people, directing sales operations at multiple locations, and solving a wide range of problems using my proven analytical, investigative, and decision-making abilities.

EXPERIENCE **Have progressed in this track record of advancement with Electronics Staffing Services, a recruiting firm which fills the personnel needs of electronics companies globally:**

2002-present: PERSONNEL RECRUITMENT SUPERVISOR. Pasadena, CA. Because of my reputation as an exceptional manager with an unusual ability to "see the big picture" while managing hundreds of operational details, was specially selected for this job which involves extensive responsibilities related to strategic planning and operations management.

- Supervise six sales/recruiting offices with 42 employees who recruit personnel while also supervising five separate offices processing new employees; in addition, manage an operations center which is the central hub of administrative control and strategic planning.
- Act as the "right arm" of the president and keep him continuously informed of trends and problems affecting the recruitment of quality employees.
- While managing the five offices processing new employees, oversee the skillful utilization of a computer bank matching employees with jobs.
- While managing the operation's "nerve center" of recruiting in the west, am extensively involved in analyzing data and in preparing charts, graphs, and other visual aids that display production and competition statistics on the sales force and on sales results.
- Conduct formal background investigations to verify applicant data and moral character.
- Conduct random analyses and investigations of all sales and processing operations.
- Have reduced costs by restructuring the computerized applicant tracking system.

1998-01: SALES MANAGER. New York, NY. Took over a recruiting operation cited for "low production and deep-rooted problems" and transformed employees with a reputation as "losers" into the #1 sales team in the parent organization; retrained, motivated, and supervised six sales professionals recruiting individuals for careers in maintenance, electronics, medical, administrative, and management fields.

- Planned and orchestrated highly effective activities related to advertising and promotion while working with print, radio, and television media.
- Led this organization to achieve or exceed all goals despite being understaffed.
- Was named **Top Sales Manager** and **Top Salesman in the Northeast.**

Other experience: SALES MANAGER. Health Staffing Services, Spokane, WA (1995-97). Trained and managed 12 people involved in recruiting health professionals including RNs, nurse practitioners, and anesthesiologists; visited hospitals and schools, created exhibits, performed phone prospecting, bought mailing lists of prospective candidates, and attended conferences and job fairs in order to meet prospects.

Other experience (1990-94). Excelled in jobs as a **Training Instructor** and as a **Personnel Recruiter** recruiting pilots, engineers, and navigators.

EDUCATION **B.A., Personnel Administration,** Kettering University, Flint, MI, 1990.

PERSONAL Am a congenial fellow who truly enjoys helping my organization grow and lending a hand to less experienced colleagues. Will travel and relocate as needed.

Date

Exact Name of Person
Exact Title of Person
Organization
Address
City, State, Zip

PERSONNEL TRAINING ADMINISTRATOR

for Golden Foods, Inc.

Dear Exact Name of Person: (Dear Sir or Madam if answering a blind ad)

I would appreciate an opportunity to talk with you soon about how I might be able to contribute to your organization through my proven leadership and management skills, my exceptional communication and problem-solving abilities, as well as through my strong personal initiative and creativity.

As you will see from my resume, I have made significant contributions to every organization of which I have been a part. I have acquired considerable expertise in the area of personnel administration, and while excelling in several "hot-seat" jobs in the personnel field, I have authored several publications related to personnel recruiting, retention, utilization, training, and other areas.

A planner and organizer who is skilled in working with budgets and controlling costs, I once excelled in a job planning meetings and negotiating contracts for International Paper Corporation. On my own initiative, I negotiated corporate rates with major hotel chains globally used for meetings, and I developed a plan to centralize the meeting planning function at corporate headquarters.

You would find me in person to be a versatile communicator who tends to become creative and tenacious in the face of stubborn problems. I am skilled in working with people and have earned a reputation as a gifted motivator and leader of people.

I can provide outstanding personal and professional references upon your request, and I would welcome the opportunity to meet with you to show you that I could become a valued part of your organization. I hope you will call or write me soon to suggest a time when we might meet at your convenience to discuss your needs and how I might serve them.

Yours sincerely,

Louise J. Gonzalez

Alternate last paragraph:
I hope you will welcome my call when I try to arrange a brief meeting to discuss your current and future needs and how I might serve them. Thank you in advance for your time.

LOUISE J. GONZALEZ

1110½ Hay Street, Fayetteville, NC 28305 • preppub@aol.com • (910) 483-6611

OBJECTIVE I want to offer an organization the extensive leadership experience I have gained along with my specialized expertise in personnel administration and proven "track record" as an innovative problem solver.

EDUCATION and TRAINING **B.S.** in **Psychology**, Aurora University, Aurora, IL, 1991.
Excelled in more than two years of graduate-level training for executives related to **personnel administration** and **operations management**.

LANGUAGES Fluent in **German** as a result of using the language while living in Germany for six years with my father, who was a military officer. Can read/understand French.

EXPERIENCE **PERSONNEL TRAINING ADMINISTRATOR.** Golden Foods, Inc., Indianapolis, IN (2003-present). For this 2,200-person plant, direct training for personnel in dozens of specialized fields.
- Supervise 12 office employees providing administrative support.
- Oversee the employee benefits and personnel managers.
- Ensured personnel availability through a computerized personnel tracking system.
- Rewrote the absenteeism policy and initiated an employee incentive program which greatly reduced absenteeism.
- Have been evaluated as a skillful communicator through my capable handling of several grievances.
- Used my strong computer skills to create an Intranet which provided information and training opportunities for employees; through this Intranet, the company is now offering courses which will be eligible for college credit from local colleges.

PERSONNEL MANAGER. Raytheon, Detroit, MI (1997-02). Performed a wide range of challenging assignments in the personnel administration field while supervising a staff of ten people.
- Screened talented applicants seeking employment at Raytheon.
- Coordinated testing and implementation of a "transition management program."
- Creatively negotiated funding for key positions from existing finances.

PERSONNEL MANAGEMENT SUPERVISOR. Bristol-Myers Squibb, Bristol, TN (1993-96). Took over this job at a time of considerable personnel turbulence and turnover; directed operations of a 21-person office processing more than 1,200 actions monthly including promotions and terminations.
- Screened, interviewed, and hired employees.
- Counseled employees with personal or professional problems.

CONTRACT NEGOTIATOR. International Paper Company, Boise, ID (1990-93). Became skilled in corporate rate negotiating while planning accommodations for board of director's meetings and regional sales meetings for a major paper manufacturer.
- Traveled 80% of the time to locations in the U.S. and abroad to select sites for training activities, conferences, and board meetings.
- Earned praise for my strong negotiating ability.

PERSONAL Tenacious problem solver who excels in finding innovative solutions to difficult obstacles. Exceptional organizer and motivator. Can provide strong references upon request.

Date

Exact Name of Person
Title or Position
Name of Company
Address (no., street)
Address (city, state, zip)

PERSONNEL TRAINING SUPERVISOR
for Rohr Industries

Dear Exact Name of Person (or Dear Sir or Madam if answering a blind ad):

I would appreciate an opportunity to talk with you soon about how I could contribute to your organization through my proven ability to motivate, lead, and supervise employees as well as through my outstanding organizational and problem-solving skills.

As you will see from my resume, I have excelled in jobs requiring skills in personnel management, training, and recruiting. I am known as a fast learner who can be depended on to find ways to ensure quality performance from others based on my own high standards. In my current position with Rohr Industries, I oversee performance and provide training and counseling for six employees as I ensure that 2,800 people qualify for and complete a variety of widely differing training programs.

I am an adaptable professional who has advanced in such diverse areas as personnel recruiting, overseeing technical operations, and ensuring the quality of training.

I hope you will welcome my call soon to arrange a brief meeting at your convenience to discuss your current and future needs and how I might serve them. Thank you in advance for your time.

Sincerely yours,

Martin I. Whitman, Jr.

Alternate last paragraph:
I hope you will call or write soon to suggest a time convenient for us to meet and discuss your current and future needs and how I might serve them. Thank you in advance for your time.

MARTIN I. WHITMAN, JR.
1110½ Hay Street, Fayetteville, NC 28305 • preppub@aol.com • (910) 483-6611

OBJECTIVE To apply my expertise in motivating and supervising employees as well as my superior organizational abilities and attention to detail to an organization that can use a mature professional who offers strong skills in guiding others to maximize their strengths.

EXPERIENCE **PERSONNEL TRAINING SUPERVISOR.** Rohr Industries, Chula Vista, CA (2003-present). Oversee performance and provide training and counseling for six employees as the coordinator of arrangements for ensuring 2,800 people qualify for and complete a variety of widely differing training programs; controlled $512,000 worth of sensitive equipment.
- Guarantee that all personnel receive the proper training in accordance with the guidelines established by the company.
- Rewrote the employee orientation manual to ensure new employees were familiar with all company policies, rules, and benefits.
- Accomplished a 20% reduction in absenteeism during fiscal year 2003.

PERSONNEL SUPERVISOR. Ford Motor Co., Detroit, MI (1998-02). Developed and oversaw training programs for all employees, to include managers; planned and directed personnel administration including promotions and terminations, safety, labor relations and grievances, and information management.
- Initiated a flex-time schedule which was credited with boosting productivity and reducing absenteeism.
- Through intensive employee pre-screening and interviewing, improved hiring techniques.
- Considered an expert in smoothly settling labor union demands.
- Updated the company manual and scripted a new employee orientation presentation.

While proudly serving my country in the U.S. Army, served in many positions in the field of human resources.
TECHNICAL OPERATIONS SUPERVISOR. Ft. Ord, CA (1995-97). Trained and directed the day-to-day performance of employees operating sophisticated weapons systems and support vehicles.
- Was singled out to provide advice to higher operational levels and to subordinates.
- Gained valuable experience in making decisions on maximizing employee's strengths through properly placing personnel within the parent organization.
- Played a major part in the company's ability to win in a performance competition on their first attempt.

PERSONNEL RECRUITER. Ft. Polk, LA (1992-94). Refined my communication and "sales" skills while contacting qualified young adults and making them aware of the advantages of a military career. Learned techniques unique to selling intangibles and developed important skills in communicating my ideas and beliefs to others.

SUPERVISOR and **TRAINING SPECIALIST.** Ft. Richardson, AK (1989-91). Earned rapid promotion and advanced in leadership roles within the company while becoming known as a technically proficient professional.

TRAINING Graduated with honors from training programs totaling 1,100 hours which emphasized personnel management, leadership, and recruiting and sales techniques.

PERSONAL Have been singled out for several awards for "meritorious service" and "outstanding achievements." Can provide excellent professional references upon request.

CAREER CHANGE

Date

Exact Name of Person
Exact Title
Exact Name of Company
Address
City, State, Zip

PLANS AND CONTRACTS MANAGER
seeks to transition into the human resources arena

Dear Exact Name of Person: (or Dear Sir or Madam if answering a blind ad):

With the enclosed resume, I would like to make you aware of my background in management and consulting. In my spare time, I have earned a Master's degree in the Human Resources field, and I am interested in transitioning into this specialized area of management.

As you will see from my resume, I have advanced within the Lockheed-Martin organization while serving in highly visible and critical roles which have required skills in negotiating, managing complex projects, and coordinating with military and civilian contractors and government agencies for services and support. At the Los Angeles location, I currently serve as Plans and Contracts Manager and am involved in providing logistics support involving hundreds of personnel and multimillion-dollar aircraft assets.

Prior to my promotion to this position, I served as a Logistics Planner and Assistant Operations Manager with the same organization. In this capacity, I developed and managed the logistics portions of operational plans while involved in contract negotiations for services and support with various contractors and agencies.

In my first assignment at Lockheed-Martin, I was handpicked as a member of a selectively staffed research and development project. For this $15 million R&D project involving 1,000 people, I provided guidance, project management support, and technical assistance. During this time I was earning a reputation as an enthusiastic and highly intelligent young professional and was selected for rapid advancement in a highly competitive environment.

If you can use an experienced professional known for high levels of drive, initiative, and energy, I hope you will welcome my call soon when I try to arrange a brief meeting to discuss your goals and how my background might serve your needs. I can provide outstanding references at the appropriate time.

Sincerely,

Andrew D. Nevins

ANDREW D. NEVINS

1110½ Hay Street, Fayetteville, NC 28305 • preppub@aol.com • (910) 483-6611

OBJECTIVE   To contribute expertise in human resources/logistics management to an organization that can use a versatile and articulate professional who offers a reputation as a diplomatic, resourceful, and intelligent leader who can be counted on for sound judgment.

EDUCATION & EXECUTIVE TRAINING

Master's Degree, Seattle University, Seattle, WA, in **Human Resources Management**, 2003.
B.A., Government and Foreign Affairs, Seattle University, Seattle, WA, 1994.
Excelled in specialized training programs with an emphasis on systems acquisition, logistics, and quality awareness management as well as logistics planning and programs.

COMPUTERS   Proficient with a wide range of popular software programs.

EXPERIENCE   *Have advanced to increasingly responsible positions at Lockheed-Martin:*
PLANS AND CONTRACTS MANAGER. Los Angeles, CA (2002-present). Cited for "superb management" and expertise, direct complex planning and contract negotiations for worldwide operations; review and coordinate logistics support.
- Coordinate 48 contracts for various types of products and services, including personnel support, with military and civilian contractors as well as government agencies.
- Earned praise for my skill in agreement processing which provided $5 million annually in reimbursements and assured costs were recovered in a timely manner.

ASSISTANT OPERATIONS MANAGER. Los Angeles, CA and Seattle, WA (1999-01). Officially evaluated as a "highly professional logistics planner with a wide range of technical skills and expertise," oversaw support services for two Lockheed plants (Seattle, WA by phone/correspondence).
- Developed and coordinated improvements while reviewing and maintaining contract agreements with military and civilian contractors as well as government agencies.
- Managed, reviewed, and coordinated the logistics sections of operations plans.
- Provided expertise in planning and managing support for training programs.

LOGISTICS MANAGER. Seattle, WA (1995-98). Handpicked to coordinate logistics support. Managed five project managers and an $8 million logistics contract.
- Provided guidance, project management support, and technical assistance in a $150 million research and development program with 1,000 people.
- Managed $3.6 million worth of new project requirements to include initiating a critical interface between project and contracting offices which reduced long processing delays.
- Established contacts which ensured the success of new contractor logistics support and vital depot support and ensured personnel understood procedures.
- Earned promotion after directing logistics support efforts on other projects and becoming known for skills in negotiating, improving program quality, and taking decisive actions.
- Reduced contract processing time from one week to 72 hours by revamping the process and developing detailed descriptions of the duties of each member of the team.

PERSONAL   Enjoy volunteering with community activities such as Habitat for Humanity and Masonic Lodge No. 318. Can provide excellent references upon request.

Date

Exact Name of Person
Title or Position
Name of Company
Address (number and street)
Address (city, state, and zip)

RETIREMENT SERVICES OFFICE SUPERVISOR
with the U.S. Department of State

Dear Exact Name of Person: (or Sir or Madam if answering a blind ad)

With the enclosed resume, I would like to make you aware of my background and experience related to office management, customer service, and administration.

My professionalism and dedication have served me well at the U.S. Department of State. Currently as Supervisor, Retirement Services Office, I supervise four employees in an office which accepts, reviews, and processes applications for retirement.

In a previous position with the Department of State as Personnel and Administrative Operations Manager, I was credited with saving the government $1 million through my resourcefulness. While supervising 34 people, I was the organization's "resident expert" on human resources, training, and personnel recruiting issues. On my own initiative, I developed a cross-training program which permitted the organization to meet or exceed all of its performance objectives despite a serious shortage of personnel in key areas.

I can provide outstanding references at the appropriate time, and I hope I will have the opportunity to meet you in person to discuss your needs. If you can use a versatile manager and office professional who would enthusiastically make valuable contributions to your business, I hope you will contact me to suggest a time when we might meet. Thank you in advance for your time.

Yours sincerely,

Chet W. Spangler

CHET W. SPANGLER

1110½ Hay Street, Fayetteville, NC 28305 • preppub@aol.com • (910) 483-6611

OBJECTIVE To offer extensive experience in office administration and computer operations, human resources management, and training and development to an organization that can use a detail-oriented professional with an excellent record of providing customer service.

EDUCATION & TRAINING

B.S., **Business Administration** with a concentration in **Human Resources Management,** Carroll College, Waukesha, WI, 1993.

A.A., Business Administration, Carroll College, Waukesha, WI, 1990.

Completed training programs in subjects including government contracting procedures, instructional techniques, as well as earlier training in office automation and logistics management.

COMPUTERS Familiar with Word, Excel, PowerPoint, and Access.

EXPERIENCE *Earned recognition for my professionalism and dedication, Department of State:*

2003-present: RETIREMENT SERVICES OFFICE SUPERVISOR. Spokane, WA. Supervise four subordinates in an office which accepts, reviews, and processes applications for retirement while maintaining close relations with peers in other government agencies.
- Refined an internal suspense system and ensured accountability and timely processing.
- Emphasized cross-training as a method of ensuring availability of human resources.

2000-03: PERSONNEL AND ADMINISTRATIVE OPERATIONS MANAGER. Washington, DC. Commended for my tireless energy, enthusiasm, and dedication, supervised 34 people as senior advisor on human relations, training, morale, and professional development issues for an organization which processed 2,600 applicants annually.
- Was credited with saving the government $1 million annually by spearheading the relocation of the unit from an expensive downtown federal building to a suburban area.
- Achieved 100% of performance standards despite personnel shortages through a cross-training program which allowed the unit to complete 12 special projects in one year.
- Cited for my initiative in identifying weaknesses in contracting issues, took over duties as the contract representative for $78,000 annually and the transition to a new site.
- Led the unit to recognition as top recruiting organization nationwide for two years.

2001: HUMAN RESOURCES AND ADMINISTRATIVE OPERATIONS SUPERVISOR. Alexandria, VA. Commended for my ability to produce results, overcome obstacles, and provide dynamic leadership, consistently exceeded standards for accuracy and timely processing of personnel, medical, and finance records for personnel leaving government service.

2000: PERSONNEL SUPERVISOR. London, England. Cited for my common-sense approach to solving problems, excelled while training and overseeing personnel.
- Handpicked ahead of more senior supervisors to oversee 94 people, initiated changes which resulted in improved morale, test scores, performance levels, and safety.

1993-00: ASSISTANT PERSONNEL MANAGER. Washington, DC. Supervised two managers while overseeing training and administrative support personnel.
- Scheduled the conference center and provided conferencing equipment when needed.
- Initiated a new employee orientation presentation for new employees.

PERSONAL Known as a tireless and dedicated employee. Enjoy working with people.

CAREER CHANGE

Date

Exact Name of Person
Title or Position
Name of Company
Address (no., street)
Address (city, state, zip)

SCHOOL OPERATIONS MANAGER

seeks to transition from an academic environment into a business setting

Dear Exact Name of Person: (or Dear Sir or Madam if answering a blind ad)

    I would appreciate an opportunity to talk with you soon about how I could contribute to your organization through my extensive management experience and administrative expertise.

    As you will see on my enclosed resume, I recently earned an M.A. degree in Personnel Management at Lewis & Clark College, Portland, OR. While my current employer, Renton Technical College, is eager to retain me, I have decided I would like to re-enter the business world in a position in Personnel.

    In my present position at Renton, I earned rapid advancement from Course Manager to School Operations Manager. I supervise a staff of up to 200 employees and oversee administrative support, legal affairs, maintenance, and logistics. I reduced the dropout rate to 15% from a previous 25% rate and, at the same time, succeeded in exceeding established performance criteria.

    If you could benefit from a creative, experienced manager who is known as a "go-getter," I hope you will call or write me soon to suggest a time convenient for us to meet and discuss your current and future needs and how I might serve them. Thank you in advance for your time.

Sincerely yours,

Juan R. Cortez

JUAN R. CORTEZ

1110½ Hay Street, Fayetteville, NC 28305 • preppub@aol.com • (910) 483-6611

OBJECTIVE To contribute to an organization that can use a talented public speaker and communicator who offers expertise in planning and coordinating along with outstanding management skills.

EXPERIENCE *Advanced in a "track record" of accomplishments, Renton Technical College, Renton, WA:*

2002-present: **SCHOOL OPERATIONS MANAGER.** Supervise a staff of up to 200 employees; oversee administrative support, legal affairs, building and equipment maintenance, and logistics.
- Coordinate various types of training subjects for classes of 80 students each.
- Reduced duplicated efforts and paperwork by developing, writing, and implementing a set of operating procedures.
- Automated logistics and administrative record keeping.

2001: **COURSE MANAGER.** Earned rapid advancement from this position supervising instructors and students and ensuring that the 11-week training cycles produced high numbers of well-trained graduates.
- Directed operations of a 100 to 150-person staff while managing legal affairs, counseling, and providing logistics support.
- Reduced the dropout rate to 15% from a previous 25% rate and, at the same time, successfully in exceeded established performance criteria. Applied my aggressive and concerned attitude in counseling students and helping them stretch their mental limits.

Other experience:
FIRST-LINE SUPERVISOR. Motorola, Portland, OR (1999-01). Oversaw 65 employees operating/maintaining $20 million of high-tech communications-electronics equipment.
- Made daily decisions on matters involving legal questions, administrative actions, and performance standards. Achieved excellent results from employees despite shortages of supplies, equipment, and training time.

SUPPLY AND SUPPORT MANAGER. Caterpillar, Des Moines, IA (1997-98). Was in charge of ensuring proper supply levels for production needs. Initiated an automated computer system for tracking inventory. Advised executives on equipment and personnel availability.
- Identified and tracked items through the repair process and stayed within the fiscal year budget. Learned to work closely with outside sources in order to maintain inventories and always have a full supply of ready equipment.

BANK RECONCILER. Allstate Insurance Company, Hartford, CT (1993-96). Became skilled in using spreadsheets for maintaining records while auditing and updating subsidiary account information and status reports.
- Automated payment systems to reduce time needed for reconciling payments and tracking transactions.

EDUCATION & TRAINING **M.A., Personnel Management,** Lewis & Clark College, Portland, OR, 2001.
B.A., Finance and Banking, Trinity College, Hartford, CT, 1992.
Excelled in more than one year of intensive training for Allstate Insurance employees with a concentration in logistics planning/management, substance abuse counseling, technical operations management techniques, and leadership.

PERSONAL Officially described as "a bright, articulate, aggressive, and enthusiastic natural leader." Can provide excellent references upon request.

Date

Exact Name of Person
Exact Title
Exact Name of Company
Address
City, State, Zip

SENIOR ADMINISTRATIVE ADVISOR

Data General Corporation

Dear Exact Name of Person (or Dear Sir or Madam if answering a blind ad):

I would like to use this opportunity to introduce you to a highly versatile and experienced management professional who excels in maximizing human resources while developing ways to increase results and performance levels.

My strongest abilities are in the areas of mentoring, supervising, advising, counseling, and training others through the application of my proven leadership skills. With a reputation as an articulate speaker and innovative manager of resources, I am highly effective in taking actions which will solve problems before they impact negatively performance and productivity.

Throughout my experience at Data General, I have been singled out for numerous honors and awards. Consistently evaluated as a results-oriented and proactive manager, I have developed a wide base of skills as varied as researching and analyzing data, utilizing automated systems, controlling budgets and payroll actions, and building teams which can be counted on to exceed standards.

As you can see from my resume, I have an M.A. in Personnel Administration from Savannah State University and a B.A. in Business Administration from Parkland College, Champaign, IL. I am known for my ability to manage time and details and to overcome personnel shortages and scarce resources through my creativity and eye for detail.

If you can use an experienced professional with knowledge of personnel administration and human resources management, please call or write me soon to suggest a time when we might have a brief discussion of how I could contribute to your organization. I can provide excellent professional and personal references at the appropriate time.

Sincerely,

Kelly L. Seneca

KELLY L. SENECA

1110½ Hay Street, Fayetteville, NC 28305 • preppub@aol.com • (910) 483-6611

OBJECTIVE A position in the management of administrative and personnel operations with an organization that can use an articulate communicator and analytical decision maker.

EDUCATION & TRAINING

M.A., Personnel Administration, Savannah State University, Savannah, GA, 2000.
B.A., Business Administration, Parkland College, Champaign, IL.
Received advanced training for personnel and administrative managers which included courses in personnel recruiting and Equal Opportunity; also attended technical training in automated systems operations and applications.

SPECIAL SKILLS

Computers: Word, Access, Excel, and Powerpoint.
Operational areas: accounting and budgeting, personnel management, counseling, computer system operations (including spreadsheets and word processing), and data collection.

EXPERIENCE

Advanced to managerial and supervisor roles ahead of my peers while with Data General Corporation, Savannah, GA.

2003-present: SENIOR ADMINISTRATIVE ADVISOR. Direct actions of an 18-person training department; determine employee benefits packages and ensure employee awareness of company policies and rules.

- Sought out for my expertise and strong knowledge, was officially cited for ability to deliver advice and guidance which resulted in above-standard performance.
- Developed a checklist used to assess training efforts which is thorough and complete, but simple enough to be used by less experienced evaluators and training specialists.
- Cited for my understanding of Affirmative Action and EEO policies.
- Revised the wage and salary schedules to reflect the current economic situation, which resulted in a cost savings for Data General.

2000-02: TRAINING AND EDUCATION ADVISOR. Planned and managed employee training programs and promoted opportunities for advancing training; controlled a $308,000 budget and directly supervised two people.

- Singled out as an innovative leader who could be counted on to share knowledge, was also described as proactive and an expert in identifying and solving problems.
- Achieved 100% enrollment rates for advanced leadership and supervisory training courses and became primary trainer for computer automation applications.

Other experience:
SUPERVISOR, PERSONNEL ADMINISTRATION CENTER (PAC). Grossard Industries, St. Louis, MO (1996-00). Advised senior management officials on personnel administrative issues; supervised and trained up to six subordinates.

- Reorganized the personnel records section which then achieved accuracy rates of 100%.
- Managed a wide range of functions including personnel retention, Equal Opportunity, records management, and drug and alcohol abuse programs.

PERSONNEL SERVICES SUPERVISOR. Dell Computers, Lawrence, KS (1990-95). Reorganized operational procedures for the headquarters of this major computer company and acted as the senior advisor to a chief executive on the status of training operations.

- Planned and managed an annual performance evaluation program.

PERSONAL Am known as an ultimate professional who is a keen observer, a motivator, and a fair and dependable manager. Can provide outstanding references upon request.

Date

Exact Name of Person
Title or Position
Name of Company
Address (no., street)
Address (city, state, zip)

STAFF SERVICES DIRECTOR
for a public utilities company.

Dear Exact Name of Person (or Dear Sir or Madam if answering a blind ad):

I would appreciate an opportunity to talk with you soon about how I could contribute to your organization through my management experience and track record of success in maximizing human and material resources through a dynamic and enthusiastic style of leadership.

While serving the City of Des Moines as Staff Services Director with the Public Works Commission, I have demonstrated my ability to organize projects and establish priorities. I am especially talented in determining the potential of each subordinate so that each person's strong points can be best utilized. I consistently find ways to improve productivity and efficiency in all areas of operations. In a prior position at Allied Industries, I earned rapid advancement because of a track record of achievements. For example, as Safety Coordinator, I directed a program which resulted in a record 12.5 million "safe work hours." I also successfully represented the company at unemployment compensation hearings and won all cases except two over a 3-1/2-year period.

Widely recognized as a mature professional with a demonstrated talent for dealing with people and strong managerial abilities, I am certain I can contribute to your organization by applying my ability to accept nothing less than the best efforts from myself and my subordinates. I would be delighted to provide outstanding personal and professional references upon request.

I hope you will welcome my call soon to arrange a brief meeting at your convenience to discuss your current and future needs and how I might serve them. Thank you in advance for your time.

Sincerely yours,

Grace Ann Owens

Alternate last paragraph:
I hope you will call or write me soon to suggest a time convenient for us to meet and discuss your current and future needs and how I might serve them. Thank you in advance for your time.

GRACE ANN OWENS

1110½ Hay Street, Fayetteville, NC 28305   •   preppub@aol.com   •   (910) 483-6611

OBJECTIVE To contribute to an organization that can use an accomplished human resources manager who offers proven ingenuity along with skills in implementing new programs and services.

EDUCATION **Bachelor of Science**, University of Northern Iowa, Cedar Falls, IA, 1986; **cum laude**. Completed graduate courses in Business Administration, University of North Carolina.

EXPERIENCE **STAFF SERVICES DIRECTOR.** Public Works Commission of the City of Des Moines, IA (2002-present). Supervise up to 10 employees, including an office supervisor, compensation and benefits specialist, training coordinator, medical nurse, safety personnel, and four others.

- Perform managerial and administrative functions, directing all human resources services to include screening, hiring, and orientation of new hires; maintain personnel records, and administer benefits programs for a utility company with over 600 employees.
- Develop, manage, and administer the division's operating budget.
- Confer with department officials and prepare recommendations for the department manager concerning human resources programs, policies, and procedures.
- Coordinate employee education programs, manage the employee grievance process, administer performance evaluation program, and conduct evaluations for personnel.

Accomplishments and achievements:
- Established the Medical Department; implemented policies and procedures in compliance with state, OSHA, and federal regulations.
- Developed "from scratch" and staffed the training section, instituting the start-up of a new Training Department and creating skill-based training courses for employees.
- Established a Compensation Section providing internal support for payroll management and employee classification. Increased employee participation from 15% to over 60% in the Deferred Compensation Program. Successfully defended numerous EEO charges.

Excelled in the following track record of promotion with Allied Industries, various locations nationwide (1986-2001):

1995-01: ASSISTANT HUMAN RESOURCES MANAGER & STAFF SERVICE DIRECTOR. Promoted to supervise personnel administrative functions for a plant with over 1,200 employees; managed personnel recordkeeping for wages, benefits, insurance, credit union activity, and vacations.

- As Safety Coordinator, directed a program which resulted in a record 12.5 million "safe work hours." Successfully represented the company at unemployment compensation hearings; won all employment compensation cases except two over a 3½ year period.

1992-94: PERSONNEL MANAGER. Handled employee relations and Affirmative Action for a 350-person plant.

1991-92: ASSISTANT PERSONNEL MANAGER. Reduced labor turnover from 150% to an industry low of 45% through skillfully screening and placing employees.

1986-90: SUPERVISOR. Was recognized for executive ability because of my achievements in the areas of safety, quality control, delivery and customer service, employment development, auditing, energy conservation, environmental protection, cost control, and maintenance.

AFFILIATIONS
- Smart Start – Board of Directors, 2000; Human Resources Committee, 2000
- Society for Human Resources Management (National, 1995 – present), charter member; served as President, 1998
- Blue Cross/Blue Shield Advisory Council, 1997
- Disability Advocacy Council of Cassius County, 1995
- American Public Power Association, HR, 1989–present; HR Planning Committee, 1993

Date

Exact Name of Person
Exact Title
Exact Name of Company
Address
City, State, Zip

STAFFING SPECIALIST

with Reliable Staffing

Dear Exact Name of Person (or Dear Sir or Madam if answering a blind ad):

With the enclosed resume, I would like to express my interest in exploring employment opportunities with your organization. I am seeking employment with a company that can make use of an outgoing and versatile individual with a proven ability to produce bottom-line results.

Most recently I have excelled in a "track record" of promotion with a personnel staffing organization with offices in Charles City, Waterloo, Cedar Rapids, and Cedar Falls. I was recruited to work for Reliable Staffing by the manager of the Waterloo, and I excelled initially as a Staffing Specialist. Subsequently I was selected to operate in an outside sales role as a Business Development Specialist, and I was very successful as I developed more than 30 new accounts and negotiated all contract details with employers. Then I advanced to manage the Waterloo office, which includes training and managing employees, maintaining liaison with employers, and overseeing production of the company's $1.3 million annual sales goal.

Prior to my work with Reliable Staffing, I served briefly in the U.S. Navy and worked in Waterloo as a Certified Chiropractic Assistant.

If you can use a highly motivated individual with a unique combination of sales ability, management skills, and strong personal initiative, I hope you will contact me to suggest a time when we might meet to discuss your needs. I offer a proven ability to produce outstanding bottom-line results through applying my aggressive customer service orientation and ability to establish excellent working relationships with people at all levels. I would certainly enjoy meeting with you to discuss your needs and how I might contribute to your business objectives, and I can provide outstanding references at the appropriate time.

Yours sincerely,

Lillian T. Dove

LILLIAN T. DOVE

1110½ Hay Street, Fayetteville, NC 28305 • preppub@aol.com • (910) 483-6611

OBJECTIVE   To benefit an organization that can use a versatile and outgoing professional with strong communication and organizational skills along with a proven ability to develop new accounts, achieve high levels of customer satisfaction, and produce outstanding bottom-line results.

EXPERIENCE   *Was promoted in the following "track record" of promotion by Reliable Staffing, Inc., Waterloo, IA (1998-present). Reliable Staffing has four offices which are in Charles City, Waterloo, Cedar Rapids, and Cedar Falls.*

2002-present: STAFFING BRANCH MANAGER. Was promoted to manage an office with an annual sales goal of $1.3 million produced through placing individuals in "select-to-hire" positions with employers in Black Hawk County.
- Continuously recruit new business clients while also training and managing the staffing personnel in the Charles City office.
- Negotiate contracts with corporations and businesses of all sizes; handle collections of accounts receivable; manage unemployment and Workers Compensation claims.
- Initiate, develop, and follow through on proposals; develop action plans for clients.

2000-2001: BUSINESS DEVELOPMENT SPECIALIST. Was specially selected to assume the responsibility of developing new business as an **Outside Sales Representative**; developed more than 30 new accounts which included Taylor Midwest (a stainless steel manufacturing facility), Midwestern Regional Medical Center, and Waterford Industries (a corrugated box manufacturer).
- Considered myself an extension of each company's business, and viewed my job as finding employees who would enhance the various company's business goals.
- Prospected for new corporate accounts; developed and presented proposals; established excellent relationships by researching all of the client's needs.

1998-00: RESOURCE SPECIALIST. Was recruited by the manager of this staffing organization to join its team in a four-person office; conducted interviews with applicants and placed qualified individuals in positions with employers.
- Tested and screened applicants in areas pertaining to skills, references, criminal records, credit history, and drug screening. Oriented new hires.
- Processed weekly payroll, prepared invoices, and negotiated contracts with employers.

CERTIFIED CHIROPRACTIC ASSISTANT. Waterloo Chiropractic Clinic, Waterloo, IA (1995-98). Relocated to Waterloo after I married a Waterloo native, and began in an entry-level position at this established chiropractic clinic; on my own initiative, pursued training which resulted in receiving my X-ray certification and certification as a Chiropractic Assistant.

U.S. Navy experience: After high school graduation, served briefly in the U.S. Navy and traveled to worldwide locations including Italy, Greece, Cuba, and the Middle East.

EDUCATION   Completed nearly two years of college courses at Hawkeye Community College, Waterloo, IA. Excelled in technical and management training sponsored by the U.S. Navy.
Completed X-ray Certification and Chiropractic Assistant, Certification, Hawkeye Community College.

PERSONAL   Strong leader who thrives on the responsibility of contributing to the bottom line. Known for my exemplary work ethic and personal initiative. Excellent references on request.

Date

Exact Name of Person
Title or Position
Name of Company
Address (no., street)
Address (city, state, zip)

STAFFING SPECIALIST
for Manpower Staffing

Dear Exact Name of Person (or Dear Sir or Madam if answering a blind ad)

I would appreciate an opportunity to talk with you soon about how I could contribute to your organization through my experience in the area of personnel management.

As you can see on my enclosed resume, in my current position as a Staffing Specialist at Manpower Staffing, I oversee operations in a temporary personnel placement agency. In this position, I manage 40 employees providing training, recruitment, and customer service. On my own initiative, I designed and implemented a new automated system that improved the sales-per-payroll ratio.

Previous positions included Support Services Manager for Eckerd Pharmaceuticals where I guided employee training programs which were credited with reducing worker accidents and improving productivity levels. As Personnel Assistant at Chrysler Motors, I exceeded standards for timely and accurate processing of personnel records while supervising 18 people preparing evaluations of employees at all levels.

My proven ability to quickly learn and adapt to both pressure and rapidly changing circumstances would allow me to contribute to your organization.

I hope you will welcome my call soon to arrange a brief meeting at your convenience to discuss your current and future needs and how I might serve them. Thank you in advance for your time.

Sincerely yours,

Raymond L. Macera

Alternate last paragraph:
I hope you will call or write soon to suggest a time convenient for us to meet and discuss your current and future needs and how I might serve them. Thank you in advance for your time.

RAYMOND L. MACERA

1110½ Hay Street, Fayetteville, NC 28305 • preppub@aol.com • (910) 483-6611

OBJECTIVE To apply my experience in planning and organizing for productivity to an organization that can benefit from my abilities in supervising/motivating employees and managing operations.

COMPUTERS Proficient with computer software including PowerPoint, Microsoft Word, and Excel.

EDUCATION Completed more than 100 hours of course work toward a degree in **Personnel Management**. Excelled in more than 600 hours of leadership and management training programs including managing transportation for hazardous materials.

EXPERIENCE **STAFFING SPECIALIST.** Manpower Staffing, Detroit, MI (2003-present). Oversee operations in a temporary personnel placement agency. Manage 40 employees providing training, recruitment, and customer service. Through my leadership and problem solving skills, the company improved its compliance with federal and state regulations.
- Designed and implemented a new automated system that improved the sales-per-payroll ratio.
- Am directing a major renovation project which will modernize a 50-year-old building and transfer the organization into the remodeled facilities.
- Evaluate forms management, worker's compensation, personnel file management, and computer documentation required as well as conducting the interviewing and orientation processes in all 26 offices.

SUPPORT SERVICES MANAGER. Eckerd Pharmaceuticals, Detroit, MI (2001-03). Provided expertise in analyzing statistical data, advising and briefing senior executives, planning and carrying out policy decisions, and supervising a staff of 25 subordinates, including the benefits administrator and personnel manager.
- Guided employee training programs which were credited for reducing worker accidents and improving productivity levels.

PERSONNEL ASSISTANT. Chrysler Motors, Detroit, MI (1999-00). Exceeded standards for timely and accurate processing of personnel records while supervising 18 people preparing evaluations of employees at all levels, promotions, and ensuring personnel availability.
- Guided training and supervised the performance of employees.
- Developed a standardized interview process used in personnel recruitment.
- Achieved a successful downsizing which decreased costs and increased productivity.

GENERAL MANAGER. Delphi Automotive Systems, Moline, IL (1996-98). Oversaw operations, personnel, maintenance, and logistics; supervised a 36-person staff and a budget of $15 million. Developed an employee retention program which resulted in lower turnover.
- Designed a new system for procuring supplies that resulted in less downtime on production lines. Learned to use computers for record keeping and word processing.

ASSISTANT TO THE TRAINING MANAGER. Exxon-Mobil, Dayton, OH (1993-95). Planned and managed employee training programs. Initiated special workshops for various groups of employees to improve productivity. Maintained personnel records on turnover and safety and made recommendations to management for improvements.

PERSONAL Excel in motivating others to work as a team and achieve management goals.

Real-Resumes Series edited by Anne McKinney

CAREER CHANGE

Date

Exact Name of Person
Exact Title
Exact Name of Company
Address
City, State, Zip

SUPPORT SERVICES MANAGER, Oscar Meyer Meats

Dear Exact Name of Person: (or Dear Sir or Madam if answering a blind ad)

With the enclosed resume, I would like to express my interest in exploring employment opportunities with your organization.

As you will see from my resume, I offer a reputation as a results-oriented professional who has consistently achieved advancement ahead of my peers. I am highly respected and have been strongly encouraged to remain at Oscar Meyer. However, I have made the decision to seek opportunities in another industry.

You will note that I have earned a bachelor's degree with a concentration in Psychology with honors and hold a master's degree in Human Resources Development.

Currently overseeing a ten-person staff at Oscar Meyer Meats as Support Services Manager, I control a $100,000 annual operating budget and provide guidance on areas where training is needed. In a previous assignment as a Personnel and Administration Manager, I was cited as the key factor in the success of efforts to solve personnel issues rooted in morale and training deficiencies. I also established a program which allowed junior employees to obtain college credits.

Throughout my career I have been singled out for praise from senior officials in recognition of my success at resolving problems and developing workable solutions, organizing activities for maximum productivity, and communicating ideas and information.

I have earned respect for my sound judgment, ability to gain the cooperation and best efforts of others, and talent for guiding and motivating personnel to excel. If you can use a mature human resources professional with a high level of initiative who thrives on meeting challenges head on, I hope you will contact me. I will provide excellent professional and personal references at the appropriate time. Thank you for your time and consideration.

Sincerely,

Frank M. Sonata

FRANK M. SONATA

1110½ Hay Street, Fayetteville, NC 28305 • preppub@aol.com • (910) 483-6611

OBJECTIVE To contribute through a proven background of solving problems, organizing activities for maximum efficiency and productivity, and persuasively communicating ideas and information to an organization in need of a results-oriented human resources professional.

EDUCATION & TRAINING **M.S., Human Resources Development,** Northwestern University, Evanston, IL, 1990.
B.S., Personnel Management with concentration in Psychology, Northwestern University, Evanston, IL, 1988; graduated *magna cum laude* with a 3.8 GPA.
Received extensive leadership training at various workshops and seminars.

COMPUTERS Proficient with Microsoft Office 2000, Word, Excel, and PowerPoint.

EXPERIENCE **SUPPORT SERVICES MANAGER.** Oscar Meyer Meats, Des Moines, IA (2002-present). Oversee a staff of ten managers and senior supervisors at headquarters, to include personnel manager and benefits administrator; interface with labor representatives to ensure production is maintained without interruption.
- Control a $100,000 annual operating budget.
- Prepare and deliver presentations on productivity, turnover, and absenteeism data to senior executives.
- Provide guidance on areas where training is needed.

Advanced with Johnson & Johnson, Dayton, OH in the following positions:
1999-02: PERSONNEL AND ADMINISTRATION MANAGER. Advised a general manager on personnel issues while coordinating training and performance of 90 employees.
- Established programs which used outside resources to transform an ineffective counseling system and established a program which allowed junior employees to obtain college credits.
- Made recommendations on medical/dental evaluation policy which greatly enhanced employee morale.

1996-98: TRAINING MANAGER. Recognized for expertise in developing and making effective presentations as well as for writing and editing skills, supervised instructors, determined areas needing further training, and prepared evaluations of subordinates.
- As subject matter expert and consultant on employee training and training standards, prepared checklists of goals for instructors to meet.
- Evaluated and analyzed training standards and strategies. Wrote a general employee orientation presentation at the request of the personnel manager.

1993-96: TRAINING SUPERVISOR. Coordinated and oversaw training and performance of 18 subordinates to include supervising instructors and preparing instructional materials.
- Was co-author of a guidebook for selection of training manuals.

Other experience: SALES AND MARKETING REPRESENTATIVE. Prudential Insurance Co. of America, Evanston, IL (1990-92). In this first job after graduation, refined a wide range of marketing, interviewing, administrative, and sales skills. Advanced ahead of my peers to supervisory and managerial roles based on my initiative, drive, and accomplishments.

PERSONAL Excellent references available upon request.

Date

Exact Name of Person
Exact Title
Exact Name of Company
Address (no., street)
Address (city, state, zip)

TEMPORARY PLACEMENT SUPERVISOR
for Premier Staffing Services

Dear Exact Name of Person (or Dear Sir or Madam if answering a blind ad):

With the enclosed resume, I would like to introduce you to an experienced management professional who excels in maximizing the effectiveness of human resources.

Currently as Temporary Placement Supervisor for Premier Staffing Services, I interview, place, and dispatch temporary labor to job sites while overseeing personnel, sales, and operations functions including recruiting/screening applications. Previously at Mercer Personnel in Olympia, WA, I was promoted to Client Services Manager after serving as Client Services Supervisor. I supervised the administrative support staff with an emphasis on marketing services to area businesses and originating new accounts through a combination of advertising, outside sales, and telemarketing.

My greatest satisfaction comes from placing the right person in the right job and pleasing both client and employee. I am skilled in all phases of this business, and I think you will find me to be knowledgeable, congenial, and a hard worker with his eye on the bottom line.

Although I am excelling in my current position and can provide outstanding references, I am in the process of relocating to Raleigh, NC, because my wife, who is an attorney, has accepted a position with a Raleigh firm.

I hope you will call or write me soon to suggest a time convenient for us to meet and discuss our current and future needs and how I might serve them. Thank you in advance for your time.

Sincerely yours,

Robert C. Person

ROBERT C. PERSON

1110½ Hay Street, Fayetteville, NC 28305 • preppub@aol.com • (910) 483-6611

OBJECTIVE To contribute to an organization that benefit from my extensive experience in the human resources industry as well as from my knowledge of computer applications.

EDUCATION & TRAINING Completed two years of college course work with a concentration in Business Administration, John Tyler Community College, Chester, VA.
Attended professional seminars emphasizing: OSHA Rules and Regulations, Management, Public Relations, and Interviewing and Recruiting

COMPUTERS Familiar with Word, Access, and the Microsoft Office Suite.

EXPERIENCE **TEMPORARY PLACEMENT SUPERVISOR.** Premier Staffing Services, Macon, GA (2003-present). Interview, place, and dispatch temporary labor to job sites while overseeing personnel, sales, and operations functions including recruiting/screening applicants.
- Utilize industry-specific software while preparing and processing daily, weekly, and monthly reports. Train and supervise the office staff.

CLIENT SERVICES MANAGER. Mercer Personnel, Olympia, WA (1998-02). Supervised the administrative support staff as the manager of a satellite office with an emphasis on marketing services to area businesses and originating new accounts through a combination of advertising, outside sales, and telemarketing.
- Prepared budgets and expense reports.
- Represented the company at Chamber of Commerce and other civic events.
- Prepared credit checks on new clients and figured their individual price rates.
- Screened, hired, counseled, and fired applicants for skilled and unskilled light industrial, clerical, administrative, and skilled technical positions.
- Recruited applicants by preparing advertising, attending job fairs, and coordinating with local colleges and state agencies. Maintained a database of employees.
- Prepared job site injury reports; followed up worker's compensation claims.
- Was promoted after excelling as a **Client Services Supervisor** (1998-99): recruited and interviewed applicants; placed temporary workers in skilled and unskilled light industrial positions; maintained accounts and recruited new ones.

TEMPORARY PLACEMENT SUPERVISOR. Wilcher Personnel Service, Miami, FL (1996-97). Interviewed applicants, administered pre-placement skills testing, and performed reference checks while researching/reviewing recruiting needs.
- Attended job fairs and prepared advertising designed to aid in locating a base of qualified applicants. Hired and assigned employees to temporary or temp-to-hire positions.
- Prepared employee evaluations; processed payroll and EDD claims.
- Assisted hiring managers with all aspects of recruitment's and selections.
- Determined and prepared client rate schedules.

EMPLOYEE STAFFING SUPERVISOR. Kelly Temporary Services, Knoxville, TN (1992-95). Screened and scheduled appointments for new applicants and interviewed applicants while also administering clerical evaluations and computer testing.
- Conducted daily safety orientations for light industrial employees.
- Prepared reference checks and verified work histories; processed payroll and claims; formatted the company newsletter; carried out other general office duties.

AFFILIATION Member, Human Resources Management Association, Macon, GA.

CAREER CHANGE

Date

Exact Name of Person
Title or Position
Name of Company
Address (no., street)
Address (city, state, zip)

TERRITORY MANAGER AND RECRUITER for the Department of Transportation. This individual seeks to join a civilian organization in a sales role.

Dear Exact Name of Person (or Dear Sir or Madam if answering a blind ad):

I would appreciate an opportunity to talk with you soon about how I could contribute to your organization through my versatile skills in sales and recruiting, management, administration, and personnel training and development, as well as in budgeting and solving a wide range of problems.

In my present position as Territory Manager/Recruiter for the Department of Transportation in San Francisco, CA, I have earned the distinction as the Top Salesman in California because of exceptional results in recruiting individuals for careers in the DOT. I took over a territory ranked #50 (near the bottom) among DOT recruiting offices and transformed it into #7 in total sales. I oversee an office of five people and have molded personnel into a high-spirited team of employees dedicated to achieving the highest results.

Although I have enjoyed serving the needs of the Department of Transportation, I have made the decision that I would like to join a civilian organization in some capacity in which I can utilize my strong sales and communication skills to maximize the company's profitability.

If you can use a versatile and adaptable professional with a reputation for integrity, dedication to excellence, and a positive attitude, I hope you will write or call me soon to suggest a time when we might meet to discuss your needs and goals and how my background might serve them. I can provide outstanding references at the appropriate time.

Sincerely,

Lamar S. Henry

LAMAR S. HENRY

1110½ Hay Street, Fayetteville, NC 28305 • preppub@aol.com • (910) 483-6611

OBJECTIVE I want to contribute to an organization that can use a dynamic and results-oriented sales professional who offers a proven ability to meet or exceed quotas while also training and developing other sales professionals.

SALES PHILOSOPHY
- Am a highly motivated individual with a winning attitude!
- Have learned how to make the best out of bad situations.
- Believe in leading by example rather than by talking.
- Understand the value of time management and the critical nature of planning in order to maximize the efficiency of each minute on the job.
- Instilled inside me is the concept of accountability, and believe in taking total responsibility for my results with a "no-excuses" attitude.
- Am thoroughly diligent in maintaining paperwork.

EXPERIENCE **TERRITORY MANAGER AND RECRUITER.** Department of Transportation (DOT), San Francisco, CA (1998-present). Have earned the distinction as the Top Salesman in California because of my exceptional results in recruiting individuals for careers in DOT.
- Became known for my ability to sell the DOT with enthusiasm and honesty; while managing other individuals, personally set the standard for performance excellence: with a personal goal of 24 recruiting contracts, achieved 43 contracts and thereby personally made 75% of the entire recruiting station's quota.
- Took over a territory ranked #50 (near the bottom) among DOT recruiting offices, and transformed it into #7 in total sales.
- Oversee an office of five people, and molded personnel into a high-spirited team of employees dedicated to achieving the highest results.
- Manage our sales and recruiting activities within prescribed budgets; solved numerous problems through skillful cost-cutting without sacrificing results or quality — for example, introduced new planning techniques which improved effectiveness even though I reduced the travel expenditures portion of the budget.

IRON WORKER. Moore Machine Company, Houston, TX (1991-98). Read blueprints and fabricated drilling rigs.

SALES HONORS In addition to nearly a dozen medals for exceptional performance, received the following:
- Received the Gold Recruiter Badge with 3 Sapphire Achievement Stars and won the Gold Recruiter Badge with 3 Gold Achievement Stars.
- In addition to the above-mentioned rarely given honors, received the Recruiter of Excellence Award presented by the President of the United States.

EDUCATION & TRAINING Completed DeVry Technical Institute, Irving, TX; developed proficiency in plate and pipe welding, 1991.
Completed more than two years of college-level training related to sales, marketing, management, and supervision, 2002.
Graduated with honors from a management program designed to refine the skills of DOT's best middle managers, 2001.
Excelled in completing an executive development program for junior managers, 2000.

PERSONAL Am an outgoing and friendly individual who enjoys meeting strangers and helping others. Am ready to help my next employer grow and prosper!

Real-Resumes Series edited by Anne McKinney

Date

Exact Name of Person
Title or Position
Name of Company
Address (no., street)
Address (city, state, zip)

TRAINING DEPARTMENT MANAGER
for Motorola

Dear Exact Name of Person (or Dear Sir or Madam if answering a blind ad):

Can you use an enthusiastic and energetic young professional who offers exceptional motivational and communication skills? With a reputation as someone "who has never met a stranger," I have become known for my insistence on exceeding high performance standards in every position I have held.

I am currently excelling in my current position as Training Department Manager with Motorola. As you will see from my resume, I was first selected to become a Personnel Recruiter involved in "selling" the idea of a career with Motorola to qualified young people. With a reputation as an articulate, enthusiastic, and dedicated professional, I have been promoted ahead of more my peers.

Since entering the sales and recruiting field, I have consistently exceeded goals and set records, and I was promoted to train new personnel and oversee the operational aspects. As a trainer and administrator, I have developed new employees while molding new personnel into "top-notch" performers.

I completed an associate's degree in Business Management and am presently pursuing a bachelor's degree in Business Management. I am proud of my reputation as a "perfectionist" and feel that I can be counted on to give 100% of my efforts to anything I attempt.

I hope you will welcome my call soon to arrange a brief meeting at your convenience to discuss your current and future needs and how I might serve them. Thank you in advance for your time.

Sincerely yours,

David D. Teaters

Alternate last paragraph:
I hope you will call or write me soon to suggest a time convenient for us to meet and discuss your current and future needs and how I might serve them. Thank you in advance for your time.

DAVID D. TEATERS

1110½ Hay Street, Fayetteville, NC 28305 • preppub@aol.com • (910) 483-6611

OBJECTIVE To contribute my energy and enthusiasm to an organization in need of an exceptional motivator and communicator who has excelled in sales, personnel recruiting, and training.

EXPERIENCE *Consistently exceeded corporate goals and set "sales" records in the areas of personnel recruiting and training with Motorola, Inc. (2000–present):*

2002-present: TRAINING DEPARTMENT MANAGER. St. Paul, MN. On the basis of my previous successes, was selected to lead the Training Department at headquarters. Plan and manage employee training programs.

- When the telecommunications industry went into a slump, I played a key role in designing Motorola's downsizing plan.
- Recognized as the subject matter expert on government policies pertaining to employment such as Affirmative Action and the EEO Act.
- Initiated special workshops for employees which were credited with improving productivity. Oversaw instructors and worked with them to prepare syllabi.
- Developed training classes for managers on management expectations; counsel supervisors in resolving employee grievances.
- Maintain records on absenteeism and safety and make recommendations on improvements to higher management.
- Was credited with achieving virtually accident-free operations due to the safety program I developed. Initiated a new attendance policy based on flex-time which was credited with reducing absenteeism and improving employee morale.

2000-02: TRAINER/RECRUITER. Brainerd, MN. Evaluated as "the best" trainer at this facility, developed inexperienced personnel into "top-notch" employees.

- Was named #1 "Recruiter" out of 16 managers throughout Motorola's branches.
- Developed and implemented a quality assurance program for the parent organization.
- Played a key role in developing a new employee orientation presentation.

Other experience:

TRAINING MANAGER. Dynegy, Columbus, OH (1997-00). Oversaw training scheduling and planning, advising department managers on training needs and requirements, and conducted one-on-one training sessions.

- Developed training improvements which resulted in a 30% increase in production.

RECRUITER. Intel, Hamilton, NY (1994-96). Earned the highest possible ratings in all evaluated areas including professional competence, performance, and standards while continuing to exceed goals after evaluating applicants, interviewing, and counseling them.

- Refined my public speaking skills while visiting area job fairs.

PERSONNEL SUPERVISOR. Honeywell International, Piscataway, NJ (1992-94). Promoted ahead of my peers and then placed in a job usually held by more experienced personnel, oversaw personnel administration.

- Managed promotions, employee performance evaluations, and personnel recordkeeping.

EDUCATION Attend Bethel College, St. Paul, working toward a **B.A. in Business Management.**
Associate's degree in Business Management, Rowan, Glassboro, NJ, 1992.

PERSONAL Known as a highly resourceful individual who thrives on developing creative solutions to problems. Proven ability to establish strong working relationships. Excellent references.

Real-Resumes Series edited by Anne McKinney **169**

TRAINING DIRECTOR
for Johnson & Johnson

Date

Exact Name of Person
Title or Position
Name of Company
Address (no., street)
Address (city, state, zip)

Dear Exact Name of Person (or Dear Sir or Madam if answering a blind ad):

I would appreciate an opportunity to talk with you soon about how I could contribute to your organization through my expertise in human resources management, as well as my exceptional analytical and decision-making abilities.

You will see from my resume that I am currently a Training Director at Johnson & Johnson. My strong public speaking and briefing skills are utilized on a routine basis while working in close coordination with senior officials at the corporate level. I am involved in all aspects of designing, coordinating, and implementing training programs and classes involving thousands of employees. I also offer experience in personnel recruitment. In an earlier position in a manufacturing firm, I managed the administration of all personnel actions for 62 employees and handled responsibilities including processing payroll, promotions, evaluation reports, workman compensation claims, and insurance..

A highly self-motivated professional, throughout my career I have attended courses and seminars on my own initiative to ensure that my skills remain "state-of-the-art" in our fast-changing world. I hold a B.S. degree in Business Administration from New York University, NY.

I offer a unique combination of creativity and vision, practical technical knowledge, and extensive experience which are transferable to many situations where I could make important contributions. I feel certain I could become a valuable resource to your organization.

I hope you will welcome my call soon to arrange a brief meeting at your convenience to discuss your current and future needs and how I might serve them. Thank you in advance for your time.

Sincerely yours,

Andrew V. Napier

Alternate last paragraph:
I hope you will call or write me soon to suggest a time convenient for us to meet and discuss your current and future needs and how I might serve them. Thank you in advance for your time.

ANDREW V. NAPIER

1110½ Hay Street, Fayetteville, NC 28305 • preppub@aol.com • (910) 483-6611

OBJECTIVE To contribute to an organization through my expertise in human resources management with a particular emphasis in organizational development, training and development, personnel, and employee relations, as well as my ability for translating concepts into action.

EDUCATION **Bachelor of Science degree in Business Administration**, New York University, NY, 1990. Completed college-level coursework, including classes in leadership, personnel management, staff operations, technical writing, public speaking, and logistics.

EXPERIENCE *During my experience at Johnson & Johnson, Cleveland, OH, have earned a reputation as an exceptionally well-qualified professional who excels in finding ways to lead groups of people of varied backgrounds, experience, and qualifications to work together:*

2003-present: **TRAINING DIRECTOR**. Utilize my outstanding human resources knowledge after selection by top-level management to design employee and manager training programs.
- Plan and direct personnel training and staff development including budgets, training needs analysis, ton-the-job training, and short-/long-term training plans.
- Develop and conduct coaching, teaching, counseling, and mentor programs to polish management potential; trained 23 managers, improving their leadership abilities.

1998-02: **HUMAN RESOURCES MANAGER**. Excelled while directing the operations of a 31-person department while also managing all training development and support programs; controlled a budget of over $2 million.
- Coordinated projects which "significantly upgraded" productivity and profitability.
- Liaised with top-level management on a variety of administrative and logistical matters.
- Planned, coordinated, and implemented various training projects, in addition to conducting weekly staff development meetings.
- Praised by superiors for consistently maintaining a high employee retention rate.

1995-97: **TRAINING MANAGER**. Refined time-management skills while creating, scheduling, and tracking all training programs.
- Planned and implemented employee and manager training programs.
- Described on official evaluations as "one who puts concern for employees ahead of his own personal interest," my confidence and enthusiasm were noted as a catalyst in building morale and molding junior personnel into effective leaders.

Other experience:
HUMAN RESOURCES MANAGER. Franklin Manufacturing, Ithaca, NY (1990-95). Managed the administration of all personnel actions for a department numbering 62 employees, including processing payroll, promotions, evaluation reports, workman compensation claims, and insurance.
- Designed an accounting tracking system that inmproved the reporting time and accuracy of all personnel records and evaluations.
- As Activities Director, organized picnics, dinners, and dances for employees and families.

Highlights of other experience: Served as a Personnel Manager at Kendall's Ford Motor Co., Santa Cruz, CA, training, supervising, and evaluating 46 personnel.

PERSONAL Am a dedicated, versatile professional with a knack for problem-solving and decision-making.

Date

Exact Name of Person
Title or Position
Name of Company
Address (no., street)
Address (city, state, zip)

TRAINING MANAGER
for Kestler
Pharmaceuticals

Dear Exact Name of Person (or Dear Sir or Madam if answering a blind ad):

   I would appreciate an opportunity to talk with you soon about how I could contribute to your organization by applying my extensive managerial and supervisory abilities as well as my proven leadership and motivational skills in the human resources field.

   In my present position as a Training Manager for a 2,500-person division at Kestler Pharmaceuticals, I have consistently been selected to assume responsibility for top-level projects which are considered of critical strategic importance to the company. My contributions to this organization have included revising wage and salary scales, automating office procedures and training clerks to use the new equipment, and emphasizing safety practices which resulted in fewer on-the-job injuries. I am known as a motivator who sets the example for professional development

   My resume will show that I also was recognized as a "subject matter expert" who has advanced as a chemical operations specialist in my previous employment. I have developed successful programs, instructed new chemical operators, and served as a consultant for organizations both overseas and in the U.S. My accomplishments have earned numerous outstanding evaluations as well as two achievement and two commendation medals for expertise as a technician, leader, and instructor.

   I hope you will welcome my call soon to arrange a brief meeting at your convenience to discuss your current and future needs and how I might serve them. Thank you in advance for your time.

Sincerely yours,

Richard T. Chin

Alternate last paragraph:
   I hope you will call or write me soon to suggest a time convenient for us to meet and discuss your current and future needs and how I might serve them. Thank you in advance for your time.

RICHARD T. CHIN

1110½ Hay Street, Fayetteville, NC 28305 • preppub@aol.com • (910) 483-6611

OBJECTIVE To contribute through my positive attitude, energy and drive, and proven expertise in organizing and managing operations as well as my training and motivational abilities.

EXPERIENCE **TRAINING MANAGER.** Kestler Pharmaceuticals, Paterson, NJ (2002-present). Provide leadership and guidance for a 2,500-person division; oversee activities with an impact in the areas of morale, professional development, health, and training.

- Took the initiative in setting up an Intranet through which employees have opportunities to participate in dozens of training programs. Morale has soared.
- Was consistently selected ahead of my peers to fill an acting senior manager's job.
- Motivated seven subordinates to excel and earn the distinction of the "Employee of the Month" for the parent organization.
- Emphasized safety practices which resulted in a significant reduction in on-the-job injuries.
- Modernized office operations: procured a computer system and had clerks trained and proficient within a month.
- Revised the wage and salary scales which was credited with improving employee morale as well as resulting in a cost savings for Pfizer. Oversaw the employee orientation presentation preparation.

Known as a "subject matter expert," advanced in positions as a chemical operations specialist in various locations, U.S. Army:

CONSULTANT and TECHNICAL ADVISOR. Ft. Ord, CA (1999-01). Advised nine separate companies which responded worldwide on short notice; provided nuclear/biological/ chemical (NBC) defense training and supervision.

- Was handpicked to set up and then oversee the organization's first-ever NBC defense program including the inspection procedures.

PROGRAM PLANNER AND COORDINATOR. Ft. Meade, MD (1996-98). Earned the respect of senior leaders and was selected to develop, review, and publish NBC plans for this base.

- Was officially evaluated as "candid and forthright" with "exceptional mental discipline."
- Developed standard operating procedures (SOP) for training and inspections.

TRAINING MANAGER. Ft. Dix, NJ (1993-95). Evaluated as a "superb performer," conducted NBC training programs for junior chemical specialists from five companies and ensured maintenance on specialized equipment; was routinely sought out to provide guidance for people from outside the organization.

- Excelled at handling multiple assignments simultaneously by breaking each project into logical steps and following through to ensure completion.
- Was personally commended for my efforts in a major inspection and oversaw four subordinate company NBC programs which earned "commendable" ratings.

EDUCATION & TRAINING **Bachelor of Science degree in General Studies,** Columbus State University, Columbus, GA, 1992. Excelled in leadership and technical training courses including the following: NBC defense management, combat chemical environment course, decontamination systems operation and maintenance, field sanitation, and an advanced chemical course.

PERSONAL Received two achievement and two commendation medals for my accomplishments. Am a good listener who contributes to team efforts. Held a Secret security clearance.

Date

Exact Name of Person
Title or Position
Name of Company
Address (no., street)
Address (city, state, zip)

TRAINING PROGRAM MANAGER
for Intel Corporation

Dear Exact Name of Person (or Dear Sir or Madam if answering a blind ad):

I would appreciate an opportunity to talk with you soon about how my human resources and personnel management expertise and experience in leadership positions could be beneficial to your organization.

With a reputation as a versatile and adaptable professional, I have consistently been evaluated as possessing "unlimited potential" with "abilities placing him head and shoulders above his peers." While serving at Intel Corp., I have risen in leadership positions where I persisted in developing teams which always performed "flawlessly" and stood out as examples to similar companies.

In my present position as Training Program Manager, I am responsible for training programs for managers, supervisors, and employees. I oversee four instructors and am considered the company's "resident expert" on government laws and regulations applicable to employment. In my previous position as General Manager, I supervised 89 employees and was responsible for training programs and administrative support operations. Consistently rated as "the best" in every performance evaluation, I supervised the personnel and labor relations managers and controlled a budget of $300,000.

I feel that I can contribute through my unique blend of concern for employees, aggressive and determined personality, and broad base of management and leadership experience.

I hope you will welcome my call soon to arrange a brief meeting at your convenience to discuss your current and future needs and how I might serve them. Thank you in advance for your time.

Sincerely yours,

Keith R. Dreyfuss

KEITH R. DREYFUSS

1110½ Hay Street, Fayetteville, NC 28305 • preppub@aol.com • (910) 483-6611

OBJECTIVE To benefit an organization through human resources and personnel management skills as a manager who has built a reputation as an aggressive communicator and motivator.

EXPERIENCE *Built a reputation as an excellent communicator and trainer of personnel with Intel Corp., Norwich, CT.*
2002-present: **TRAINING PROGRAM MANAGER.** Responsible for training programs for managers, supervisors, and employees. Am considered the organization's "resident expert" on government laws and regulations.
- Oversee four instructors and monitored classes to ensure quality training of employees.
- Prepared several syllabi for training courses; schedule personnel for training.

1997-01: **GENERAL MANAGER.** Developed 89 people into a team consistently rated as "the best" by wide margins in every performance evaluation and training program.
- Supervised the personnel and labor relations managers. Controlled a budget of $300,000.

1996-97: **PERSONNEL MANAGER.** Earned rapid advancement to General Manager on the basis of my performance in supervising a staff of 48 and coordinating and assessing ongoing training for 785 employees.
- Developed training programs for the management team.
- Rewrote the policy regarding attendance and created a flex-time schedule which was credited with decreasing absenteeism and improving productivity.
- Polished my time management skills "juggling" a variety of projects.

Advanced in technical management roles, U. S. Army, Ft. Hood, TX:
OPERATIONS MANAGER. (1995). Coordinated administrative and logistics support as the "second-in-command" of a 105-person company.
- Directed all aspects of running the organization's training program which earned official praise for "setting the standards."

TECHNICAL AND ADMINISTRATIVE OPERATIONS MANAGER. (1993-94). Supervised two departments: a 24-person administrative support staff and 45 employees maintaining and operating more than $2 million in vehicles/weapons systems.
- Earned praise for the quality of work my employees accomplished.

FIRST-LINE SUPERVISOR. (1991-92). Developed training programs for a 150-person company while supervising performance of 12 employees.

Other U.S. Army experience: Earned rapid promotion and was singled out for attendance at advanced leadership development programs after excelling as the training manager for a 120-person company.

EDUCATION B.A., Business Administration, Bentley College, Waltham, MA, 1991.

TRAINING Excelled in more than ten months of training including executive management programs.

PERSONAL Was honored with many commendation and achievement medals for "meritorious service."

Date

Exact Name of Person
Title or Position
Name of Company
Address (no., street)
Address (city, state, zip)

VICE PRESIDENT FOR HUMAN RESOURCES

with a prominent credit union

Dear Exact Name of Person (or Dear Sir or Madam if answering a blind ad):

I would appreciate an opportunity to talk with you soon about how I could contribute to your organization through my extensive management experience in most functional areas of human resources, operations, and banking.

As you will see from my resume, I have enjoyed a track record of promotion with the Charleston Federal Credit Union, one of the leading minority-owned financial institutions in the South. I have often worn multiple "hats" and am known for my ability to oversee complex responsibilities in numerous areas simultaneously. For example, in my current position as a vice president, I oversee the Operations, Human Resources, and Compliance areas for the credit union, and I actually developed the credit union's Deposit Compliance Program.

If you feel your management team could benefit from my in-depth experience, creative problem-solving style, and reputation as a strategist and visionary, I would be delighted to make myself available at your convenience to discuss your needs and goals and how I might help you achieve them. I will be relocating to the Atlanta area in order to be closer to my family, and I am exploring employment opportunities with local area firms.

I hope you will welcome my call soon to arrange a brief meeting to discuss your current and future needs and how I might serve them. Thank you in advance for your time.

Sincerely,

Patricia Ann Silver

PATRICIA ANN SILVER

1110½ Hay Street, Fayetteville, NC 28305 • preppub@aol.com • (910) 483-6611

OBJECTIVE To benefit an organization that can use an innovative manager who believes that "the sky is the limit" when persistence, creativity, and attention to detail are combined with superior planning, time management, organizational, communication, and problem-solving skills.

EDUCATION & TRAINING

B.S., **Accounting**, College of Charleston, SC, 1990.
Excelled in the following courses:

Accounting	Introduction to Computers	Business Communication
Banking and Finance	Supervision	Principles of Management

Attended seminars on sexual harassment, interviewing & hiring, state and federal wages, personnel policies (developing/implementing), public speaking, and check processing.

SUMMARY OF EXPERIENCE

Have built a "track record" of accomplishment in positions of increasing responsibility at Charleston Federal Credit Union, Charleston, SC; have earned a reputation as a dynamic motivator, skilled trainer, and creative organizer.

EXPERIENCE

VICE PRESIDENT FOR HUMAN RESOURCES. (2003-present). Was promoted to handle responsibilities related to human resources while continuing to handle responsibilities described in the Assistant VP job below.

- On my own initiative, undertook a major project which involved analyzing all company job descriptions. One result has been a new Position Description Manual which clarifies employee responsibilities.

ASSISTANT VICE PRESIDENT, OPERATIONS & HUMAN RESOURCES. (2000-03). In this highly visible, fast-paced position reporting to credit union president, am wearing "three hats," balancing responsibilities in human resources, operations, and investments.

- **Human Resources**: Applied my expert knowledge to develop, maintain, and administer all personnel policies as they applied to 35 credit union employees; oversaw EEO compliance, recruitment, safety & health.
- **Benefits Administration**: Oversaw all salary and benefit functions, including 401(k) pension plan and Blue Cross/Blue Shield health plan.
- **Training**: In addition to coordinating in-house programs on personnel policies, organized and conducted training on compliance with demand deposit, regular direct deposit, credit union privacy, and other credit union regulations.
- **Management:** Directly supervised five people.
- **Operations**: In coordination with top management, developed and implemented plans and policies that affected accounting, bookkeeping, and data processing.
- **Finances**: Managed an investment portfolio utilizing excess funds per day while efficiently planning and administering the department's budget.

OPERATIONS OFFICER. (1996-00). Excelled in directing all aspects of the Operations Department because of my versatile management skills.

HEAD BOOKKEEPER. (1993-1995). Ensured the highest standards of customer service while supervising and reviewing the work of five assistants.

PROOF OPERATOR. (1990-1992). While learning the basics of office management, acquired precise habits balancing, encoding, endorsing, and filming all items related to deposits.

PERSONAL Have a working knowledge Word, Excel, and Access. Am a self-motivated, dedicated professional with a reputation as a team leader. Will cheerfully relocate.

ABOUT THE EDITOR

Anne McKinney holds an MBA from the Harvard Business School and a BA in English from the University of North Carolina at Chapel Hill. A noted public speaker, writer, and teacher, she is the senior editor for PREP's business and career imprint, which bears her name. Early titles in the Anne McKinney Career Series (now called the Real-Resumes Series) published by PREP include: *Resumes and Cover Letters That Have Worked, Resumes and Cover Letters That Have Worked for Military Professionals, Government Job Applications and Federal Resumes, Cover Letters That Blow Doors Open,* and *Letters for Special Situations.* Her career titles and how-to resume-and-cover-letter books are based on the expertise she has acquired in 20 years of working with job hunters. Her valuable career insights have appeared in publications of the "Wall Street Journal" and other prominent newspapers and magazines.

PREP Publishing Order Form

You may purchase any of our titles from your favorite bookseller! Or send a check or money order or your credit card number for the total amount*, plus $4.00 postage and handling, to PREP, 1110 1/2 Hay Street, Fayetteville, NC 28305. You may also order our titles on our website at www.prep-pub.com and feel free to e-mail us at preppub@aol.com or call 910-483-6611 with your questions or concerns.

Name: _____

Phone #: _____

Address: _____

E-mail address: _____

Payment Type: ☐ Check/Money Order ☐ Visa ☐ MasterCard

Credit Card Number: _____ Expiration Date: _____

Put a check beside the items you are ordering:

☐ Free—Packet describing PREP's professional writing and editing services
☐ $16.95—REAL-RESUMES FOR RESTAURANT, FOOD SERVICE & HOTEL JOBS. Anne McKinney, Editor
☐ $16.95—REAL-RESUMES FOR MEDIA, NEWSPAPER, BROADCASTING & PUBLIC AFFAIRS JOBS. Anne McKinney
☐ $16.95—REAL-RESUMES FOR RETAILING, MODELING, FASHION & BEAUTY JOBS. Anne McKinney, Editor
☐ $16.95—REAL-RESUMES FOR HUMAN RESOURCES & PERSONNEL JOBS. Anne McKinney, Editor
☐ $16.95—REAL-RESUMES FOR MANUFACTURING JOBS. Anne McKinney, Editor
☐ $16.95—REAL-RESUMES FOR AVIATION & TRAVEL JOBS. Anne McKinney, Editor
☐ $16.95—REAL-RESUMES FOR POLICE, LAW ENFORCEMENT & SECURITY JOBS. Anne McKinney, Editor
☐ $16.95—REAL-RESUMES FOR SOCIAL WORK & COUNSELING JOBS. Anne McKinney, Editor
☐ $16.95—REAL-RESUMES FOR CONSTRUCTION JOBS. Anne McKinney, Editor
☐ $16.95—REAL-RESUMES FOR FINANCIAL JOBS. Anne McKinney, Editor
☐ $16.95—REAL-RESUMES FOR COMPUTER JOBS. Anne McKinney, Editor
☐ $16.95—REAL-RESUMES FOR MEDICAL JOBS. Anne McKinney, Editor
☐ $16.95—REAL-RESUMES FOR TEACHERS. Anne McKinney, Editor
☐ $16.95—REAL-RESUMES FOR CAREER CHANGERS. Anne McKinney, Editor
☐ $16.95—REAL-RESUMES FOR STUDENTS. Anne McKinney, Editor
☐ $16.95—REAL-RESUMES FOR SALES. Anne McKinney, Editor
☐ $16.95—REAL ESSAYS FOR COLLEGE AND GRAD SCHOOL. Anne McKinney, Editor
☐ $25.00—RESUMES AND COVER LETTERS THAT HAVE WORKED. McKinney. Editor
☐ $25.00—RESUMES AND COVER LETTERS THAT HAVE WORKED FOR MILITARY PROFESSIONALS. McKinney, Ed.
☐ $25.00—RESUMES AND COVER LETTERS FOR MANAGERS. McKinney, Editor
☐ $25.00—GOVERNMENT JOB APPLICATIONS AND FEDERAL RESUMES: Federal Resumes, KSAs, Forms 171 and 612, and Postal Applications. McKinney, Editor
☐ $25.00—COVER LETTERS THAT BLOW DOORS OPEN. McKinney, Editor
☐ $25.00—LETTERS FOR SPECIAL SITUATIONS. McKinney, Editor
☐ $16.00—BACK IN TIME. Patty Sleem
☐ $17.00—(trade paperback) SECOND TIME AROUND. Patty Sleem
☐ $25.00—(hardcover) SECOND TIME AROUND. Patty Sleem
☐ $18.00—A GENTLE BREEZE FROM GOSSAMER WINGS. Gordon Beld
☐ $18.00—BIBLE STORIES FROM THE OLD TESTAMENT. Katherine Whaley
☐ $14.95—WHAT THE BIBLE SAYS ABOUT... *Words that can lead to success and happiness* (large print edition) Patty Sleem

_____ TOTAL ORDERED

_____ (add $4.00 for shipping and handling)

_____ TOTAL INCLUDING SHIPPING

*PREP offers volume discounts on large orders. Call us at (910) 483-6611 for more information.

> THE MISSION OF PREP PUBLISHING IS TO PUBLISH BOOKS AND OTHER PRODUCTS WHICH ENRICH PEOPLE'S LIVES AND HELP THEM OPTIMIZE THE HUMAN EXPERIENCE. OUR STRONGEST LINES ARE OUR JUDEO-CHRISTIAN ETHICS SERIES AND OUR REAL-RESUMES SERIES.

Would you like to explore the possibility of having PREP's writing team create a resume for you similar to the ones in this book?

For a brief free consultation, call 910-483-6611
or send $4.00 to receive our Job Change Packet to
PREP, 1110 1/2 Hay Street, Fayetteville, NC 28305. Visit our website to find valuable career resources: www.prep-pub.com!

QUESTIONS OR COMMENTS? E-MAIL US AT PREPPUB@AOL.COM